THE BORDER BALLADS

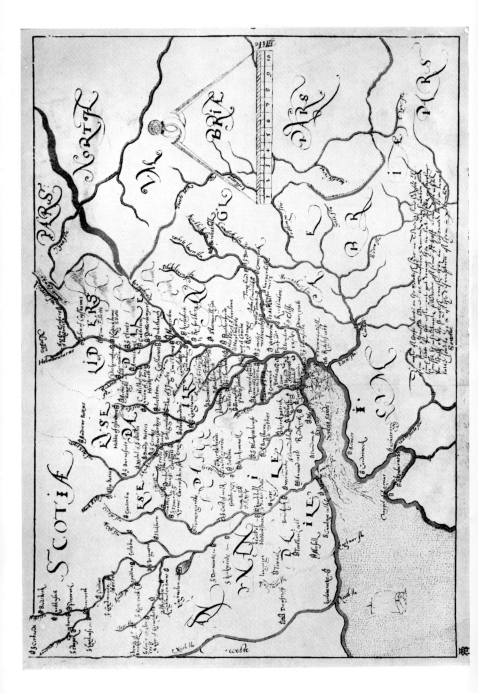

THE BORDER BALLADS

JAMES REED

UNIVERSITY OF LONDON
THE ATHLONE PRESS
1973

Published by
THE ATHLONE PRESS
UNIVERSITY OF LONDON
at 4 *Gower Street, London* WC1

Distributed by
Tiptree Book Services Ltd
Tiptree, Essex

U.S.A. and Canada
Humanities Press Inc
New York

ISBN 0 485 11144 6

Printed in Great Britain by
T. & A. CONSTABLE LIMITED
Edinburgh

For Carol
'My lady is my warld's meed'

Time, which antiquates antiquities, and hath an art to make dust of all things, hath yet spared these minor monuments.

Sir Thomas Browne, *Hydriotaphia*

ACKNOWLEDGEMENTS

A writer who attempts to explore the relationships between literature and its environment accumulates many debts, not all of them academic: mine are to librarians and shepherds, booksellers and publicans, photographers, students and singers, the distinguished and the anonymous, and to patient friends. I hope this book will not do them injustice.

In the completing of it, I owe most to Dr William Beattie and Dr Thomas I. Rae, both of the National Library of Scotland, who read the manuscript and with searching but kindly scholarship informed my ignorance.

My friends Harry Foster and John Brown of Alnwick have also been generous, ready to help with books, pictures and discourse at the drop of a steel bonnet.

But the pages that follow would probably never have been written, had it not been for the true Border hospitality of Madge Anderson, once Madge Hall of Elsdon, many years ago at Blakehopeburnhaugh, not so very far from the spot where Parcy Reed was murdered by the fause Ha's o' Girsonsfield.

I wish to thank the Royal Commission on Historical Monuments, England, the Royal Commission on the Ancient and Historical Monuments of Scotland, the Scottish Tourist Board, the Society of Antiquaries of Scotland and the Trustees of the British Museum for permission to reproduce photographs. The chapter tail-pieces are woodcuts by Thomas Bewick reproduced from *1800 Woodcuts by Thomas Bewick and his School* (Dover Books).

J. R.

CONTENTS

PLATES

MAPS

INTRODUCTION

Francis Jeffrey, reviewing *The Lay of the Last Minstrel* in 1805, confessed himself baffled, and indeed offended, by Scott's use of specifically environmental elements in a poem offered to the public as literature. 'We really cannot so far sympathise with the local partialities of the author', he wrote, 'as to feel any glow of patriotism or ancient virtue in hearing of the Todrig or Johnston clans, or of Elliots, Armstrongs, and Tinlinns; still less can we relish the introduction of Black John of Athelstane, Whitslade the Hawk, Arthur-fire-the-Braes, Red Roland Forster, or any other of those worthies who

> Sought the beeves that made their broth
> In Scotland and in England both

into a poem which has any pretensions to seriousness or dignity. The ancient metrical romance might have admitted those homely personalities; but the present age will not endure them: and Mr Scott must either sacrifice his Border prejudices, or offend all his readers in the other parts of the empire.'[1] For Jeffrey and most of his eighteenth-century predecessors true literature could not be made out of the commonplace and the homely, though as early as 1761 William Shenstone, recommending Percy's *Reliques* to a friend, could write, 'The public has seen all that art can do, and they want the more striking efforts of wild, original, enthusiastic genius.'

The chronology of taste is interesting, and in the case of Border Ballads may be plotted at three points. In *The Compleat Angler* of 1653, Isaak Walton could write, without obvious condescension:

Piscator. I pray, do us a courtesy that shall stand you and your daughter in nothing, and yet we will think ourselves still something in your debt; it is but to sing us a song that was sung by your daughter when I last passed over this meadow, about eight or nine days since.

Milk-woman. What song was it, I pray? Was it 'Come, Shepherds, deck your herds'? or, 'As at noon Dulcina rested'? or, 'Phillida flouts me'? or, 'Chevy Chase'? or, 'Johnny Armstrong'?, or, 'Troy Town'?

But a century later, when such songs become the prey of the antiquary, taste trembles. William Warburton, Bishop of Gloucester, writing on 29 July 1734 to a reverend friend in Stamford, comments scathingly on the activities of the antiquary Francis Peck: 'he is at present busy upon a collection of our ancient English ballads; which, I understand, he intends to give with notes and emendations. With all this he thinks he is serving the world. May it always be thus served! its neglect of merit, its ingratitude, and universal corruption deserving no other devotees.'[2]

The prevalence of such views makes the publication in 1765 of Bishop Percy's *Reliques of Ancient English Poetry* an event of considerable significance in social as well as literary history. On both sides of the border, for a century or more, men had collected the songs of the people, but it was the *publication* in London of Percy's work that exercised such a compelling influence on an age in which Dr Johnson could say that 'Chevy Chase pleased the vulgar, but did not satisfy the learned; it did not fill a mind capable of thinking strongly'.[3] Percy had rescued a folio manuscript of ballads which were being used as firelighters in the house of Humphrey Pitt of Shifnal, and used it as the basis of the *Reliques*. It is an uneven work, but made a strong impression on the mind of 13-year-old Walter Scott:

I forgot the hour of dinner, was sought for with anxiety, and was still found entranced in my intellectual banquet. To read and to remember was in this instance the same thing, and henceforth I overwhelmed my school-fellows, and all who would hearken to me, with tragic recitations from the Ballads of Bishop Percy. The first time, too, I could scrape a few shillings together, which were not common occurrences with me, I bought unto myself a copy of these beloved volumes; nor do I believe I ever read a book half so frequently, or with half the enthusiasm.[4]

Introduction

Scottish interest had already developed: Allan Ramsay's collection of Scots and English songs in *The Tea-Table Miscellany* first appeared in 1724, with '*The Evergreen*, being a collection of Scots poems, wrote by the ingenious before 1600'. David Herd, too, published in 1776 *Ancient and Modern Scottish Songs, Heroic Ballads*, etc., *collected from Memory, Tradition, and Ancient Authors*, and Henderson speaks for all critics in describing him as 'one of the most trustworthy of the old collectors . . . almost incapable not merely of writing, but of altering or amending verse'.[5]

Neither Herd nor Percy offer circumstantial accounts of how they obtained their ballads; ballad scholarship in this respect was pioneered by the meticulous but unlovable Joseph Ritson. He attacked Percy violently, and of John Pinkerton, who published in 1781 and 1783 collections of Scottish Ballads containing much forged and spurious work, he wrote, 'Your success has doubtless fully gratified your expectations, and the dexterity of a pickpocket may vie with the impudence of a highwayman.'[6] Scott, too, was severe on Pinkerton, but more kindly. Curiously, Ritson and Scott, antipathetic in personality, very different in their antiquarian methods, did achieve a respect for one another's work. 'While industry, research, and antiquarian learnings are recommendations to works of this nature, few editors will ever be found so competent to the task as Joseph Ritson',[7] is how Scott himself puts it. Lockhart writes uncompromisingly: 'This narrow-minded, sour, and dogmatical little word-catcher had hated the very name of a Scotsman, and was utterly incapable of sympathising with any of the higher views of his new correspondent. Yet the bland courtesy of Scott disarmed even this half-crazy pedant.'[8]

The major original work, however, in this field, is undoubtedly the product of Sir Walter Scott's scholarship, *The Minstrelsy of the Scottish Border* (Vols. 1 & 2, Kelso 1802, Vol. 3 Edinburgh 1803). Though influenced by his predecessors, Scott differed from them both in motive and in method. 'By such efforts, feeble as they are', he writes in his introduction,

I may contribute something to the history of my native country; the peculiar features of whose manners and character are daily melting and dissolving into those of her sister and ally. And, trivial as may appear such an offering to the Manes of a kingdom, once proud and independent, I hang it upon her altar with a mixture of feelings which I shall not attempt to describe.[9]

Scott lived in the Borders, and collected his ballads either directly from singers or from neighbouring Borderers like William Laidlaw, James Hogg and John Leyden. He had a fine ear for genuine ballad rhythms, though it played him false when he accepted the forgeries of his friend Surtees who had not the heart to disillusion him. (These were *Barthram's Dirge, Lord Ewrie* and *The Death of Featherstonehaugh.*) His ear also led him to improvise, elaborate and generally tinker with much of what he collected, though he escaped censure by Ritson. *The Minstrelsy* really is the work of a minstrel rather than a scholar, and one would not wish it otherwise.

One interesting account of his methods survives in a record by J. E. Shortreed of 'Conversations with my father on the subject of his Tours with Sir Walter Scott in Liddesdale', written in June 1824.[10] Their first expedition was made in the Autumn of 1792, when Scott was 21, and the excursions continued annually for seven years.

JES And how did Sir Walter obtain all the Liddesdale Ballads? Was it from recitation or how?

Father Not one o' them was got from recitation but the 'Fray o' Suport'. Dr. Elliot of Cleuch-head had a great turn for that kind o' lore himsel, and had collected a vast deal o' the old Ballads o' the Country for his own amusement, and when Sir Walter came in quest o' that kind o' thing, he got all that the Doctor had then collected, and seeing his great fondness for them, the Doctor was induced to exert himself in gathering a great many more. I think with the exception o' the Fray o' Suport (and he had an imperfect set of it too) and a very few that had been printed before in the *Hawick Museum* they war all gotten in MS from Dr. Elliot—All our raids were made in the autumn season, but the one we undertook one year in the Spring—(and blirting, snawy weather it was I mind) for the express purpose o' hearing the air o' the Fray o' Suport, frae auld Jonathan Graham, the lang quaker as he was called. We went to Newlands, where Dr. Elliot was then living, and a man and a horse were sent ance errand for Jonathan, who came accordingly. He was a man upwards of eighty year auld I dare say. I'll never forget his appearance, tall, and sae thin as to be mair like a walking skeleton than a living being. Indeed ye wadna hae said, to have lookit at him, that he *was* a living creature, till he began to recite and then he fired up and got prodigiously animated. He spoke, or rather *skraughed*, in a loud stentorian voice, which formed the oddest contrast imaginable wi' his worn and emaciated figure. He had been a great repository o' Ballads and traditions in his day, but his memory and other faculties war nearly gane by the time *we* saw him. He could eat little or nane, poor creature, *but he drank* weel, and the Dr. and Sir Wr. filled him exeedingly fou o' brandy—oh he was ill! Faith I thocht he wad die i' our hands ance athegither, for he fainted clean away—but we got him carried out into the fresh air, and threw water onto his auld wizened face, and rubbit him, and wrought on till he came about again, and nae sooner was he better than he set to roaring the outlandish lilt again. He made the awfuest and uncoest howling sound I ever heard. It was a mixture o' a sort o' horrible and eldritch cries, and to hae lookt at him ye wad hae thocht it impossible they could come out o' that dead trunk. He wad sune hae been as ill as ever again wi' liquor, if we had let him, but we got him to his bed. He gaed his ways hame the neist mornin', as he had come, after getting a gratuity from Sir Walter. He had gotten a sair fleg wi' the quaker's *swarfin'* the night before, and was in an unco taking about him till he came round again.

JES   How far had the quaker come?

Father   It wadna be less than 15 mile o' gate, and it was just to hear him sing the Fray o' Suport that we baith *gaed* into Liddisdale that time and *sent* for him. We had gotten the words of it from him before. That was the time too, that Sir Walter made one of his sketches of Hermitage Castle. It was taken from the side o' Earnton fell, and he stood all the time he took it to his knees in snow. But nothing then did him any harm.

JES How long did you stay in the Country when you went on these journeys?

Father Four or five days commonly, though I have seen it a week.

JES Then how did you occupy your time, for seeing Sir Wr. was saved the trouble of going about to collect the Ballads, you must have had a good deal on hand?

Father Oh, we rade about visiting the scenes o' remarkable occurrences, and *roved away amang the fouk* haill days at a time, for Sir Walter was very fond o' mixing wi' them, and by that means he became perfectly familiar wi' their character and the manners o' the Country . . .

JES How did you get the *Musick* of Jock o' the Side, and Dick o' the Cow?

Father From the laird o' Whithaugh—but I mind o' our ridin' away ae forenoon, may be 6 or 7 mile to auld Thomas o' Twizelhope (pronounced Couzelhope) who was a great hand for musick, for no other reason than to see gin I had the right *lilt* o' Dick o' the Cow, for Whithaugh wasna vera sure about it. Sae away we gaed to uncle Thamas, as he was called, and after finding that I had the genuine *lilt* o' the air, we had a gude snaiker o' whisky punch wi' him i' the forenoon, out o' a bit stroopit mug that he ca'ad *Wisdom*, and which he had for mair than 50 year. It *made* only tway or three spoonfuls o' spirits, I forget which. He used to say that naebody could get drunk out o' his wisdom, but he filled mae fouk fou wi' it, than ony other body i' the haill parish, for a' that. Oh, aye! that was a kind o' spree that we thocht naething o' . . .

JES Did Sir Walter keep a memorandum-book or take any notes, during your tours?

Father None that I ever saw. We had neither pens, nor ink, nor paper. But we had *knives* and they served the turn just as weel, for we took bits o' Cuttings wi' them, frae a broom Cowe, or an aller, or a hazel-bush, or whatever else might be at hand, and on thae bits o' stick (maybe tway or three inches lang they were) he made a variety o' notches, and these were the only memoranda I ever saw him take or have, of any of the memorable spots he wished to preserve the recollection of, or any tradition connected wi' them. And when he had notched them they were just slipt into our pockets, a' heads and thraws. When we cam hame frae some o' our trips, I hae seen us have a'maist haill wallets fu' o' them—wud aneuch to mend a mill as Burns says. I coudna think what he meant by this at first, and when I asked him what a' thae marked sticks were for, he said, 'these are my log-book, Bob!'

JES This is most amazing—and are you aware that he ever made after use of them?

Father Yes I can satisfy ye on that point too. For I was frequently wi' him at his father's house in Edinr. when he was preparing the Minstrelsy for publication, and I know, *for I saw it*, that as he went along he very often had recourse to *the notched sticks*. He had them a' hanging in their order above him, by a string alang the ceiling o' his room—(as you'll see Rhubarb in a gardener's house)—wi' mony mae o' the same kind about the Highlands . . . I never saw a pen in his hand nor a piece o' paper a' the times we were in Liddesdale the-gither, or in any other o' our Border rides, but twice, and that was when he took the two sketches that he made o' Hermitage Castle; and the one sheet o' paper he got frae Dr. Elliott, and the other frae Willie o' Millburn.

Without any doubt, Scott was the pioneer in seeing Border Ballads as a vital record, however distorted by time, chance and the individual singer, of the way of life of a definable region. Through his intimate knowledge of the Border, of Borderers and their history, of Border law and Border families, of witchcraft, superstition, and local legend and landscape, he brought to these songs an understanding and sensitiveness which still far outgoes that of the mere anthologist, the mere literary critic or the mere performer, essential though these may be to the life of the songs now that the communities from which they sprang no longer exist. He was followed by collectors of distinction and scholar-ship, like William Motherwell, whose *Minstrelsy Ancient and*

Modern first appeared in 1827 and who wrote there: 'It has become of the first importance to collect these songs with scrupulous and unshrinking fidelity . . . It will not do to indulge in idle speculations as to what they once may have been, and to recast them in what we may fancy were their original moulds.'[11]

During the nineteenth century such collections continued to be literary rather than musical; imitations, 'ballad-poems', became popular, and volumes of these, often embodying themes of parochial history, proliferated. The most scholarly collection of original ballads, however, a most impressive work of international scholarship, was *The English and Scottish Popular Ballads* edited by Francis James Child of Harvard between 1882 and 1898. It contains variant versions of 305 ballads, with copious notes, and I have used it, with Scott's *Minstrelsy*, as the main source of my material here. It has not yet been superseded.

In referring to Child ballads, I have followed his system of indicating variants: capitals (A, B, C etc.) denote versions obtained from different sources; lower case letters indicate minor variant forms within the former. Thus, he gives six versions of *Earl Brand*, A from Robert White, B from Scott etc; four variants of A are given as a, b, c, d.

Only towards the end of the period was the music extensively recorded, largely as a result of the scholarly enthusiasm of Cecil Sharp; but all our sensitive and sophisticated recording systems cannot draw from the air words and music which, for their originators, were so much more than mere songs. The true ballad communities of the Border died with the way of life which produced them. To quote Edwin Muir's *Complaint of the Dying Peasantry*,

> The singing and the harping fled
> Into the silent library,

where they remain now in B. H. Bronson's monumental volumes of *The Traditional Tunes of the Child Ballads*.

The following pages are an attempt to understand Borderers and the Border, up to the union of the crowns, through their ballads seen not merely as folksong, nor simply as poetry, but as a unique record of the life, in all its joy, superstition, savagery and grief, of a remote and precarious frontier community.

CHAPTER 1
THE BORDERS AND THE BALLADS

Falling steeply south-west from Berwick to the Solway Firth, the Scottish border crosses the map like a cartographic symbol of the wrangle and battle that left it unresolved for almost a millennium. Hadrian's Wall, uncompromising and unequivocal along the high ridges from Solway to Newcastle, was thirty miles shorter and territorially much simpler, but in the end it did not serve. The Wall was imposed, the true border grew, fought out and negotiated between 1018, when Malcolm of Scotland, victorious after the Battle of Carham, claimed the whole country north of the Tweed, and 1838 when the last local dispute was peacefully settled. Malcolm also held Cumberland and much of Westmorland, which did not become part of England until 1157, the first date of an uncertain line from Solway to Tweed.

From its eastern end at Marshal Meadows, just north of Berwick (which has been in England since its capture by Richard III in 1482), the border runs south to join the Tweed near Paxton; it follows the river by the ancient stronghold of Norham (whose description opens *Marmion*), past Wark ('Auld Wark upon the Tweed / Has been mony a man's dead') to Carham where it turns abruptly south to the Hanging Stone on Cheviot. From here it wriggles along the watershed of the Cheviot range between Roxburgh and Northumberland, crossing the heads of Redesdale (where Parcy Reed was murdered) and Tynedale to follow south-west the Kershope Burn and Liddel Water (Armstrong country) into the Debatable Land, whose name explains the historical twist the line endures west along the Scots Dyke to the River Sark, and thence to the Solway Firth at Sark Bridge, just south of Gretna.

Across this frontier, even today, only three main routes lead from England to Scotland: one in the eastern coastal plain joining Newcastle to Edinburgh; one in the centre leading to

Jedburgh over Carter Bar from Redesdale; one in the west running through the lowlands of Carlisle and Solway Moss.

I have described the border thus far, simply because it would be misleading to confuse a political boundary with The Borders which is the heart of this book. The Borders is not a line but an area, in many respects historically and traditionally almost an independent region, certainly so in the eyes of the inhabitants who gave us the Ballads. It exists within a rough rectangle with corners at Newcastle, Penrith, Dumfries and Edinburgh, concentrated in the wild open hills of Northumberland, Cumberland, Roxburgh and Selkirk. Here lived the Borderers: the Armstrongs, Telfers, Nobles, Graemes, Reeds, Halls, Rutherfords, Elliotts, Crosiers and the rest, whose names not only people the ballads but enrich business directories and school registers in the area today, and the ubiquitous ruins of whose dwellings evoke the memory of song and bloodshed which flourished there from the middle ages until well into the seventeenth century. These were Borderers before they were either Scots or English; their allegiance was first to the family, the Surname, not to the Crown; they would marry, or steal, or kill among their own countrymen as well as across the border. 'They are a people', wrote a harassed official in 1583, 'that will be Scottishe when they will, and Englishe at their pleasure.'[1] They lived apart.

The violence and intensity of life in the Borders, up to and beyond the union of the crowns, is implicit in the language of the region, its laws, administration and domestic architecture, as well as explicit in that complex, cryptic, fascinating and incomplete body of words and music, corrupt in text, unsure of provenance, subject to skilful forgery and romantic elaboration, that we inadequately refer to as Border Ballads. Twentieth-century comment on these songs has been so obsessed by scholarship in language, folklore and literary criticism that we are in danger of forgetting that the works are unique in their representation, however distorted by time and chance, of the way of life of a medieval-Elizabethan frontier community tenuously surviving in a world of poverty, violence and superstition, yet singing down the centuries their strange and melancholy tales of love and hate and longing, of thieving and killing, of jealousy, incest, witchcraft and revenge. The ballads, in the words of Edwin Muir, 'are almost the only Scottish dialect poetry extant in which the poet both thinks and feels in the dialect he uses. Scottish folk song is pure feeling; but the Ballads express a view of life which is essentially philosophic, though completely devoid of reflection.'[2]

We have lost much in seeing these ballads as literature, rather than hearing them as songs, and the censure of the Ettrick Shepherd's mother upon Scott has lost none of its sting: 'There was never ane o' my songs prentit till ye prentit them yoursel', and ye hae spoilt them a'togither. They were made for singin' an' no for readin', but ye hae broken the charm now, an' they'll never be sung mair.' The music of the ballads has been discussed and reproduced with scholarly enthusiasm and insight by B. H. Bronson; it is a complex and technical subject if one wishes to verbalise it rather than simply listen. I have contented myself, therefore, with providing a discography of current recordings in the hope that the present popularity will increase to such a degree that it will ultimately be impossible to think of the ballads primarily as poems, and that they will have been rescued, still alive, from the mortuary slabs of the school anthology.

My first concern here, however, is with the ballads as the products of a particular environment at a particular period of history. Let men more eloquent than I speak the prologue.

William Dunbar was a Lothian man, and in *The Twa Merrit Wemen and the Wedo* he has left us a sensitive and evocative picture of a summer dawn:

> The morow myld wes and meik, the mavis did sing,
> And all remuffit the myst, and the meid smellit;
> Silver schouris doune schuke as the schene cristall,
> And berdis schoutit in schaw with thair schill notis;
> The goldin glitterand gleme so gladit ther hertis,
> Thai maid a glorius gle amang the grene bewis.
> The soft sowch of the swyr and soune of the stremys,
> The sueit savour of the sward and singing of foulis,
> Myght confort ony creatur of the kyn of Adam,
> And kindill agane his curage, thocht it were cald sloknyt.

This could, of course, be almost anywhere, but there is a whisper of 'Border' in 'The soft sowch of the swyr'.

Almost a century later, in 1586, Camden writes that the western border:

> nourisheth a warlike kind of Men, who have been infamous for Robberies and Depredations; for they dwell upon *Solway Firth*, a foordable Arm of the Sea at Lowwaters through which they made many times outrodes into *England* for to fetch in Booties, and in which the inhabitants thereabout on both sides with pleasant Pastime and delightful sight on Horseback with spears hunt salmons whereof there is abundance.[3]

(Scott has a fine description of this salmon-spearing in *Redgauntlet*, Letter IV.)

An eighteenth-century Scot, Alexander Pennycuick, remained unimpressed by the Yarrow valley:

> This country is almost everywhere swelled with hills, which are, for the most part, green, grassy, and pleasant, except a ridge of bordering mountains, betwixt Minchmuir and Henderland, being black, craigie, and of a melancholy aspect, with deep and horrid precipices, a wearisome and comfortless piece of way for travellers.'[4]

The range he describes here runs east and west to the north of St Mary's Loch. Scott in the second Canto of *Marmion*, gives a very different view of the same landscape a century later, a landscape which has changed little since his time:

> Oft in my mind such thoughts awake,
> By lone St. Mary's silent lake;
> Thou know'st it well—nor fen nor sedge
> Pollute the pure lake's crystal edge;
> Abrupt and sheer, the mountains sink
> At once upon the level brink;
> And just a trace of silver sand
> Marks where the water meets the land.
> Far in the mirror, bright and blue
> Each hill's huge outline you may view;
> Shaggy with heath, but lonely bare,
> Nor tree, nor bush, nor brake is there,
> Save where, of land, yon slender line

Bears thwart the lake the scatter'd pine.
Yet even this nakedness has power,
And aids the feeling of the hour:
Nor thicket, dell, nor copse you spy
Where living thing concealed might lie;
Nor point, retiring, hides a dell
Where swain, or woodman lone, might dwell;
There's nothing left to fancy's guess,
You see that all is loneliness:
And silence aids—though the steep hills
Send to the lake a thousand rills;
In summer tide, so soft they weep;
The sound but lulls the ear asleep;
Your horse's hoof-tread sounds too rude,
So stilly is the solitude.

What, for Pennycuick, is merely wearisome and comfortless becomes for the Romantic the very scene whose 'nakedness has power / And aids the feeling of the hour'. External nature in the ballads has little philosophical significance; its appearance evokes neither Augustan horror nor Romantic introspection, yet its presence is never ignored, and one becomes aware in time of its power, sometimes as an isolating wilderness like Bewcastle Waste, sometimes as a source of simples for weal or woe, as at Carterhaugh, sometimes reflected in the landscapes of the next world in *Tam Lin* and *The Daemon Lover*.

Thomas Bewick, the engraver of Cherryburn on the Tyne, recalls in his memoirs how, during his childhood

The winter evenings were often spent in listening to the traditionary tales and songs, relating to men who had been eminent for their prowess and bravery in the border wars, and of others who had been esteemed for better and milder qualities, such as their having been good landlords, kind neighbours, and otherwise in every respect bold, independent and honest men. I used to be particularly affected with the warlike music, and with the songs relative to the former description of characters; but with the songs regarding the latter, a different kind of feeling was drawn forth, and I was greatly distressed, and often gave vent to it in tears.[5]

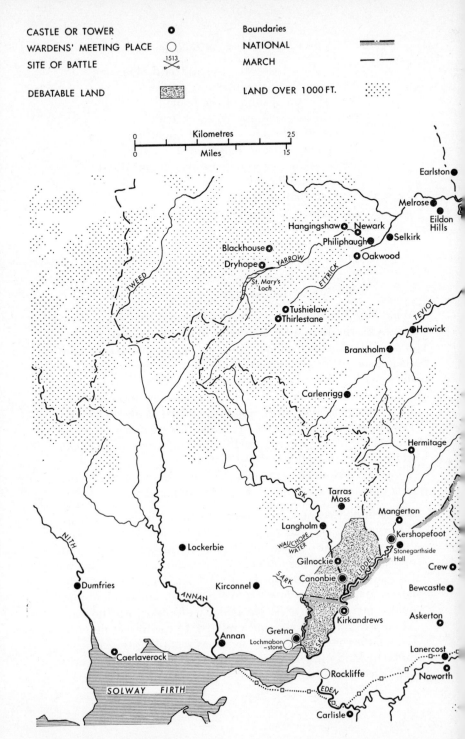

Map 1. The Borders

Later, in 1776, he made a journey through the Borders:

I had been, in this short tramp, particularly charmed with the Border scenery; the roads, in places, twined about the bottoms of the hills, which were beautifully green, like velvet, spotted over with white sheep, which grazed on their sides watched by the peaceful shepherd and his dog. I could not help depicturing in my mind the change which had taken place, and comparing it with the times of old that had passed away, and inwardly rejoicing at the happy reverse. It is horrid to contemplate the ferocious battles of that day, between men descended from the same stock, and bearing the same names on both sides of the Border, only divided from each other by a river, a rivulet, a burn or strip of ground—that they should have been, at the nod of their chieftains, called out to the wild foray by the slogan horn, or the shrill notes of the bugle; that they should have been led to meet and slaughter each other, to manure the ground with their blood, amidst the clash of arms and the thrilling music of the pipes, which helped to excite them on to close their eyes in death. These transactions, which are handed down to their descendants of the present generation in traditionary tales, and kept in remembrance by the songs and tunes of old times, serve now only as food for reflection or amusement.[6]

To move from the unsophisticated to the scholar, another distinguished Borderer will sum up the tale, perhaps over-romantically, with an eloquent comment on the people and their songs:

Like the Homeric Greeks, they were cruel, coarse savages, slaying each other as the beasts of the forest; and yet they were also poets who could express in the grand style the inexorable fate of the individual man and woman, the infinite pity for all the cruel things which they none the less perpetually inflicted upon one another. It was not one ballad-maker alone but the whole cut-throat population who felt this magnanimous sorrow, and the consoling charm of the highest poetry. A large body of popular ballads commemorated real incidents of this wild life, or adapted folklore stories to the places and conditions of the Border. The songs so constructed on both sides of the Cheviot Ridge were handed down by oral tradition among the shepherds, and among the farm girls who, for centuries, sang them to each other at the milking. If the people had not loved the songs, many of the best would have perished. The Border Ballads, for good and for evil, express this society and its quality of mind.[7]

History and ballad in the Borders emerge from the valleys, from the waters of Sark, Esk, Wauchope and Liddel flowing into the Solway; from Teviot, Ettrick and tragic Yarrow, tributaries of the Tweed; from Tynedale, Redesdale, and from Bewcastle Waste, west of the River Irthing. Here lived the names that occur so frequently in Border musters and in Border song; who fought and loved, built and burned, farmed and thieved regardless of patriotism or law, and whose animosities and intricate allegiances were only slowly resolved after James VI became James I and 'prohibited the name of *borders* any longer to be used, substituting in its place that of the *middle shires*. He ordered all the places of strength in these parts to be demolished except the habitations of noblemen and barons; their iron gates to be converted into plough-shares, and the inhabitants to betake themselves to agriculture, and the other works of peace.'[8]

Wild in terrain, sparsely populated, remote and difficult of access, the Borders in the Tudor period was not an attractive outpost for the administrator, and the correspondence of the English Wardens repeatedly reveals their anxiety, their sense of isolation and neglect, as they attempt to bring home to their superiors in the capital the true nature of life in the Border Marches. None of you, they seem to say, ever understand; routine letters and formal reports are punctuated explosively with personal outbursts against the disordered nature of the region and its tempestuous inhabitants, a condition in no way ameliorated by what they clearly see as parsimonious procrastination by civil servants living secure lives in metropolitan comfort.

In 1580 Norham and Wark, the two principal strongholds on the east Border were 'so greatly in ruyne and decay, as no man dare dwell in them, and if speedy remedy be not had, they will falle flatte to the ground'.[9] Delays in getting on with repairs result in higher costs,[10] ready money is lacking,[11] troops remain unpaid and discontented. At Christmas, 1597, the unpaid Berwick garrison must either sell their horses to the Scots 'or els knocke them on the headde for want of meat', and are like to have 'a brave Crismas, neither meat, nor drinke, nor money, nor good clothes'. On both sides it seems that there is too much talk, and too little action taken over 'the ruenous state of this beggerly border',[12] 'for this side do nothing but thus hold councils, every day altering'.[13]

Their grievances were real enough, yet to some extent the Wardens were deluded. By the end of the sixteenth century there was little chance of open warfare between the two countries, and the earlier near autonomy of the Wardens had been much reduced by the increasing centralisation of administration in London. The kind of Border exploit recorded in the ballads was of little international significance, and the office of Warden was being deliberately run down. It is from this situation that the uneasiness of the Wardens grows, and their reports consequently express a view of frontier life not wholly reliable.[14]

One of the most poignant cries concludes a lengthy and detailed report on the Border Riders made to Burghley by Thomas Musgrave, Captain of Bewcastle, at the end of 1583. The letter is an attempted explanation of his own condition, as well as an official communication, and ends:

> I my selfe have sene the Grames assayle my Lord Scrup being wardin and have put him and the gentlemen of the cuntrey in great perill, and manie of his companie hurte, yet never anie execucion done for it, but all remytted and forgeven, besydes manie other heighe crymes done, and never anie that lost his lyf for whatsoever they did. Hardly deare anie gentleman of the cuntrey be of any jury of lyfe and death yf anie of them be indyted, as the justices of that circuit can testefie, they are growne so to seke bloode, for they will make a quarrell for the death of their grandfather, and they will kyll any of the name they are in feade with. So I (my good lord), ame banyshed my cuntrey for feare of my lyfe, and from my place of service, where I have served this x yeres, and I doe but report my doinges to the gentlemen and trewe

people of the cuntrey, and my behavyour to my neighbours. And seeing my lord, I ame banished from my frendes and forst to stande on my gard in land of pease, havinge tyed my selfe to all the Queenes lawes which they dare not answer, my onely trust resteth in your honor to be my helpe, trustinge your lordship will pittie my estate and my olde fathers, and I shal be bounde daly to pray to God for your good health long lyfe and incresce of much honor.[15]

But another correspondent, John Fern, after parading before Burghley the required statistics, seizes on one of the most significant features of Border life and throws it like a knife into the middle of his report, where it sticks, vibrating: 'Deadly foed', he writes, 'the word of enmitye in the Borders, implacable without the blood and whole family distroied.'[16] The succinctness of his expression is a fair measure of the intensity of his feeling. Indeed, our attitude (as well as Burghley's) to Musgrave's plight in the above letter may well be qualified by the information that he and Scrope were at feud with the Grames. Here we reach one of the central motifs of the ballads. The feud relationship is assumed or implicit in many of these Border songs; natural enough in a society where it was endemic. In some tales, however, like *The Death of Parcy Reed*, it is made explicit, whether originally or from the zeal of an editorial hand it is impossible to say. Such lines as the following amply confirm the fears of Musgrave and his contemporaries that the law is ineffective:

> Now Parcy Reed has Crosier taen,
>   He has delivered him to the law;
> But Crosier says he'll do waur than that,
>   He'll make the tower o' Troughend fa.

> And Crosier says he will do waur,
>   He will do waur, if waur can be;
> He'll make the bairns a' fatherless,
>   And then, the land it may lie lee.

And a refrain later adds

> The Crosiers haud thee at a feud,
>   And they wad kill baith thee and me.

Such a condition arises from and is a clear indication of the importance to the Borders of family loyalties, and its place in their lives is well seen from the following passages:

There is in many dales, the chief are Tynedale and Reedsdale, a countrey that William the Conqueror did not subdue*, retaining to this day the ancient laws and customs, (according to the county of Kent), whereby the lands of the father is equally divided at his death amongst all his sonnes. These Highlanders are famous for thieving; they are all bred up and live by theft. They come down from these dales into the low countries, and carry away horses and cattell so cunningly, that it will be hard for any to get them or their cattell, except they be acquainted with some master thiefe, who, for some mony, (which they call saufey-mony), may help them to their stoln goods, or deceive them.

There is many every yeare brought in of them into the gaole of Newcastle, and at the assizes are condemned and hanged, sometimes twenty or thirty. They forfeit not their lands, (according to the tenure in gavelkind) the father to bough, the sonne to the plough.

The people of this countrey hath had one barbarous custome amongst them; if any two be displeased, they expect no lawe, but bang it out bravely, one and his kindred against the other and his; they will subject themselves to no justice, but in an inhumane and barbarous manner fight and kill one another; they run together in clangs [clans], as they terme it, or names.

This fighting they call their feides [feuds], or deadly feides, a word so barbarous that I cannot express it in any other tongue. Of late, since the union of both kingdoms, this heathenish bloody custom is repressed, and good laws made against such barbarous and unchristian misdemeanours and fightings.[17]

Throuch al the provinces of Scotland, quhilkes ar upon the bordouris foranent Ingland takes to thame selfes the grettest libertie and licence, quairthrouch thay reioyse that unpuniste ay thay chaipe. ffor quhen in tymes of weirs throuch invasione

* Northumberland, Cumberland, Westmorland and Durham were excluded from the Domesday Survey.

of ennimies daylie thay ar brocht til extreime povertie, in
tyme of peace, the ground albeit fertil anuich feiring that
schortlie the weiris oppresse thame, thay alutterlie contemne
to tile. quhairthrouch cumis to passe that be steiling and reif,
thay rayer seik thair meit, for fra scheding of blude thay
greitlie abhor; Nathir gyve thay mekle betwene, quhither the
Scottis or the Inglesmen, steil or reive or dryve away prayis
of horse, oxne and scheip behind baks. upon fleshe, milk, and
cheis, and sodne beir or orgmount, principallie thay lyve.
Thay have verie lytle use of breid, evin as thay have of gude
beir, amaist na wine, ჳe quhen baith ar present, thay ar
seine in nouther of thame to delyte mekle. Thair castelis and
palices ar scheiphouses and luges, quhilkes thay commonlie
cal pailes, of quhais burning thay ar nocht sair solist. Bot thay
far starker do make, four nuiked, of earth only quhilke nathir
can be burnte, nor without a gret force of men of weir, doune
can be castne, or without sum travel, with the sweit of thair
browis, thir ar thair pailes . . .
   . . . Bot I returne agane to our bordir men in quhome sum
things ar seine, nocht verie meikle nocht to thair prais,
sum things agane rare, sum things finalie mervellous. ffor
quhen thay spoyle behind backes al thair nychtbouris feildes,
thay intend thairby to seik thair leiving, nochtwith standeng
thay ar war with al possible diligens that thay sched nocht
thair blude quha ar in thair contrare. for thay ar persuadet
that all the gudes of al men in tyme of necessitie, be tha lawe
of nature, ar commoune to thame & uthiris: bot slauchtir and
sik iniures be the lawe of God forbidne. Bot gif thay commit
ony voluntarie slauchtir, to be maist in revenge of sum
iniure; and cheiflie for the slauchtir of sum cosing or freind to
sum man. fra quhilke thay wil nocht absteine, thoch the lawes
of the Realme commandet: quhairof ryses deidlie feid, nocht
of ane in ane, or few in few bot of thame ilk ane and al, quha
ar of that familie stock or tribe how ignorant sa evir thay be
of the iniure. This pest albeit it be commoune to the hail
Realme and a grevous calamitie, to thir nochtwithstanding it
is cheiflie proper.
   Lat this mairover be eiket to thair first vertue that quhomto
ance thay gyve thair faith thoch til ane ennimie it be, thay

keip it maist surelie, In sa far that quha ance brek his faith nathing is thocht mair ungracious than he. Bot gif ony amang thame be fund giltie of sik a crime he quha suffiris the iniure uses, or sum in his name, in a solemne conventioune, quhen present to mend and bind up al materis on baith the handes ar baith the warderis of the bordiris,—eftir this maner thay use, I say, to put a gluve upon the poynte of ane speir in exprobration and schame of him quha crakit his creddence, rydeng of sik a maner throuch al the people, schaweng it out, na infamie is compared to this, his companiouns wissis oft that God take him out of this lyfe be ane honest deith. Nathir have thay nochtwithstandeng, now vanelie fallin frome the faith of the Catholik Kirk, as mony uthiris have done. Thay delyt mekle in thair awne musick and harmonie in singing, quhilke of the actes of thair foirbearis thay have leired, or quhat thame selfes have invented of ane ingenious policie to dryve a pray and say thair prayeris. The policie of dryveng a pray thay think be sa leivesum and lawful to thame that nevir sa ferventlie thay say thair prayeris, and praythair Beides, quhilkes rosarie we cal, nor with sick solicitude and kair, as oft quhen thay have xl or l myles to dryve a pray . . .

finalie gif thay be takne, thay ar sa eloquent, & sa mony fair and sweit wordes thay can gyve, that thay move the Juges ᴣe and thair adversaries how seuir saevir thay be, gif nocht to pitie, at leist to woundir vehementlie.[18]

There can be no doubt of the importance of surnames in the Borders. Feudal landowners such as the Kers in Scotland and the Dacres in England form a significant political element, but as far as ballads are concerned it is the kinship groups that matter; lesser men in social dignity and political influence, but often great in power locally, widespread and complex in social loyalty and dispute. Such groups are the Armstrongs of Liddesdale on the Scots side, the Halls of Redesdale on the English. A report by Robert Bowes, 'lord Warden of all the thre marches of England for enempst Scotland' contains the following:

The countrie of Tyndale situate upon two waters one called northe Tyndale, the other southe Tyndale, the countrie of north Tindale which is more plenished with wilde and mis-

demeaned people may make of men upon horsebacke and
foote vj hundreth whereof commonlye there be aboute two
hundrethe able horsemen to ride with there keaper unto any
service into Scotland.

They stand most by surnames whereof the Charletons are
the cheife and in all services or chardge imposed upon that
countrye, the Charletons and suche as ar under ther rule be
rated for the one halffe of the countrye. The Robsons for a
quarter, and Dodds and Milburnes for an other quarter.

Of everye surname ther be sundrie famylies or traines as
they call them, of everye of which there be certen hedesmen,
yt [that] leadeth and answereth for all the rest, and doe laye
pledges for them when neade requireth, for good rule of the
countrie . . .[19]

Names are used, often intimately, in the formal accounts and
reports of the period, and evidence for allegiances and hostilities
is not hard to find.

In a letter to Walsingham dated May 1582, for example, John
Forster, Warden of the Middle March, wrote ('from my house
nigh Alnwicke'), 'I have had nothing worthy to write,—the
estate of the Borders standinge so tyckelye and daungerous as yt
nowe dothe, and of late there is great feedes and slaughters risen
among the surnames of the Borders of Scotland, which cawseth
greate disobedience there.'[20]

In July 1583 we find 'A note of the gentlemen and surnames
in the Marches of England and Scotland'.

EAST MARCHES.—England; gentlemen—Forsters, Selbies,
Graies, Strowders, Swiners, Mustians. Surnames.—John-
sons, Vardes, Ourdes, Wallisses, Stories, Armestronges,
Dunnes, Flukes. Scotland; gentlemen—Humes, Trotters,
Bromfeilds, Dixons, Craws, Crinstons.

WEST MARCHES.—England; gentlemen—Musgraves, Loders,
Curwenes, Sawfelde. Surnames.—Graemes, Rutlitches,
Armestrongs, Fosters, Nixons, Tailors, Stores. Scotland;
Maxwells, Johnsons, Urwins, Grames, Bells, Carlills,
Battison, Litles, Carrudders.

MIDDLE MARCHES. — England; gentlemen — Ogeles,
Fenickes, Hernes, Withringtons, Medfords, Shafters,

C

Ridleis, Carnobies. Surnames;—Ridesdale—Halls, Hedleys, Andersons, Potts, Reades, Dunnes, Milburnes. Tindale—Charletons, Dodds, Milbornes, Robsons, Yaroes, Stapletons. Scotland; gentlemen—East Tividale—Carrs, Yongs, Pringles, Burnes, Davisons, Gillcries, Tattes. Lidesdale—Rudderfords, Carrs, Dowglasses, Trombles, S(c)ottes, Piles, Robsons, Halls, Olivers, Ladlers, Armestrongs, Elwoods, Nixons, Crosers, Turners, Fosters.

We shall become further acquainted with a number of these in the chapters that follow, particularly in the West and Middle Marches. One practical difficulty does arise, however: with such a limited number of names, how does one distinguish individuals of one extensive family who bear the same Christian name? The Borderer's answer was the common solution of the small community or family: the nick-name, or to-name, deriving from parentage, dwelling, or (often cruelly) from physical deformity or mutilation.

To-names indicating parentage are still the most familiar form of distinction in closely-knit communities; in the Borders we find *Nellies Johne, Mungoes Arthur, Sandies Rinyons Archie, Paties Geordies Johnie*. All are harmless, neutral forms; mere signs. Close to these in tone and accuracy, with some humour, come the names involving personal features: *Jock of the long brand, Wyde hoise, Bony buttis, John with the one hand. John with the jak* occurs after the union of the crowns, when the Borderers were not permitted to wear 'jaks', jackets made of two layers of strong canvas, or of a quilted material with small metal plates enclosed. Less reputably we find *George Elliott alias buggerbacke, Arche Ellott called dog pyntle, Hob Ellott of the Staneshelle alias bane prycke*.

Names tied to places of residence cover significantly a much wider area: *Sandy of Rowaneburne, Jock o' the Side*. The map of 1590 (frontispiece) records several, including *Archie of Whithaughe, Kinmonts Tower, Ffrancie of Canobie*, and *John of Copshaws*. Sometimes dwellings are used in place of proper names, as in *Jamie Telfer*:

> Warn Gaudilands and Allanhaugh,
> And Gilmanscleugh and Commonside.

Occasionally, the names are unashamedly offensive or reproach-ful: *David na gud priest, Curst Eckie, Evilwillit Sandie, Flie the Gaist Scabbit*; others possess an almost narrative power of suggestion: *Dand the man, David the lady, Unhappy Anthone, Ill-drowned George, Fire the brais, Ower the moss.* R. B. Arm-strong gives an extensive list of the politer forms.

They are indigenous, an accepted part of the language of the country, and especially common in the Riding Ballads. They give a curiously intimate character to the recurrent bills of complaint enrolled before the warden clerk by all those who wished to seek redress for loss sustained in a Border incident.

Complaint Michaell Wanles of Stewardsheiles in Ryddes-dale, upon Arche Elwet of the Hill, James Elwet his brother, younge John Elwet of the Parke, Hob Elwet of the Parke, sonne to James, Jock Elwet of the Parke, son to Scots Hob, Martyne Elwet of the Hewghouse called Red Martyne, and their complices to the number of ane hundred persons, for that they came to Eleshawe and there reft, stale and took away lxxx kye and oxen, vj horses and meares and howsehold stuf, to the value of xl^{li} sterlinge, a slew dog, and then murdered and slewe Roger Wanles and John Wanles, the xxjth of August 1852. Whereof he does ask redres.[21]

Compleyenes Bartrame Mylburne of the Keyme, Gynkyne Hunter of the Waterhead in Tyndale, upon William Arme-stronge of Kinmowthe, Ecky Armestronge of the Gyngles, Thome Armestronge of the Gyngles, Thomas Armestronge called Androwes Thome, of the Gyngles, Johne Forster sone to Meikle Rowie of Genehawghe, George Armestronge, called Renyens Geordie, and his sons of Arcleton in Ewesdale, and there complices, for that thay and others to the nomber of thre hundrethe parsons in warlyke maner ranne one opyn forrowe in the daye tyme, on Frydaie in the mornynge last, being the xxxth of August, in Tyndale unto certen places that is to say the Keyme, the Reidhewghe, the Black Myddynes, the Hillhowse, the Waterhead, the Starr head, the Bog head, the High feelde, and ther raysed fyer and brunte the most pairte of them, and maisterfullie refte, stale and drove awaye fowre hundrethe kyen and oxen, fowre hundrethe sheip, and

goate, xxx horses and mears, and the spoyle and insyght of
the howses to the walewe of towe hundrethe pounds, and
slewe and murdered crewellie six parsons, and maymed and
hurte ellevin parsons, and tooke and led away xxx presoners,
and them do deteigne and keip in warlyke maner, myndinge
to ransom them contrarie the vertewe of trewes and Lawes of
the Marches. Whereof they aske redres.[22]

For the most part, the Borderers were farmers, though this
side of their lives lends itself less to spectacular commemoration
in history and ballad than their more violent exploits. But the
land produced barely enough to sustain its people, and the
position deteriorated towards the end of the sixteenth century,
when, in the changing pattern of English agriculture, pastoral
farming was more profitable to the landowner than arable.
Sheep were reared for wool and mutton, and food production in
the Borders was inevitably affected. At the end of the sixteenth
century the situation was aggravated by the ravages of the
Scots, as in Leslie's description, and by the systematic destruction of crops harvested by the thieves of the Scottish marches,
an operation undertaken by Scottish government forces to
deprive the malefactors of food during the winter months.[23] In a
letter to Burghley in May 1597, the Dean of Durham writes:

> The decay of tillage in this country and in Northumberland
> is very great and dangerous. In the bishopric within these 20
> years there are said to be laid down above 500 ploughs,
> whereon dwelt and lived many an able man with wife,
> children, and servants . . . these are now converted to a few
> private men's benefit, the poor are multiplied, and hospitality,
> which was much regarded, greatly decayed. If corn were not
> in this dearth supplied both here and elsewhere from foreign
> nations—many thousands who might have it growing at their
> own doors would perish for bread.[24]

In 1582 one Clement Reed of Elsdon made his will, at the end of
which appears the following inventory:

> An ENVITORI of the gudys of clement red prased be jhon
> red of trowen and roger red of the hoold tovn. fyrst vj oxson
> pris iiij povnd Item vj ky pris iiij povnd Item iiij stotys pris

xl[s] Item iiij ky pris iiij mark Item iiij yong novt pris xxxvj[s]. viij[d]. Item inseth gere x[s].[25]

The list is a melancholy corrective to romanticised accounts of Border raids; 'insight gear' or the entire household goods of Clement Reed amount to only ten shillings, about half the price of a cow. Since the insight valuation here is so slight, it suggests an honest assessment, and further arouses the suspicion that the values recorded in the bills of complaint just quoted, are exaggerated in the hope of profit to the complainers. Such attempts at gain are hardly surprising when one considers the prevailing poverty. As late as 1662 John Ray, travelling in East Lothian, observed that 'the ordinary country houses are pitiful cots, built of stone, and covered with turves, having in them but one room, many of them no chimneys, the windows very small holes, and not glazed'.[26]

In quiet times, the Borderers bred mainly horses, cattle and sheep, practising what is now called transhumance, as Camden records in 1600:

> Here every way round about is the *wasts* as they tearme them, as also in Giliesland, you may see as it were the ancient *Nomades*, a martiall kind of men, who frome the moneth of Aprill unto August, lye out scattering and summering (as they tearme it) with their cattell in little cottages here and there which they call *Sheales* and *Shealings*.

In place-names this word usually appears as *shiel*, *shield*, or, in Cumberland and Westmorland, *scale*. An interesting comment is made in Johnson and Goodwin's *Survey* of 1604 where we find that in Redesdale 'each man knoweth his sheilding steed, and they sheylde together by surnames'. Indeed it was probably in such a hut that Hobbie Noble slept, at Foulbogshiel, the night before his capture. The word 'shield' is sometimes equivocally used of any hut or dwelling, as it is perhaps in the following letter from Lord Eure to Cecil on 29 April 1597—one of a series complaining of the vicious and murderous cruelty of Buccleuch:

> My opposite the laird of Baclughe has revived with cruel revenge, his malicious 'feede' against the Queen's subjects of Tindale—'the conceived greife growing upon the taking of his

father prisoner in former tyme by them' . . . and now the last on the 17th where he himselfe was an actor, murdered, burned and drowned almost 30 persons, and burned the 'fayrest houses of the ordinarie yeoman men within Tindaile', to the number of 3 or 4, with 20 out houses attached. This barbarous cruelty and ancient enmity to the English, has prevented these poor people from venturing to their 'sheilding' for fear of their lives, without some help which I humbly beg your honor to procure by her Majesty's pleasure from the garrison of Berwick. For they fly from their winter dwellings 5 or 6 miles into the country, so that the March lies waste and uninhabited, through the 'unchristianlie usage' of this officer in time of peace. Carlisle. Ra. Eure.

And he adds a laconic postscript, which cannot really have been an afterthought to the worried Warden, so familiar is its theme: 'The number of 100 foot would do much good for Tindayle sheild'.[27]

A further entry in the Papers, perhaps by Sir Robert Carey, throws an interesting light on the annual cycle. Border thieves, he says,

will never lightly steale hard before Lammas [1 Aug.], for feare of the assises, but beeing once past, they returne to their former trade: and unless in such yeares as they cannot ride upon the wastes by reason of stormes and snowes, the last moneths in the yeare are theyr cheife time of stealing: for then are the nightes longest, theyr horse hard at meate, and will ride best, cattell strong, and will drive furthest: after Candlemas [2 Feb.] the nightes grow shorter, all cattell grow weaker, and oates growing dearer, they feed their horses worst, and quickly turne them to grasse.[28]

Though some shielings were turf-built, many were of dry-stone with walls about two feet thick, rectangular, varying in length from seventeen to forty-one feet and in width from less than nine feet to twenty-five feet; they were about eight feet high to the roof ridge. No doubt they were used sometimes as permanent dwellings, but they are not typical. Apart from the houses of the very poor ('such', wrote Andrew Boorde, 'as a man may build in three or four hours'), probably of wood thatched with straw or heather, the principal forms of Border domestic architecture are the closely related bastle, pele and tower-house, though the names can be confusing since they are differently, and inconsistently, applied on each side of the border. Of course the region had its magnificent castles: Alnwick, the Percy fortress, and Bamburgh, the spectacular and legendary Joyous Gard, both survive; Dunstanburgh has been a vast, haunting ruin since the fifteenth century, Norham since the sixteenth, and Berwick, allowed to decay after James I's accession, was ignominiously blown up in 1843 to make room for a railway station. In the English West March, Carlisle and Naworth stand. To the north, Caerlaverock in Dumfriesshire is an impressive, elegant shell, but little remains of Roxburgh, once the most powerful of Border holds, razed in 1460; in East Lothian, Dirleton and Tantallon stand nobly in their ruin. But these are not characteristic of the Ballad country, and exist mainly in those areas which are relatively easy of access by land or sea, and likely to be involved in large scale military activity. The dwellings of the ballads are the bastles, peles and tower-houses built largely along the valley folds of the Middle and West Marches where they supply still a grim punctuation to most Border prospects. Some towers, like Kirkandrews on the Esk, and the former vicarage at Elsdon in Redesdale, are still inhabited; many English bastles remain in use as farm buildings, but most towers, in spite of their formidable strength, have decayed, pillaged for stone, and stand in farmyards or on open pasture and fell, clung about with moss and turf and lichen like giant tombs. And yet . . . something endures in the stones, and the memory is rich:

> While Johnie lived on the Border Syde,
> Nane of them durst come near his hauld!

The English bastle was essentially a defensible farmhouse consisting of two floors, where the family lived above and the animals sheltered below (see diagram and Plates 1, 2 and 3). Originally, there appears to have been no access to the first floor from the outside, only by ladder or steps through a trap from the ground floor. The distribution south of the border is significant, all the surviving examples being within twenty

PLATES 1-8

1, 2. HOLE BASTLE AND BASEMENT On the River Rede near Bellingham, Northumberland. An English example of a simple fortified dwelling. It measures 32×20 ft with walls 4 ft thick. The barrel vault of the ground floor contains a ladder-hole which would provide the normal means of communication between the two levels. The external stone stairway is probably a later refinement introduced when security was not a prime consideration.

3. MELKRIDGE TURRET The bastle stood two miles east of Haltwhistle in Northumberland but was demolished about 1954. It measured 38×24 ft with walls 4 ft thick. The watch turret is more elaborate than usual in such a small building.

4. MERVINSLAW TOWER Stands in the remote valley of the Peel Burn, a tributary of the Jed Water in Roxburghshire. A very simple 'stone-house' or 'pele-house', 25×21 ft with walls 4 ft thick. It consists of two storeys and a garret, with neither vaulting nor fire-places.

5. GREENKNOWE TOWER Near Gordon, Berwickshire. A good example of a tower developed on domestic rather than on merely military or defensive lines. It is L-shaped in plan, with 4 ft walls; the larger wing is 24×15 ft, the smaller 15 ft wide and projecting 10 ft eastwards. The entrance has a fine example of an iron 'yett'. The vaulted basement is a kitchen, not a byre, and the whole building more generously and elegantly conceived, with windows and fire-places, than is common in earlier towers. It dates from 1581.

6. SMAILHOLM TOWER A romantic impression by J. M. W. Turner, made on a visit with Scott in 1831. The early sixteenth-century tower is still roofed, though hollow within, and well preserved, standing on a rocky outcrop near Kelso. It measures 39 ft 9 ins $\times$ 32 ft with walls averaging 7 ft in thickness, and has five storeys. The parapet-walk has a watchman's seat with a recess for his lantern, and looks across to Hume Castle, about five mile away in Berwickshire.

7. ELSDON TOWER A vicar's pele in the former capital of Redes-dale, the tower was built by the Umfraville family, whose arms it still bears, in the fourteenth century. It was used as a vicarage from the early fifteenth century until 1962. It has a vaulted basement with walls over 8 ft thick, and measures overall about 30×20 ft.

8. EDLINGHAM CHURCH A Norman building near Alnwick, Northumberland. The tower is early fourteenth-century and probably was used for a 'lock-up' as well as for defence. In a field to the east are the remains of a fine fourteenth-century tower house.

1, 2. Hole Bastle (*left*) and Basement

3. (*above*) Melkridge Turret   4. Mervinslaw Tower

6. Smailholm Tower

5. Greenknowe Tower

7. (*above*) Elsdon Tower   8. Edlingham Church

miles of the border line, with the southernmost limit of distribution running closely parallel to it. This perhaps accords with Acts of 1555 and 1584 which specified twenty miles as the distance from the border within which castles and forts were to be put in order, and open ground enclosed with ditches and quickset hedges to impede the movements of raiders. The dimensions of these strongholds are roughly 35 feet by 25 feet,

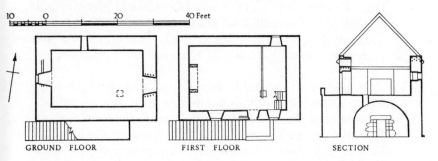

GROUND FLOOR   FIRST FLOOR   SECTION

with walls about four feet thick built of large blocks of stone; their position, distribution and construction clearly identify them as defensive dwelling houses, a basic necessity in such an unsettled society, though their use would be restricted to the small farmer and some of his stock. In Scotland, the bastle was the least substantial form of refuge, similar to the stone-house, pele-house or pyle, small, gable-ended and lower than a tower; some interesting examples survive, such as Mervinslaw on the Jed Water (Plate 4). These were built only in the absence of the stronger tower-house, the classic type of laird's dwelling throughout the sixteenth century, varying in style from the austere vertical fortress like Smailholm to the larger L-shaped houses with pretensions to elegance as well as strength, like Greenknowe (Plate 5); they were used for the protection of tenants as well as to house the family. In the Records of the Parliament of Scotland, 1535, occurs the following entry:

FFOR BIGGING OF STRENGTHIS ON THE
BORDOURIS
Item it is statut and ordanit for saiffing of men thare gudis and gere upon the bordouris in tyme of were and all uther trublous tyme that every landit man duelland in the inland or

upoun the bordouris havand thare ane hundreth pund land of
new extent sall big ane sufficient barnikyn apoun his heretage
and landis in the place maist convenient of stane and lyme
contenand thre score futis of the square ane eln thik and vi
elnys heicht for the resset and defenss of him his tennentis and
thair gudis in trublous tyme with ane toure in the samin for
himself gif he thinkis it expedient. And that all uther landit
men of smaller rent and revenew big pelis and gret strenghis
as thai pless for saiffing of thare selfis men—tennentis and
gudis. And that all the saidis strenthis barnikynnis and pelis
be biggit and completit within twa zeris under ye pane.[29]

This kind of stronghold dwelling developed throughout the
Borders, and to the south, in Northumberland, it persisted long
after the rest of England had changed over to the more comfort-
able manor house. The survey of 1541 describes the Tynedale
peles as: 'very stronge houses whereof for the most parte the
utter sydes or walles be made of greatt sware [square] oke trees
strongly bounde & Joyned together with great tenons of the
same so thycke mortressed [morticed] that yt wylbe very harde
withoute greatt force & laboure to breake or caste downe any of
the said houses the tymber as well of the said walles as rooffes be
so greatt & covered most parte with turves & earthe that they
wyll not easyly burne or be sett on fyere'. This wooden structure,
however, appears to have been generally superseded by the kind
of stone tower described above. The *barmkin* described here too,
a defensive enclosure about sixty feet square with walls a yard
thick and eighteen feet high, appears as an independent refuge,
but commonly it was attached to the tower itself. A Border
tower is normally rectangular, measuring about thirty feet by
forty feet and rising to about fifty feet, usually with battlements
of more or less elaboration. As a rule, the ground floor is tunnel
vaulted, with a spiral staircase in one corner leading to the two,
or even three, upper storeys. As in the English bastle, the
vaulted ground floor was used for beast and storage, the upper
floors as the family dwelling, with the top floor internally as a
last refuge for women and children during the fighting, externally
equipped for defence within the crenellations, and having at one
corner a bartizan, a kind of crow's nest for the look-out, to

which was attached a fire-pan filled with pine roots and peat: 'Every man that hath a castle or a towre of stone shall, upon everie fray raysed in the night, give warning to the countrie by fire in the topps of the castle or towre in such sort as he shall be directed from his warning castle, upon paine of 3s 4d.' (An order issued in 1570 by the Earl of Sussex, Lord President of the Council of the North, to Wardens of the East, and Middle Marches of England.)[30] The walls are of immense thickness for a relatively small building, varying between five and ten feet.

One of the most severe and interesting is Smailholm Tower (Plate 6). Here at Sandyknowe, his grandfather's farm, Scott spent some of the most impressionable weeks of his early childhood, and here, even so early, seems to have begun that intimacy with Border lore and history which thirty years later gave us the *Minstrelsy*. He recalls the experience in *Marmion*:

> And still I thought that shattered tower
> The mightiest work of human power,
> And marvelled as the aged hind
> With some strange tale bewitched my mind,
> Of forayers who, with headlong force,
> Down from that strength had spurr'd their horse,
> Their southern rapine to renew,
> Far in the distant Cheviots blue;
> And home returning fill'd the hall
> With revel, wassel-rout, and brawl.
> Methought that still with trump and clang
> The gateway's broken arches rang;
> Methought grim features, seam'd with scars,
> Glared through the window's rusty bars,
> And ever, by the winter hearth,
> Old tales I heard of woe or mirth,
> Of lovers' slights, of ladies' charms,
> Of witches' spells, of warriors' arms;
> Of patriot battles, won of old
> By Wallace wight and Bruce the bold.

Sixty feet high, empty, stone-roofed and gaunt, the tower still dominates the landscape, offering from its narrow parapet what is probably the finest view in the Borders.

Perhaps they were not always so mournful as their ruins suggest. Did the stones of Hangingshaw, between Yarrow and Selkirk, ever correspond to the picture in *The Outlaw Murray*?

> There's a feir castelle, bigged wi' lyme and stane;
>   O! gin it stand not pleasauntlie!
> In the forefront o' that castelle feir,
>   Twa unicorns are bra' to see;
> There's the picture of a knight, and a ladye bright,
> And the grene hollin abune their brie.

It is doubtful. The tower-house was the product of a society at once politically unstable and economically straitened; in its compromise between the claims of domestic comfort and those of defence it admits neither civil embellishment nor military sophistication, and its dark, vertically disposed units give little encouragement to cheerful conjecture. Even when we look through the eyes of one of the original occupants we see a pride in strength rather than in beauty: Sir Richard Maitland writes of his own tower of Lennoxlove, in East Lothian:

> Thy tour and fortres, lairge and lang
> Thy neighbours does excell;
> And for thy wallis thick and strang,
> Thou graitly beirs the bell.
> Thy groundis deep, and topis hie,
> Uprising in the air,
> Thy vaultis pleasing are to sie,
> They are so greit and fair.

Some of the vicarages and church towers in Northumberland and Cumberland were also built for purposes of defence, or refuge. Embleton, Shilbottle and Elsdon (Plate 7) have fine vicar's peles, still in use, while Edlingham (Plate 8) near Alnwick is a dramatic example of a fortified church. Tomlinson quotes from a survey of Longhoughton parish made in 1567: 'The chirche and steple of this towne is the great strenth that the poore tenants have to drawe to in the tyme of warre, wherefor it were neadfoull the same be, for that and other causes, kepit in good reparations.'[31]

Our primary interest as far as Border Ballads are concerned is with the environment rather than with military activities, but the following passage from an account of Somerset's expedition to Scotland in 1547 is not without its relevance in demonstrating the attack and defence of one of these strongholds.

In the way we should go, a mile and a half from Dunglas northward, there were two Piles or Holds, Thornton and Anderwick [*Innerwick*] set both on craggy foundation, and divided a stone's cast asunder, by a deep gut, wherein ran a little river. Thornton belonged to the Lord Home, and was kept then by one Tom Trotter. Whereunto, my Lord's Grace over night, for summons, sent Somerset, his Herald. Towards whom four or five of this captain's prickers with their gads ready charged, did right hastily direct their course: but Trotter both honestly defended the herald, and sharply rebuked his men; and said, for the summons, 'he would come speak with my Lorde's Grace himself'. Notwithstanding he came not, but straight locked up a sixteen poor soldiers like the soldiers of Dunglas, fast within the house, took the keys with him, and commanding them they should defend the house and tarry within (as they could not get out) till his return, which should be on the morrow, with munition and relief, he with his prickers pricked quite his ways.

Anderwick pertained to the Lord of Hamilton, and was kept by his son and heir, (whom by custom they call the Master of Hamilton,) and eight more with him; gentlemen for the most part, we heard say. My Lord's Grace, at his coming nigh, sent unto both these Piles; which, upon summons, refusing to render, were straight assailed; Thornton by a battery of four of our great pieces of ordinance, and certain of Sir Peter Mewtys's hackbutters to watch the loopholes and windows on all sides, and Anderwick by a sort [*company*] of these hackbutters alone. Who so well bestirred themselves, that when these keepers had rammed up their outer doors, cloyed and stopt up their stairs within, and kept themselves aloft for defence of their house about the battlements, the hackbutters got in and fired the underneath, whereby being greatly troubled with smoke and smother, and brought in desperation of defence, they called pitifully over their walls, to my Lord's Grace, for mercy; who, notwithstanding their

great obstinacy, and the ensample others of the enemy might
have had by their punishment, of his noble generositie, and by
these words making half excuse for them, 'Men may sometimes do that hastily in a gere [*business*] whereof, after, they
may soon repent them', did take them to grace, and therefore
sent one straight to them. But, ere the messenger came, the
hackbutters had got up to them, and killed eight of them
aloft. One leapt over the walls, and, running more than a
furlong after, was slain without, in a water. All this while, at
Thornton, our assault and their defence was stoutly continued:
but well perceiving how on the one side they were battered,
mined at the other, kept in with the hackbutters round about,
and some of our men within also occupying all the house under
them, for they had likewise shopped [*shut*] up themselves in
the highest of their house, and so to do nothing, inward or
outward, neither by shooting of base [*small cannon*], whereof
they had but one or two, nor tumbling of stones, the things of
their chief annoyance, whereby they might be able any while
to resist our power or save themselves; they plucked in a
banner that afore they had set out in defiance and put out
over the walls, a white linen clout tied on a stick's end, crying
all with one tune, for 'Mercy!' but having answer by the whole
voice of the assailers, 'They were traitors! It was too late!'
they plucked in their stick and sticked up the banner of
defiance again, shot off, hurled stones, and did what else they
could, with great courage on their side, and little hurt of ours.
Yet then, after, being assured by our earnesty that we had
vowed the winning of their hold before our departure, and
then that their obstinacy could deserve no less than death,
they plucked in their banner once again, and cried upon
'Mercy!' And being generally answered, 'Nay, nay! Look
never for it, for ye are arrant traitors!' then made they
petition that 'If they should needs die, yet that my Lord's
Grace would be so good to them as they might be hanged,
whereby they might somewhat reconcile themselves to GOD,
and not to die in malice, with so great danger of their souls!'
A policy surely in my mind, though but of gross heads, yet of a
fine device. Sir Miles Partridge being nigh about this Pile at
that time, and spying one in a red doublet, did guess he

should be an Englishman; and therefore, they rather came and furthered this petition to my Lord's Grace. Which then took effect. They came and humbled themselves to his Grace: whereupon, without more hurt, they were but commanded to the Provost Marshal.

It is somewhat here to consider, I know not whether the destiny or hap of man's life. The more worthy men, the less offenders, and more in the Judge's grace, were slain; and the beggars, the obstinate rebels, that deserved nought but cruelty, were saved.

To say on now, the house was soon after so blown with powder, that more than one half fell straight down to rubbish and dust, the rest stood all to be shaken with rifts and chinks. Anderwick was burned, and all the houses of office [*servants' rooms*] and stacks of corn about them both.[32]

This is one kind of fighting, but the Scots had a traditional approach to confrontations with the 'auld enemy', austerely presented by King Robert in the fourteenth century (see Fordun's *Scotichronicon*):

> On fut suld be all Scottis weire
> Be hyll and mosse thaimself to weire:
> Lat wod for wallis be, bow and speir
> That innymeis do thaim na dreire;
> In strait places gar keip all stoire,
> And byrnen the planer land them before;
> Thanen sall thai pass away in haist,
> Quhen that they find nothing but waist.
> With wyllis and waykenen of the nicht,
> And mekill noyes maid on hicht.
> Thanen sall they turnen with great affrai,
> As thai were chasit with swerd awai.
> This is the counsall and intent
> Of gud king Robert's testament.

The plea for holy dying in Patten's account is interesting. Religion in the Borders during the sixteenth century was scantly observed; and little wonder. For centuries the great Border abbeys at Kelso, Melrose, Dryburgh and Jedburgh had survived repeated sackings by Danes and English. But Henry VIII had them irreparably pillaged and burnt, a process completed by Hertford in 1545, about which he wrote from Kelso to the royal vandal with inhuman complacency. He has resolved to raze and deface the house of Kelso, so as

> the enemye shall have lytill commoditie of the same, and to remain encamped here for five or six days, and in the meane seasone to devaste and burne all the country hereabouts as farre as we maye with our horsemen. As to-morrowe we intend to send a good bande of horsemen to Melrose and Dryburghe to burne the same, and all the cornes and villages in their waye, and so daylie to do some exploytes here in the Mershe, and at the end of the said 5 or 6 dayes to remove our campe, and to marche to Jedworthe to burne the same, and thus to marche through a great part of Tyvydale, to overthrow their piles and stone houses, and to burne their cornes and villages.[33]

In many parishes, according to Tough, especially in Northumberland, the vicars had to serve from two to five chapels, and some of the parish churches had no vicars at all, but were served by vagabond Scots exiles. Indeed, a tradition exists that it was once the custom in the Scottish Border to leave the right hand of male children unchristened, so that it might deliver more unhallowed blows upon the enemy:

> At the sacred font, the priest
> Through ages left the master-hand unblest,
> To urge with keener aim the blood-encrusted spear.
> (Leyden, *Ode on Visiting Flodden*)

Borderers were slow to accept the reformed religion, as Sir William Bowes wrote to Burghley from Newcastle in November 1595:

> True religion hath taken verie little place, not by the unwillingness of the people to heare, but by want of meanes, scant three able preachers being to be found in the whole country. False and disloyall religion hath taken deipe roote, and that in the best howses, increasing daily by the number

and diligence of the semynaries, with more libertie resorting hither, being driven from other places of both the realmes.[34]

Lord Eure, Warden of the Middle March, wrote to the Queen in April of the following year to report on the poor state of affairs there: 'Another most grievous decay is "want of knowledge of God" whereby the better sort forget oath and duty, let malefactors go against evidence, and favour "a parte" belonging to them or their friends. The churches mostly reuined to the ground, ministers and preachers "comforthles to com and remaine where such heathenish people are", so there are neither teachers nor taught.'[35] He writes to Burghley on September 1 of the same year that the parson of Simonburn has left, and suggests that a Mr Crackenthorpe, his chaplain and tutor of his son, should fill the vacancy, 'for the better instruct of the people, who standeth in greate need thereof'. But the task apparently proved too burdensome for Crackenthorpe, 'master of Arte in Oxenforde', since on October 24 Eure writes again asking that the living be given to Mr George Warwick, because Mr Crackenthorpe 'haithe made refusall thereof, deaminge his body unable to live in so troublesome a place, and his nature not well brooking the perverse nature of so crooked a people'.[36]

Wherever we look, at farming, architecture or Church, the same picture forms of a turbulent, unregenerate race on both sides of the borderline, and it is hardly surprising that religion figures little in the ballads; so little, in fact, that when we do meet with it we suspect the intervention of some later moralising hand, as in *Dick o' the Cow*. But the church did not sleep. On 28 October 1525, Thomas Magnus wrote from Edinburgh to Cardinal Wolsey; priest and diplomat, Magnus acted as Henry VIII's agent in Scotland with the status but, for political reasons, not the title of ambassador:

> The Kingges high pleasure and youres I shall folowe, as it shall or may lye in my little power; advertissing your Grace I send unto youe also the copy of a terrible cursing, whiche, by the autorite of your gracious writing adressed to the Archebusshop of Glasco, I have procured to be executed in every notable place upon the Bordours of Scotland.

The curse follows, in Latin and Scots. After bewailing the

violence on the Borders, and specially mentioning areas 'sic as
Tevidale, Esdale, Liddisdale, Ewisdale, Nedisdale, and Annan-
derdaill', he goes on:

And thairfor my said Lord Archbischop of Glasgw hes
thocht expedient to strike thame with the terribill swerd of
Halykirk, quhilk thai may nocht lang endur and resist; and
hes chargeit me or ony uther chapellane to denunce, declair,
and proclame thaim oppinly and generalie cursit, at this
market croce, and all utheris public places. Heirfor throw the
auctorite of Almighty God the Fader of Hevin, his Son our
Salviour Jhesu Crist, and of the Haly gaist; throw the
auctorite of the Blissit Virgin Sanct Mary and [here a list of
all the saints, angels, prophets etc. etc.] I denunce proclamis
and declaris all and sundry the commitaris of the said saikles
murthuris, slauchteris, birnyng, heirschippis, reiffis, thiftis,
spulezeis, oppinly apon day licht and under silence of the
nicht . . . generalie cursit, waryit, aggregeite, and reaggregeite,
with the greit cursing. I curse thair heid and all ye hairis of
thair heid; I curse thair face, thair ene, thair mouth, thair
neise, thair toung, thair teith, thair crag, thair schulderis,
thair breist, thair hert, thair stomok, thair wame, thair armes,
thair legges, thair handis, thair feit, and everilk part of their
body fra the top of thair heid to the soill of their feit, befoir
and behind, within and without. I curse thaim gangand, I
curse thame rydand; I curse thaim standand, I curse thaim
sittand; I curse thaim etand, I curse thaim drinkand; I curse
thaim walkand, I curse thaim slepand; . . . I curse thaim within the house, I curse thaim without the house; I curse thair
wiffis, thair barnis, and thair servandis participant with thaim
in thair deides . . . All the malesouns and waresouns that ever
gat worlie creatur sen the begynnyng of the warlde to this
hour, mot licht upon thaim. [Here follows wishes for afflictions
similar to those that lit upon Lucifer, Adam, Cain, Noah,
Sodom and Gomorrah, Babylon, etc. etc. The victims are
deprived of all Christian company and rights.] . . . And finaly
I condempn thaim perpetualie to the deip pit of Hell to re-
mane with Lucifer and all his fallowis, and thair bodeis to
the gallowis of the Burrow Mure, first to be hangit, syne revin

and ruggit with doggis, swyne, and utheris wyld beistis, abhominable to all the warld. And, as thir candillis gangs fra zour sicht, sa mot thair saulis gang fra the visage of God, and thair gude fame fra the warld, quhill thair forbeir thair oppin synnys forsaidis, and rise fra this terribill cursing, and mak satisfaction and penaunce.[37]

Scott (of course) realistically assesses the situation: 'Upon the religion of the Borders there can very little be said. We have already noticed that they remained attached to the Roman Catholic faith rather longer than the rest of Scotland. This probably arose from a total indifference upon the subject.'[38] Ecclesiastical malediction, especially from places as remote as Glasgow, seventy miles from Selkirk, had, one imagines, little effect on everyday life, and indeed it is not difficult to accumulate evidence which indicates the ineffectiveness of the Church in restraining the Borderers in their excesses. Three years after his excommunication, for instance, Simon Armstrong, laird of Whitaugh ('Sym the larde') boasted to the English Warden of how he and his followers had destroyed thirty parish churches. So raiding, fray and feud continued while the civil authorities and government representatives did what they could to check the incessant 'murtheris, slauchteris, birnyng, heirschippis, reiffis, thiftis and spulzeis'.

One can be in no doubt, after all this, that the Borders were a matter of some governmental concern. It was easy for family feuds to develop into political conflicts between the nations; it was equally easy for troops to be outwitted by hostile Borderers of either realm in a region where local knowledge of both family and terrain was indispensable to the success of any project. Both governments enlisted the help of the Border chiefs and their followers to protect the frontier, and by the sixteenth century an intricate system of Border administration had evolved, based largely on the appointment of the leaders of powerful feudal families as Wardens, responsible to the Crown, of three districts or Marches, East, Middle and West, on each side of the frontier.

In both countries, the East March is of least interest to a reading of the ballads, and the reason is clear when one looks at the map. North-east Northumberland and south-east Scotland are low-lying, easily traversed by armies, and accessible by sea. Here the logistical problems are least difficult, policing easier, and consequently military architecture more prominent than bastle or pele. G. M. Trevelyan calls it 'the spacious Thermopylae of the war between the two great Kingdoms, studded with famous castles—Etal, Wark, Norham; and famous battlefields —Homildon Hill and Flodden'. Activity in this area is dominated for centuries by the fortunes of the military garrison at Berwick.

The English Middle March comprised most of the rest of Northumberland south-west of a line running roughly from Cheviot through Alnwick, though no precise boundaries existed. Its most unruly regions were North Tynedale and Redesdale, from where important passes opened into Scotland.

The West March centres on Carlisle. Again, it is cut by a main route to Scotland, and was the scene of much military movement, but the land was less easy to traverse than that of the East March, partly because of the morasses of Solway Moss, partly because of the Debatable Land, a tract of country between the Rivers Esk and Sark whose nationality was not officially established until 1552. It was a small but troublesome place, about ten miles by four, stretching roughly from Gretna to Langholm, with Canonbie in the middle, and is first called Debatable in a truce document of 1450. It had been the custom for both Scots and English to pasture cattle on the land, but as soon as any building was set up a battle over ownership began. Naturally, the area attracted fugitives, criminals and outlaws of all kinds, and this to such a degree that in 1551 the Wardens of both countries issued a proclamation: 'All Englishmen and Scottishmen, after this proclamation made, are and shall be free to rob, burn, spoil, slay, murder and destroy all and every such person or persons, their bodies, buildings, goods and cattle as do remain or shall inhabit upon any part of the said Debatable land, without any redress to be made for same.'[39] However, in 1552, as an alternative to the first proposal that the district 'should be wholly evacuated and laid waste', the land was divided between the kingdoms by an earth rampart called the Scots Dyke, though the old name lingered. The rescuers of Kinmont Willie, it may be remembered, 'cross'd the Bateable Land' on their way to Carlisle.

Wardens of the English Marches were drawn from a few powerful families, such as Dacre and Scroope in the West, Percy, Bowes, Eure and Forster in the Middle, Carey in the East. Family influence and pride did not always make for smooth administration, but such considerations were even more important in Scotland where, in the three Marches, family power and local leadership were more influential than across the border. Fewer names appear in the lists of Wardens, Home dominating in the East, Ker in the Middle, and Maxwells in the West. Technically, Liddesdale was part of the Scottish Middle March, but its remoteness and the extreme lawlessness of its inhabitants, chiefly Armstrongs, led to the appointment of a Keeper for that district alone. Sir Walter Scott of Buccleuch (or Branxholme) held this office from 1550 to 1552, and again from 1594 to 1603; it was he who led the attack on Carlisle Castle, held by Scroope, to rescue Kinmont Willie in 1596. We find Scroope too in *Dick o' the Cow* and *Hughie the Graeme*.

From time to time Commissioners were appointed by the Crown to examine Border affairs and make recommendations for their regulation. The administration of the Border evolved partly out of such recommendations, partly through international treaty, partly from tradition and custom. In balancing these three factors, the Warden needed both an astute mind, local support and an integrity equal to most of the problems of moral judgment which came his way, especially where expediency, family feeling or personal ambition conflicted with national policies. A keen governmental eye was indeed kept on these custodians, as a letter to Sir John Forster, Warden of the English Middle March, testifies:

20 Aug. 1595. We doubt not but it is too well known to you that pitiful complaints of the outrages in the Bishopric of Durham have been laid before her Majesty, and that if better order be not speedily taken by you as her Warden there, her Majesty must of very necessity make choice of some other to have that place which you of so long time have held. And though it may be presumed that by reason of your great

years and infirmity you are not able in person to follow and prosecute the recovery of justice by frequent keeping of the truce days, or by personal prosecution of the offenders; yet as you have sundry officers under you and gentlemen of good value for service, who might under your direction preserve the Queen's subjects from outrage, we require your speedy answer what may be done by you herein: for this misgovernment can no longer be suffered, and her Majesty will continue you as her officer no longer than you can repress these disorders by Border-Law.[40]

It is a neat and realistic letter for those who still believe that Border life was romantic, and court life a charade. 'For blood', Nicolson reminds Cecil in 1598, 'there must be some course.'

The Warden and his deputies, Captains, Land Serjeants, frequently appear in the ballads, where their problems in the administration of Border Law are mainly concerned with theft and the recovery of stolen goods (e.g. *Jamie Telfer, The Lochmaben Harper*), the treatment of fugitives, outlaws, banished men (*Hobbie Noble*) and the organisation and supervision of days of truce (*The Raid of the Reidswire*). The formalisation of unwritten tradition and custom appears to have been first undertaken at a meeting in 1249 of twelve English and twelve Scottish knights, presided over by the Sheriffs of Northumberland, Berwick, Roxburgh and Edinburgh, 'for to know the lawis and the customs of the marchis'. They devised thirteen statutes, of which the eighth typifies the mode of procedure before Wardens Courts were created, justice being done through oaths and combat:

If any Scots thief shall have stolen a horse in England, or oxen, or cows or anything else and leads the same away into Scotland the owner, in whatsoever place he finds his gear, shall recover it in the Court of the Feudal Lordship where he has found his gear.

And this he shall recover in the aforesaid Court by the oath of six men—his own making the seventh—unless it chance that he who retains the gear says it is his own, in which case a contest may issue on the Marches.[41]

Later, the Wardens were given considerable powers to administer the laws, and the laws themselves made more elaborate while they continued to allow for traditional methods:

And if any inhabitant within eyther realme have there goddes stolen or spoild they may lawfullye followe there goddes either with a sleuthe hounde the trodde thereof, or ells by such other meanes as they best can devise, so that when they shall entre the opposite realme they come to a house and desire some honest person of these marches into which they followe there goods, to accompany them in the pursuite of the same, and to testifye with them that they did not minde or intende to doe any unlawfull acte within that realme but onlye to serche and inquear for his own goddes taken or spoyled, declaring ther the certentie and nombre of his saide goddes lackinge.[42]

A treaty of 1563 confirms the legality of the 'Hot Trod', or immediate pursuit of stolen goods over the border: 'permitting to Pairties greved to follow thair lauthfull *Trode with Hund and Horne, wyth How and Cry* and all uthir accustomed manner of fresche Persute for Recoverie of thair Goodes spoilzeit.'[43]

This was allowed up to the union of the crowns, together with 'cold trod', or pursuit within six days of the offence. The victim could also appeal for justice to a Warden of the opposite kingdom. If a Warden pursued fugitives or thieves across the border, he was not only granted safe conduct, but allowed to recruit help, having given notice of his quest to the 'first town he cometh by or the first Person he meeteth with'. Other than this, the Warden's Raid such as opens *Jamie Telfer* was forbidden in 1596.

One of the most important features in Border legislation was the Border Meeting, two kinds of which Bowes distinguishes in a letter to Burghley in 1598: '1st. Ordinary, between the wardens or deputies for common justice, 2nd. The other, the more solemn, as between commissioners sent for leagues, treaties of peace, or misconduct of wardens.' Our concern is with the first of these, the Warden's Meeting, or Day of Truce, which was held at a point on the border agreed between the Wardens; Forster wrote in 1598: 'Sometime I went to him into Scotland, sometime

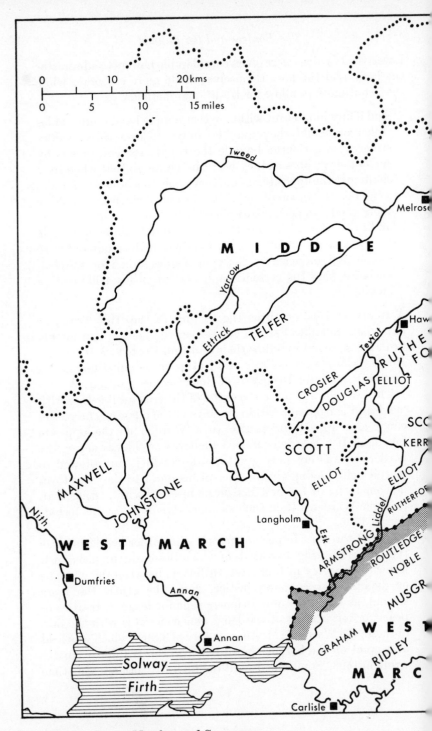

Map 2. Border Marches and Surnames

hee to me as the convenience of the place served: in winter if the weather served not, sometime I sent my deputy to Yatam, sometime he sent to Kirkneuton, ther to determine of causes.'[44]

The procedures at such 'Days of March', at least on paper, were formal and complex, devised and elaborated over the years for the mutual redress of grievances between the subjects of both kingdoms. Usually the formalities were observed, though, as *The Raid of the Reidswire* records, such meetings could conclude in mutual recrimination and affray; it was after such an occasion too that 'the fause Sa'kelde', Scroope's deputy in the West March, pursued Kinmont Willie across the border and captured him, in defiance of one of the March Laws which stated that the truce should last 'fra the hour of their meeting (for samonie persons as thay have in cumpanie for that time) to the nixt morning of the sone rising', though apart from this it had been a successful meeting.

It will have become clear from the foregoing pages that an appreciation of the ballads in their environmental and historical context is, linguistically, not a simple matter of glossing dialect words by their English equivalent: *know* for *ken*, *much* for *muckle*, *bear* for *drie*. Such problems are easily overcome, possibly without enlightenment; their solution is of too general a nature, and does not further our understanding of the words and phrases peculiar to Border life for which no direct English equivalent exists. Most of these terms arise from conflict, reprisal and Border Law, their significance frequently taken for granted in the ballads, the tacit acknowledgement of common experience and a common tongue in singer and audience.

For example, on the alarm being given of an imminent raid, the owner of the tower under attack would follow a routine whose general nature seems fairly clear. Beast near enough to the building he would drive into the barmkin, perhaps even into the tunnel-vaulted basement, and secure as far as possible. The women and children of his family, as well as those of dependants, would take refuge on the top floor within the battlements round which their men would be stationed, having lit the beacon in their bartizan fire-pan at the first sign of danger, and in some cases tolled a bell. These were not only distress signals; they were a summons to more powerful families to whom the victim of the raid had paid *black mail,* or protection money, to honour their bond. This is a significant motif in, for example, *Jamie Telfer,* where we see that such agreements were not always fulfilled; indeed the practice was often ruthlessly dishonoured, with distressing, impoverishing consequences, as Sir Richard Maitland makes dramatically clear in his *Complaynt* (see Chapter 2). Nicolson and Burn point out that 'Black maile seems to have been commonly paid in cattle, as white maile was paid in silver, vulgarly (but improperly) styled *quit rent'.*[45] The arrangement was common in the Borders, but became so corrupt as to be condemned by the Wardens and ultimately made a felony.

On the alarm being given by fire, bell or rider, it was the duty of neighbours, whether they were in the protection ring or not, to *follow the fray,* that is, to rise in arms and either help to repel the assault or to pursue the *reivers* and retrieve the stolen goods. Failure in this was a serious offence:

> whosoever hydes fra the Fray, or turns again so long as the Beaken burns, or the Bell rings, shall be holden as Partakers to the enemies, and used as Traitors to the Head Burgh of the Shyre, upon the Court day, and thereafter intimation made in the Parish Kirk, and published on ane Sunday, in presence of the People, and fra thenceforth to be used as a fugitive and disobedient person.[46]

When Sir John Forster was under censure for incompetence in the 1590s, he was accused of just such an offence in a letter from Eure to Burghley:

> On Tuesday, 28th December 27 horse whose headsmen and leaders were Sir Robert Kerr's servants, spoiled the Earl of Northumberland's tenants in Ruggley 'hard by Alnewicke'. They were above two hours in the town, the fray came to Alnwick at 7 p.m., the bell was rung and the fray continued till 10, as I am credibly informed. Yet though there were numbers of strangers in Sir John Forster's house that night, and 30 horse in his stable, as Mr. Fenwick of Wallington tells me—Captains Carvell and Twiford with 100 men on their way to Lord Scrope—none rose to aid the town or follow the fray, but 2 men of Sir William Reade's, and one of Mr. Beadnell's,

who meeting one of the poor men 'in his shirt naked', running there for aid, told him to complain, or they would find means to let your lordship know.[47]

But the raid was not always a parochial, family affair. Heights such as Penrith's Beacon Hill indicate an ambitious marauding distance, though major Scottish incursions penetrated as far south even as Ripon and Skipton in Yorkshire. Large or small, these ridings, especially at night, would require of the leaders a consummate knowledge of the country, its drove roads, passes, friendly and hostile townships, and corruptible men; moreover, as border fords and hill tops on the known thieves' routes were watched night and day, both scouting and pathfinding would have to be undertaken with some skill, as we see in *Hobbie Noble*.

It is obvious that the man of strong family and loyal allies would be least vulnerable as well as most effective in defence; whereas *broken men*, those who had so far declined in outlawry as to have no responsible chief, were every man's prey. They had no one to stand surety for their good conduct and often became outlawed by both nations, denizens of the Debatable Land. Ultimately, even the Armstrongs were reduced to a broken clan.

Raiders and reivers travelled light and moved fast; leader and led, mounted, clothed and armed alike would wear a reinforced coat or *jak*, with a steel cap, and carry a spear. Firearms were rare. Muster rolls typically read like this extract from Esdale Ward, Cumberland, 1580/81:

In jackes and steale cotes	lx^{c}xxij (?)
In steale capes	ccclij
In spears or lances	dccxv
In bowes	lxxiij
In gunes	one

or from Allerdale, Cumberland: 'In this township go able men; 20 furnished with steel coats or jacks and caps, bows and arrows or bills—40 with only a bill or lance staff, the rest with nothing.'[48]

After the fighting, the silence; slow smoke rising from the charred wooden huts where women searched for their men among the debris:

> I took his body on my back,
> And whiles I gaed, and whiles I sat;
> I digg'd a grave, and laid him in,
> And happ'd him with the sod sae green.

Then the process of rehabilitation would begin, with a formal complaint to the Warden describing the raid and the losses in *gear* and *insight* (possessions, and contents of the house), like these made to Burghley against Buccleuch for attempts on the West March of England:

August

Leonard Corbett of the Orchard howses, upon Arche Ellot of the Hill, his 2 brothers, Arche 'doge pintle', and his 2 brothers, for 12 kye, 2 nags, burning 4 houses and 100l. sterling insight.

8 Sept.

The wife of Andrew Routledge *alias* Leatche, in Bewcastle, upon the Armstrongs of Whittleye for wilful murder of her said husband.

Aug. 1

Richard and William Armstrong etc., the Queen's tenants in Gilsland, upon said Watt of Harden, young Whithaugh, John and Gib Ellot sons to Martine with 400 men 'arrayed in most warlike manner', running a day foray, taking 300 kye and oxen, 20 horses etc., burning 20 houses, taking and burning gold money 'apperrell' etc., worth 400l., and mutilating many of them.[49]

And so to the Warden's Meeting 'for common justice'; but no legislation can undo bereavement or mutilation, no romantic colouring hide the hideous reality of the 'Lockerbie Lick' (a gashed face, the phrase arising from the Johnstones' slaughter of the Maxwells in Lockerbie after the Battle of Dryffe Sands), or complaints like 'all maymed and hurt in perill of death, whereof one hath his legs cut of'.[50] Too often one finds 'and no redress' at the end of it all.

But the ballads rise above even this; they are frequently regretful, often melancholy, never self-pitying, as we shall see in turning from the bald, though evocative, statements of the

Wardens to the songs of the people, whose combining of landscape, love and violence is perhaps nowhere more succinctly or poignantly expressed than in an ancient Scottish prophecy:

> A Raven shall comme ouer the moore,
>   And after him a Crowe shalle flee
> To seeke the moore, without(en) rest
>   After a crosse is made of stane
> Ouer hill & dale, bothe easte & weste;
>   Bot wiete wele, Thomas, he sall find nane.
> He sall lyghte, whare the crose solde bee
>   And holde his nebbe vp to the skye;
> And drynke of gentill blode and free;
>   Thane ladys waylowaye sall crye.[51]

CHAPTER 2
BALLADS OF THE WEST MARCHES

Of all the ballads, none are more informed with the spirit of place and character than the Riding Ballads, the tales of reiving, treachery, foray and rescue raid which record memorably, if decoratively, some of the more lurid episodes of life in the Borders before the union of the crowns. With the distinguished exception of *Jamie Telfer of the Fair Dodhead*, they derive mainly from the Scottish West March; from the country northeast of the Solway Firth, where the action is played out in the wilderness of the Tarras Moss and the Debatable Land, and along the waters of Esk, Sark, Wauchope, Liddel and Hermitage. (Though administratively, Liddesdale above Kershopefoot was not part of the West March, in ballad terms it is difficult to separate.) On both sides of the border, Liddesdale was a name of terror in the marches, and the vivid impression of its significance given by the sixteenth-century Scots judge, Sir Richard Maitland, is well confirmed by history and ballad. His *Complaynt Aganis the Theivis of Liddisdail* is a rare example of contemporary literary comment on Border violence by one who had no small part in the legislation which attempted to bring order to the land. This is the version which Scott gives in his *Minstrelsy*: 'From Pinkerton's edition, collated with a MS of Maitland's Poems, in the Library of Edinburgh College.'

> Of Liddisdail the commoun theifis
> Sa peartlie steillis now and reifis,
> That nane may keip
> Horse, nolt, nor scheip,
> Nor yett dar sleip
> For their mischeifis.
>
> Thay plainly throw the country rydis,
> I trow the mekil devil thame gydis!
> Quhair they onsett,

Ay in thair gaitt,
Thair is na yet
Nor dor, thame bydis.

Thay leif rich nocht, quhair ever thay ga;
Their can na thing be hid them fra;
For gif men wald
Thair housis hald,
Than wax they bald,
To burne and slay.

Thay theifis have neirhand herreit hail,
Ettricke forest and Lawderdail;
Now are they gane,
In Lawthiane;
And spairis nane
That they will waill.

Thay landis ar with stouth sa socht,
To extreame povertye ar broucht,
Thay wicked scrowis
Has laid the plowis,
That nane or few is
That are left oucht.

Bot commoun taking of blak mail,
Thay that had flesche, and breid and aill,
Now are sae wrakit,
Made bair and nakit,
Fane to be slakit
With watter caill.

Thay theifis that steillis and tursis hame,
Ilk ane of them has ane to-name;
Will of the Lawis,
Hab of the Schawis:
To make bair wawis
Thay think na schame.

Thay spuilye puir men of their pakis,
Thay leif them nocht on bed nor-bakis
Baith hen and cok,

With reil and rok,
The Lairdis Jok,
All with him takis.

Thay leif not spindell, spoone, nor speit;
Bed, boster, blanket, sark, nor scheit;
Johne of the Parke
Ryps kist and ark;
For all sic wark
He is richt meit.

He is weil kend, John of the Syde;
A greater theif did never ryde.
He never tyris
For to brek byris;
Ouir muir and myris
Ouir guide ane gyde.

Thair is ane, callet Clement's Hob,
Fra ilk puir wyfe reifis the wob,
And all the lave,
Quhatever they haife,
The devil recaive
Thairfor his gob.

To sic grit stouth quha eir wal trow it,
Bot gif some great man it allowit?
Rycht sair I trew,
Thocht it be rew;
Thair is sa few
That dar avow it.

Of sum great men they have sic gait,
That redy are thame to debait,
And will up weir
Thair stolen geir;
That nane dare steir
Thame air nor late

Quhat causis theifis us ourgang,
Bot want of justice us amang?
Nane takis cair,

Thocht all for fear;
Na man will spair
Now to do wrang.

Of stouth thocht now thay come gude speid,
That nother of men nor God has dreid;
Yet, or I dee,
Sum sall thame sie,
Hing on a tree
Quhill thay be deid—
            Quo' Sir R. M. *of* Lethington, *knicht.*

Son of Sir William Maitland of Lethington, who was killed at Flodden, the 'auld laird' was essentially feudal in his outlook. 'Patriot rather than partisan', writes Henderson,

> he regarded political and religious questions mainly from the standpoint of an administrator of the law. Throughout the political and religious commotions of his time . . . he kept so aloof from party disputes that he continued in his office of judge whichever party was in power; and having, in the words of James VI, served the king's 'grandsire, goodsire, goodame, mother, and himself', was permitted, when he resigned his judgeship in July 1584, to enjoy, by special favour, its emoluments during the remainder of his life.[1]

He died in 1586 at the age of 90. Considering his character and background, one may reasonably doubt John Speirs' view that there is in this poem 'a certain glee in the rhythms which suggests a partial identification of the old judge with the thieves'.[2]

Many of the names Maitland mentions will turn up again in the following pages, particularly that of Armstrong.[3] This family dominated the West March in both England and Scotland during the greater part of the sixteenth century, operating where they pleased from their strongholds along the Liddel and Esk waters, and carrying on an unremitting guerrilla warfare against the Establishment in Carlisle. Evidence of the conflict is not far to seek, and the excitement underlying the following letter from the Warden of the English West March is as understandable as the occasion for it is uncommon. Scrope writes to Walsingham in January 1583-4, concerning the capture of Armstrong of Mangerton:

> This man is the chief and principal of his surname and also the special evildoer and procurer of the spoils of this March . . . His taking is greatly wondered at here, for it was never heard of that a laird of Mangerton was taken in his own house either in peace or war without the hurt or loss of a man. Now I have him, I trust it will be to good effect and keep the others quiet.[4]

He was, however, the following September, to seek reinforcements of 100 horsemen against the Scots, 'Specially Kynmont his sonnes and complices'.

Veitch quotes a manuscript Tract addressed to Lord Burghley, of 1590: 'In Lyddesdale the chief surnames are Armestrongs and Elwoods (Elliots). The chiefe Armstrong is of Mangerton, and the chiefe Elwoode at Cariston. These are two great surnames, and most offensive to England at this daie, for the Armestronges, both of Annerdale and Lyddesdale, be ever ryding.'[5]

Three of the most striking of the West March ballads tell closely similar tales of raid, capture and rescue, all of them in one way or another involving the Armstrongs: *Jock o' the Side*, *Archie of Ca'field*, and *Kinmont Willie*. Child prints four versions of *Jock o' the Side*; I have taken as my text the one which appears in Scott's *Minstrelsy*.

There is some evidence for the existence of John of the Side, apart from Maitland's commemorative stanza; R. B. Armstrong prints two bonds in which John Armstrong of the Syde is a party, dated 1562 and 1563.[6] He also appears, or at least the name appears, first about 1550 in a list of marauders against whom complaint was made to the Bishop of Carlisle 'presently after' queen Mary Stuart's departure for France. 'Syid' is marked on Blaeu's map of Liddesdale opposite Mangerton, but is unmentioned in the map of Liddesdale of 1590 (frontispiece). The place is noticed in an account quoted by Scott of an episode in which Jock o' the Side helps the Earl of Westmorland to escape after his rebellion with the Earl of Northumberland in 1560: 'the earls being gone, the Lady of Northumberland was left there on foot, at John of the Side's house, a cottage not to be compared to many a dog-kennel in England.'[7]

The ballad begins with a vigorous introduction of event and personality upon which the narrative is to develop:

> Now Liddesdale has ridden a raid,
>> But I wat they had better hae staid at hame;
> For Michael o' Winfield he is dead,
>> And Jock o' the Side is prisoner ta'en.
>
> For Mangerton house Lady Downie has gane,
>> Her coats she has kilted up to her knee;
> And down the water wi' speed she rins,
>> While tears in spaits fa' fast frae her e'e.

The energy of the opening stanza seems at a first reading to be generated by simple means; by abruptness of statement, and by an economy of expression which excludes almost all adjectival and adverbial qualification. But the lines have at the same time a more complex organisation which avoids the danger of dullness inherent in simplicity; here, the line structure contains a tension which counterpoints the rhythmical speed with some strain. Essentially, this derives from the enclosing of two passive phrases by two active ones:

> . . . ridden a raid
> . . . staid at hame
> . . . he is dead
> . . . prisoner ta'en.

The second word, too, as Maitland's poem indicates, would be heavy with significance for its original audience, place names to them being often a matter of life or death, rather than simply the means of generalised literary evocation such as a more literate people is used to. The power of place in Border Ballads is very different from what is exerted in Marlowe or Milton.

By the end of the second stanza, not only has the location (and therefore the Surname involved) been clearly established (Mangerton is about three miles below the confluence of the Hermitage and Liddel waters), but also the narrative mode common to so many of these songs. The appeal for help is there too, implying the response, the gathering, and the ensuing rescue foray (like *Kinmont Willie, Jamie Telfer*), all in accordance with Border lore and loyalties.

More representative techniques follow, sustaining the urgency as the narrative details are developed:

> Then up and spoke our gude auld lord—
> 'What news, what news, sister Downie, to me?'
>   'Bad news, bad news, my Lord Mangerton;
>   Michael is killed and they hae ta'en my son Johnie.'

The laird responds by choosing three men to send as a rescue party, and promising to sacrifice all he owns before he sees Johnie die. The three men chosen are called by the usual to-names (see above p. 24): the Laird's Jock, the Laird's Wat (i.e. sons of the Laird of Mangerton) and Hobbie (Halbert) Noble, of whom we shall hear a good deal more. ('Lards Jockes' is marked on the 1590 map. He, too, is remembered by Maitland, while Hobbie has a ballad to himself.) For the next seven stanzas the narrative is concerned with the scheme for the three men to penetrate deep into enemy territory by disguising themselves as corn dealers. From Mangerton to Newcastle where Jock is imprisoned is about fifty miles as the crow flies. As in *Archie o' Ca'field* they have their horses shod in reverse. When they reach Chollerford, on the North Tyne, they cut trees down to help them over the town walls of Newcastle (over twenty miles distant), but when they arrive, they find them too short and decide to force the gates. (In Spottiswoode's account of Kinmont Willie the ladders are too short and they adopt the same tactics; in the ballad, the ladders are used.)

It is at this point that they kill their first man. What has, since the opening stanzas, been a lively and apparently harmless adventure (we are, after all, detached from the killing of Michael o' Winfield), now reveals its seriousness in characteristic Border fashion; ruthless, direct, unsentimental yet unhorrific. The porter at the gate opposes them:

> His neck in twa the Armstrangs wrang;
>   Wi' fute or hand he ne'er play'd pa!
> His life and his keys at anes they hae ta'en
>   And cast the body ahind the wa'.

(A similar episode occurs in *Kinmont Willie* where Buccleuch, coming to rescue Willie,

> . . . has ta'en the watchman by the throat,
> He flung him down upon the lead—
> 'Had there not been peace between our land,
> Upon the other side thou hadst gaed!'

But in contrast to the incident in *Jock o' the Side*, we see Buccleuch here, the responsible official, seeking to avoid slaughter. He throws his watchman, stunned, on to the roofleads of his turret, not, dead, over the castle wall.)

The men ride off after the rescue, all tension gone, realistically exchanging relaxed banter over the still shackled ex-prisoner:

> 'O, Jock, sae winsomely's ye ride
> Wi' baith your feet upon ae side;
> Sae weel ye're harneist, and sae trig,
> In troth ye sit like ony bride!'

The four return in a storm and reaching Chollerford again are confronted with the North Tyne in flood. The crossing of water is a recurrent motif in the ballads, often, as here, a crossing to freedom, but also a test of courage, loyalty, steadfastness of purpose:

> Then out and spoke the Laird's saft Wat,
> The greatest coward in the cumpanie;
> 'Now halt, now halt! we need na try't;
> The day is come we a' maun die!'
> 'Puir faint-hearted thief!' cried the Laird's ain Jock,
> There'll nae man die but him that's fie.'

A similar incident occurs in the companion ballad, *Archie o' Ca'field*. In Scott's version of this, when the party have to cross the swollen Annan Water, the laird, 'coarse Ca'field' suggests jettisoning the prisoner to save their own lives, and is rebuked:

> 'Shame fa' you and your lands baith!
> Wad ye e'en your lands to your born billy?'

Jock's rescuers safely reach the other bank and, as in the other two ballads, cock a snook at their pursuers who, though 'A' English lads baith stout and true', see the impossibility of crossing and so resign their prisoner; but they ask for the fetters back, and are refused. The tale ends with Jock, freed of his shackles, by his own fireside.

The mixture in this ballad of violence, humour, narrative and dialogue is such that each element modifies the others to provide a balance in the whole which allows (in a manner characteristic of this form of literature, though not always so well achieved) each to make its mark without tedium, sentimentality, or a self-indulgent lingering over bloodshed and brutality.

In the main, the narrative of *Archie o' Ca'field* is very close to that of *Jock o' the Side*, the Halls of Calfield playing the part of the Armstrongs in the latter ballad. Calfield is near the Wauchope Water, about two miles west of Langholm, but it appears that in the sixteenth century it was a stronghold of the Armstrongs. Scott identifies it with Calfhill which occurs in the following document:

A breviate of the bills of England fouled at Berwick upon the Westmarches of Scotland, by the commissioners according to the indenture.

Jan. 1582. Thomas Rootledge of Todholes, and his neighbours complain upon Kynmont Jock, Eckie of Stubholme, Jock of Calfhill, and their complices 40 kine and oxen, 20 sheep and gaite, a horse, insight 300l sterl.

Jan. 1582. Dick's Rowie Rootledge, complains upon Kynmont Jock, Jock of Calfhill, and their complices 30 kine and oxen, a horse, insight and spoil 60l.

Sept. 1582. James Rootledge and his neighbours, complain upon Geordie Armstrong of Calfhill, and Jock his brother, with their complices; for 100 kine and oxen.*

Nov. 1586. Cuddie Taylor and his neighbours of Hullethirst (against) Young Christopher Armstrong of Awghing gill, Jock of Calfhill, Eckie's Richie, Willie Cany (Gait warden) 60 kine and oxen, 4 horses, armour, and insight 200l sterling.[8]

The most famous exploit, however, in which an Armstrong takes part is that recorded in *Kinmont Willie*, 'one of the last

---

* It is worth noting that this bill has no valuation. Only 'insight gear' is valued in bills; cattle, etc. were valued on a traditional standard.

and most gallant achievements performed upon the Border',
according to Scott. Critics have looked wryly at this version,
since its only printed source is the *Minstrelsy*, where Scott
writes: 'This ballad is preserved, by tradition on the West
Borders, but much mangled by reciters; so that some conjectural
emendations have been absolutely necessary to render it in-
telligible. In particular, the *Eden* has been substituted for the
Eske, the latter name being inconsistent with geography.' Child
comments: 'It is to be suspected that a great deal more emenda-
tion was done than the mangling of reciters rendered absolutely
necessary. One would like, for example, to see stanzas 10-12 and
31 in their mangled condition.' The escapade is historically well
documented, and it is hardly surprising to find Scott saying that
Spottiswoode's account 'is less different from that contained in
the ballad than might perhaps have been expected'. A contemporary account of the incident is given in The Newbattle
Manuscript, *The Historie of James the Sext*:

In the end of this aforesaid moneth of Januar, Sir Walter
Scott of Branxholme, knyght, Barron of Balclewch, and Lord
of Liddesdaill, nevoy to Archebald earle of Angus that last
deceist, and narrest ayre of blude to that earledome, he held a
day of trewis be his deput, Walter Scott of Gowdelands, at the
marche of Kershope; and the lord Scroope, lord warden of the
west Marches of Ingland, met be his deputeis at that same
marche, for performance of justice, as use is; and in the end
of that meating, it fortunat [happened that] sum insolent
Scottish borderers to be ryding nar these bounds, doing
violence in Ingland, and the veritie thareof being notefeit to
the Inglish deputeis, they immediatelie complenit to the
deputie of Scotland; and he with great humanitie and reasoun
maid answer, that geve [if] it could be fundin that thais
Scots war any indwellers within his bounds, he sould with all
diligence apprehend thayme, and sould send thayme with
diligence to the lord warden, without any restraynt of condi-
tioun; and this answer was taikin in very gude part; sa that
the deputeis the mair willinglie maid an end of that thair
meating; and indeed the deputie of Scotland was scantlie
accumpaneit with 20 men in nomber; amang whais was,

Williem Armestrang of Morton, als callit Will of Kynmonth.
At ilk meating on the borders, the use is, that the deputeis do
crave to have trewis, ane of another, fra the hour of thair
meating (for samonie persons as thay have in cumpanie for
that time) to the nixt morning of the sone rising. But the
parties being thus departit asunder, and the deputie of
Ingland, being then accumpaneit with the nomber of thre or
four hundreth armit men, they followit upon the insolent
Scottish-men aforetauld, and chaisit thayme within Scotland
a great way; during the whilk tyme Kynmonth was ryding on
his hie way hayme to his awin hous; and the great cumpany of
Ingland rynning that same way, dang him to the ground,
perforce wittinglie and willinglie, notwithstanding of any
crying or showting that he might mak for his saiftie, and
convoyit him preasoner perforce to Carlisle castle, aganis the
nature of the general peax, and of the contractit trewis for that
day; wharin thay detenit him almaist be the space of thre
moneths, for any wryting that ather the king of Scotland,
Mr. Bowes ambassador for Ingland, or the noble lord of
Liddisdaill for Scotland, could send. The lord Scroope behavit
himself so straitlie in that matter, that he wald do na kind of
reason. And notwithstanding that last of all, the Queyne of
Ingland was sufficientlie adverteist heirof, and in dew time be
hir ambassador, yit the answer was sa slaw in deliberatioun,
that the noble lord finding sik delay on all hands, and sik
strait disloyaltie on the part of the lord Scroope, he thocht
gude to essay ane extreme meane, whilke was, be a stratageme
to recover the preasoner, thus unlaughfullie detenit, whais
restitution had bene sa aft lauchfullie requirit.[9]

The morning after the raid, which took place on 13 April 1596,
Scroope wrote to Elizabeth's Privy Council:

Yesternighte in the deade time thereof, Walter Scott of
Hardinge, the cheife man about Buclughe, accompanied with
500 horsemen of Buclughes and Kinmontes frendes, did come
armed and appointed with gavlockes and crowes of iron,
handpeckes, axes, and skailing lathers, unto an owtewarde
corner of the base courte of this castell, and to the posterne
dore of the same—which they undermyned speedily and

quietlye and made themselves possessores of the base courte, brake into the chamber where Will of Kinmont was, carried him awaye, and in their discouerie by the watch, lefte for deade two of the watchmen, hurt a servante of myne, one of Kynmontes keperes, and were issued againe oute of the posterne before they were discried by the watche of the inner-warde, and ere resistance coulde be made. The watch, as yt shoulde seeme, by reason of the stormye night, were either on sleepe or gotten under some covert to defende them selves from the violence of the wether: by means wherof the Scottes atchieved their entreprise with lesse difficultie. The wardinge place of Kinmonte, in respect of the manner of his takinge, and the assurance he had given that he woulde not breake away, I supposed to have bin of sufficient suretie, and little looked that any durst have attempted to enforce in the tyme of peace any of her Majestys castells, and a peece of so good strength.[10]

The affray developed into an international incident, since Elizabeth, having notice sent her of what was done, 'stormed not a little', and her ambassador was instructed to say that peace could not continue between the two realms unless Buccleuch were delivered to England, to be punished at the queen's pleasure.

One or two elements in the ballad seem to strike a more self-conscious literary note than is commonly apparent in this form. With ballads, as with other forms of writing, what is taken for granted is often as important to a reading as what is made explicit. There seems, in *Kinmont Willie*, an attempt to intro-duce factors in a mildly explanatory way, which attracts attention to them disproportionate to their narrative signifi-cance. Such intrusions as I suspect here would also be charac-teristic of Scott with his own vast legal and historical knowledge of Border life. In stanza 5.3, for example, 'Or answer by the Border Law', is taken up again in stanza 11.2 'Against the truce of Border tide'. Such direct reference to the legislation of the Border is rare indeed in the ballads. This placing of the treachery which captured Kinmont Willie within a neat framework has some counterpart in the imagery of the poem. Simile is infrequent in the Riding Ballads; it is uncommon in all Border Ballads. When this figure does occur, it is usually colloquial and presented in direct speech. So, in *Archie o' Ca'field*, *Dick o' the Cow*, *Johnie Armstrong*, *The Lochmaben Harper*, *Johnie o' Breadislee* (*Johnie Cock*), *The Fray of Suport*, no similes occur at all. In *Jock o' the Side* we find three: 'lighter than a flee' (st. 23); 'ye sit like ony bride' (st. 25); 'the water ran like mountains hie' (st. 26). Only the third approaches the nature of the true literary / rhetorical simile, and it is given to the narrator, not, like the other two, put into the mouth of an individual character. Similarly in *Hobbie Noble*, the only two similes are direct and colloquial: 'dark the night as pick and tar' (st. 12); 'I'm but like a forfoughen hound' (st. 28). When we look at *Kinmont Willie*, however, the figures have a different quality. In stanza 10, for example, Scott of Branksome, Laird of Buccleuch, is speaking:

> 'O is my basnet a widow's curch?
>   Or my lance a wand of the willow tree?
> Or my arm a lady's lilye hand,
>   That an English lord should lightly me?'

This has a self-conscious, structural elegance uncommon in ballad verse, and suggests a more literary hand at work. Dobie disagrees, but his evidence is equivocal. He says 'This is certainly in Scott's best romantic vein, and the attribution would have been plausible enough, if a letter of Scott to Heber had not turned up, in which he says "Some of the ballads I have recovered are very fine indeed—what think you of this verse?"—and gives the four lines exactly as they are printed in the Minstrelsy'.[11] Indeed, the stanzaic correspondences interwoven in stanzas 18-24 suggest almost purely literary composition. Moreover, for what it is worth, the *OED* records 1627 as the earliest date for 'gang' in the sense of 'a company of workmen'; but since the language of the ballads is mainly, as John Speirs argues, that of the eighteenth century, linguistic evidence is of little value. Perhaps we can only prefer to believe, with Hustvedt echoing 'Lang and many others', that Scott 'did not foist upon the public as traditional any ballad wholly of his own fabrication'.[12]

If we turn away the searching and speculative eye, and read the ballad simply as we have it, there can be no doubt of its appeal. Its vigour and imaginative scope are in the genuine tradition of the Border Ballad, and in the balance of forces we are characteristically expected to throw our weight on the side of Kinmont, the betrayed outlaw, and forget his own brutalities. From the first stanzas:

> O have ye na heard o' the fause Sakelde?
>> O have ye na heard o' the keen Lord Scroope?
> How they hae ta'en bauld Kinmont Willie,
>> On Hairibee to hang him up?
>
> Had Willie had but twenty men,
>> But twenty men as stout as he,
> Fause Sakelde had never the Kinmont ta'en,
>> Wi' eight score in his cumpanie.
>
> They band his legs beneath the steed,
>> They tied his hands behind his back;
> They guarded him, fivesome on each side,
>> And they brought him over the Liddel-rack.
>
> They led him thro' the Liddel-rack,
>> And also thro' the Carlisle Sands;
> They brought him to Carlisle castell,
>> To be at my Lord Scroope's commands.

we are in the middle of a fray between the treacherous English (Salkeld was Scroope's deputy at the Warden's truce meetings), and the dashing mosstrooper, 'bauld Kinmont'. The place-names, too, localise without tedium or irrelevance; Hairibee was the place of execution at Carlisle, the Liddel-rack a ford on that river, which in itself indicates how far the English were over the border, following no lawful trod.

Historically, Salkeld did play false, unable to resist the chance of taking Kinmont, in spite of the truce. Historically, it is apparent that Buccleuch behaved properly but, unable to obtain redress, took matters into his own hands; there is an interval of almost a month between Scroope's report of the lodging of Kinmont in Carlisle Castle and his report of the attack on 13 April. Buccleuch moreover seems to have laid his plans shrewdly. The ballad represents a direct attack on the castle, a stunning of

the watchman, and even a mocking trumpet call (O wha dare
meddle wi' me?') to announce their entry. But if Scroope is not
merely finding scapegoats, Buccleuch had spies within the castle
to prepare the way. On 2 May 1596 the Warden examined two
witnesses 'concerninge the breckeing of Carlisle Castle', and
reported to the Council that the two men 'had sworn that one
Thomas Carlton, Launcelat Carlton, and Ritchie of Breckenhill
with others did agree and sett doune the plot how the castell
shoulde be broken, and that Thomas Carlton did undertake to
make the watchmen of the said castell sheure'.[13] The lines,

> He has call'd him forty Marchmen bauld,
> Were kinsmen to the bauld Buccleuch,

are supported by the contents of a letter intercepted by Scroope
in which Buccleuch writes: 'I could nought have done that
matter without great friendship of the Grames of Eske; and
speciallie of my guid frind Francis of Cannabie, and of his
brother Langton, frinds to my brother Bothewell: and of Walter
Grame of Neytherbie who were the chief leaders of that clan.'[14]
Kinmont's wife was a daughter of 'Base Hutchen', a Graham of
Esk. Another factor which could have made Kinmont's rescue
slightly easier than it appears in the ballad is that he may have
been unfettered. From Scroope's report, he appears to have been
on parole: 'The wardinge place of Kinmont, in respect of the
mannar of his takinge, and the assurance he had given that he
would not breake away, I supposed to have bin of sufficient
suretie.' Such reasoning, however, shows the Warden either as
extremely gullible, or as thoroughly rattled, as he well might be,
about what to say for the best to his superiors in distant,
civilised and relatively secure London.

The killing of Salkeld is also a ballad fabrication, but tidies up
the dispensation of outlaw justice very well. Salkeld is the first
man they meet when they cross the border:

> And as we cross'd the Bateable Land,
> When to the English side we held,
> The first o' the men that we met wi',
> Whae shuld it be but fause Sakeld?

*   *   *

'Where be ye gaun, ye broken men?'
Quo' fause Sakelde; 'come tell to me!'
Now Dickie of Dryhope led that band,
And the never a word o' lear had he.

'Why trespass ye on the English side?
Row-footed outlaws, stand!' quo' he;
The nevir a word had Dickie to say,
Sae he thrust the lance through his fause bodie.

(In the first of these stanzas, the narrative changes from 'they'
to 'we', and maintains this until the penultimate stanza;
consciously or not as far as composition is concerned, this
provides an interesting shift in both places from observer to
participant.)

Dickie of Dryhope, the hero of this episode, appears in a
'Breviate of the attempts of England committed upon the West
Marches by the West borders of Liddesdale, and fouled by the
commissioners of Berwick for lack of appearance':

July 1586
Thomas Musgrave, deputy warden of Bewcastle complains
upon the Lard's Jock, Dick of Dryupp and their complices;
for 400 kine and oxen, taken in open forrie from the Drysyke
in Bewcastle.

Sept. 1587
Andrew Rootledge of the Nuke, complains upon Lard's Jock,
Dick of Dryupp, Lancie of Whisgills, and their complices;
for 50 kine and oxen, burning his house, corn, and insight,
100l sterling.[15]

As in the rescue of Jock o' the Side, the tension of the fray and
the freeing is released in humour. Kinmont, still fettered, is
carried out of the castle by Red Rowan, 'the starkest man in
Teviotdale':

Then shoulder high, with shout and cry,
We bore him down the ladder lang;
At every stride Red Rowan made,
I wot the Kinmont's airns play'd clang!

'O mony a time,' quo Kinmont Willie,
   'I have ridden horse baith wild and wood;
But a rougher beast than Red Rowan,
   I ween my legs have ne'er bestrode.

'And mony a time,' quo' Kinmont Willie,
   'I've pricked a horse out oure the furs;
But since the day I backed a steed,
   I never wore sic cumbrous spurs!'

Just as Buccleuch had announced his arrival with a trumpet call,
so Kinmont calls an ironic farewell to Scroope:

   'Farewell, farewell, my gude Lord Scroope!
     My gude Lord Scroope, farewell!' he cried—
   'I'll pay you for my lodging maill,
     When first we meet on the Border side.'

And he did:

West March: 20 March 1600.
The queen's tenants of Scotby township complain of Christie
Armstrong of Barnleyce, Will Armstrong of Kynmont (and
others) 7 score Scotsmen, for burning houses, barns etc., and
taking prisoners, besides 60 kye and oxen, 50 horse and
mares etc.
The same night: The inhabitants of 'Ricardgate of the
suburbbs of Carlyle' complain of the above named to the
number of 130 persons, with Thome Carlton and John
Carlton 'Inglish disobedients, who after the attack at Scotby',
brack and cutt upp the postes that conteyned the yron
cheynes (made for the keepeing and streingth of Eadenbrigg
by night), and cutt up their doores, toke prisoners, &c., and
some of them came to the city walls near the castle crying,
'upon them, upon theym, a Daker, a Daker, a read bull, a read
bull', with the naming of Johnston, Armstrong, Bell and
Carlyll, forcing the citizens in their defencyve arrayes, for to
repayre to the walls, and the beacon to be sett in fyre, for the
warning of the wardenry.[16]

Of the origin of *Hobbie Noble* Child says, referring to the
Minstrelsy, 'the source is not mentioned, but was undoubtedly

Caw's Museum, though there are variations of the text, attributable to the editor'. Dobie, however, speaking of Scott's early raids into Liddesdale, is more circumspect:

> *Jock o' the Side, Dick o' the Cow,* and *Hobbie Noble* were current in those parts—the lilts of them were piped to him by Auld Thomas o' Twizzlehope and fiddled to him by the Laird of Whithaugh—and he probably picked up variants on the spot. Dr. Elliot of Cleughead, who already had a large manuscript collection, and for several years hunted for more ballads for Scott, may have given him these three ballads, or referred him to the complete versions in Caw's *Poetical Museum,* to which he had perhaps himself supplied them.[17]

The ballad celebrates the last adventure of the man who figured so heroically in the rescue of Jock o' the Side, betrayed to execution by Sim o' the Mains, an Armstrong of Whithaugh, a few miles up the Liddel from Mangerton. Certain elements here one finds common to other ballads of betrayal and execution, notably *Johnie Armstrong* and the Northumbrian tale of *The Death of Parcy Reed.* In the latter, especially, the betrayal motif is close to that of *Hobbie Noble,* as is the heroic farewell of the dying man which closes the ballad; it appears also in *Hughie the Graeme.*

Beyond what we learn of him from this ballad and from *Jock o' the Side,* little is known of Hobbie Noble. A 'Hobbe Noble' is mentioned as dwelling 'within the Nyxsons' in a letter to Burghley of 1583, and Edmund Bogg (without offering evidence) says that he was born at Crew Tower, a pele about two miles north of Bewcastle.[18] It is just possible that he is the 'Hobbe of Cumcrooke, an English outlaw "resett" some times in both countries—for whose apprehension I shall do my diligence'.[19]

This piece is rich in place-names, and suitably so, since in the beginning it is Noble's knowledge of the country which leads him back to his native land.

> Now Hobie he was an English man,
>   And born into Bewcastle dale,
> But his misdeeds they were sae great,
>   They banished him to Liddesdale.

It is from a tryst at Kershopefoot that Noble is to guide Sim
o' the Mains and his treacherous companions into England
ostensibly to steal horses. Sim o' the Mains is mentioned in the
Register of the Privy Council of Scotland for 1569: 'Lancy
Armstrong of Quhithauch obliged him . . . for Sim Armistrang
of the Mains and the rest of the Armistrangis of his gang. Syme
of the Mains was lodged in Wester Wemys.' Kershopefoot was
well known as a crossing point on the border. In Sir Robert
Bowes' Survey of 1550 we find the following:

> Albeit at Kershope hath been some alteration or doubt
> what part thereof is the true boundary between the west
> marches of England and the middle marches, for the borderers
> of the middle marches of England affirm that the division
> between the said west and middle marches of England is at
> Kershope Rig or Cassenbury Crag. And both the Scots and the
> borderers of the West marches of England, affirm that the
> bounds between the said marches is at the foot of Kershope or
> Kershope Bridge which is a common passage as well for the
> thieves of Tynedale, Bewcastle and Gillsland in England, as
> for the thieves of Liddesdale in Scotland with the stolen goods
> from the one realm to the other.[20]

Since he is a banished man, Noble insists on going by night:

> But will ye stay till the day gae down,
> Until the night come o'er the grund,
> And I'll be a guide worth ony twa
> That may in Liddesdale be fund.
>
> Tho dark the night as pick and tar,
> I'll guide ye o'er yon hills fu' hie,
> And bring ye a' in safety back,
> If you'll be true and follow me.'

Then the place-names follow, tightening the tale by contracting
the terrain within clear bounds. There was good reason, moreover, for them to travel by night, quite apart from Noble's
apprehensions; the border was systematically guarded at the
significant points, as we find in the following 'Articles devised at
Newcastle the 12th and 13th of September, in the 6th year of the
reign of our sovereign lord king Edward the sixth'.

First, that watches be appointed for the inhabitants of the said marches, and the places, with the numbers of the watches, with setters, searchers, and overseers, according to the ancient customs of the marches.

Also, that every man do rise and follow the fray, upon blowing of horn, shout or outcry; upon pain of death . . .

The orders of the Watches upon the West Marches made by the lord *Wharton*, upon the instructions aforesaid . . .

. . . From *Hathwate* burn foot unto the foot of *Cryssop*, five several watches, and four men in every watch. And these watches nightly to be searched by two men appointed at the assignment of *John Musgrave*, the king's highness's servant.

From the foot of *Cryssop* unto the head of *Cryssop*, three several watches, and in every watch four men; whereof one to be at *Craighill* foot, and the other two beneath: and the searchers for every watch nightly to be appointed by the said *John Musgrave*.[21]

The activity appears to have left its mark in Border place-names; among the Northumbrian hills, for example, we find *Watch Hill, Spy Law, Look Out, Keekout, View Law, Viewley*, not to mention *Scots Gap*.

The marauders rest at Foulbogshiel while word goes to the Land-sergeant at Askerton, who immediately rouses support along the Hartlie Burn, and from Willeva, and Spear-Edom (now Spade Adam, ironically a rocket site) where Noble's pursuers were warned to 'sharp their arrows on the wa' '. Assembling his men at Rodrie-haugh, the Land-sergeant anticipates meeting Noble at Conscouthart Green.[22] Meanwhile the latter:

> . . . has dreamed a dream,
> In the Foulbogshiel where that he lay:
> He thought his horse was 'neath him shot,
> And he himself got hard away.
>
> The cocks could crow, and the day could dawn,
> And I wat so even fell down the rain:
> If Hobie had no wakened at that time,
> In the Foulbogshiel he had been tane or slain.

But he wakes in the rain, and optimistically urges his companions across the fell:

> 'And the warst clock of this cumpanie
> I hope shall cross the Waste this day.'

He is, of course, surrounded and taken, after a fight in which he breaks his 'laddies sword' across Jersawigham's head. Betrayed and bound, he is led to Carlisle, and there is a laconic, bitter irony in the line: 'They asked him if he knew the way', emphasising the pathos of his earlier eager promise,

> 'And I'll be a guide worth ony twa . . .
> . . . If you'll be true and follow me.'

As he is led up the Ricker Gate (again, a typical explicit localisation), the women recognise him as the hero of Jock o' the Side's rescue, but he is not comforted by their adulation; his present humiliation is unbearable:

> 'Fy on ye women, why ca' ye me man?
> For it's nae man that I'm used like;
> I'm but like a forfoughen hound—
> Has been fighting in a dirty syke.'

Finally, when he is offered his life in return for a confession to having stolen 'my lord's horse', he refuses, with dignity, and utters his last farewell:

> 'Now fare thee weel sweet Mangerton;
> For I think again I'll ne'er thee see.
> I wad betray nae lad alive,
> For a' the goud in Christentie.
>
> And fare thee weel now Liddesdale,
> Baith the hie land and the law—
> Keep ye weel frae traitor Mains;
> For goud and gear he'll sell ye a'.
>
> I'd rather be ca'd Hobie Noble,
> In Carlisle where he suffers for his faut,
> Before I were ca'd traitor Mains,
> That eats and drinks of meal and maut.'

Noble was obviously a rogue, yet in the ballad there is about him an air of gentle, almost innocent heroism and pathos most unusual in this genre. 'Brave Noble is seld away', ironically sold to the gallows by an Armstrong, whose family he had so nobly served. For the reader who needs more comfort, and who desires full justice, there is always Scott: 'Sim o' the Mains fled into England from the resentment of his chief; but experienced there the common fate of a traitor, being himself executed at Carlisle about two months after Hobbie's death. Such, at least, is the tradition of Liddesdale.'[23]

Two further ballads concern the Armstrongs; *Dick o' the Cow* and *Johnie Armstrong*. The first of these characters is mentioned as early as 1596 in Nashe's *Have With You to Saffron Walden*: 'Dick of the Cow, that mad demi-lance northern borderer, who plaied his prizes with the lord Jockey so bravely.' Scott quotes in the *Minstrelsy* another possible allusion to it in Parrot's collection of epigrams *Laquei Ridiculosi*, or *Springes for Woodcocks* of 1613:

> Owenus wondreth since he came to Wales,
>> What the description of this isle should be,
> That nere had seen but mountains, hills, and dales,
>> Yet would he boast, and stand on pedigree,
> From Rice ap Richard, sprung from Dick a Cow,
> Be cod, was right gud gentleman, look ye now!
>
> (Epigr. 76)

Child also points out that 'Cow' in Dick's name can not refer to his cattle, otherwise he would have been called Dick o' the Kye; he suggests that the word may mean 'the hut in which he liv'd; or bush or broom'. This is unconvincing, but it is worth noting incidentally that the word 'cows' hardly appears before 1600, 'ky(e)' being the regular plural.

Three versions of this ballad are given in Child, but they differ in unimportant respects. Johnie Armstrong and his brother plan a raid over the border, but their attempt on Hutton Hall is foiled because the laird has secured all his beasts within, leaving only six sheep to be stolen, which the brothers feel is beneath them. They therefore rob Dick of three cows and three coverlets from his wife's bed. Dick seeks Scroope's permission to retrieve his goods, and this is granted on the condition that 'Thou'lt steal frae nane but wha sta' frae thee'. Dick here is appealing not simply to his master, but to the Warden of the March, and in Border terms, his lone foray would appear to have about it some legality, since he accepts the condition:

> 'There is my trowth, and my right hand!
>   My head shall hang on Hairibee;
> I'll ne'er cross Carlisle sands again,
>   If I steal frae a man but whae sta' frae me!'

But the arrangement is dubious; the following of stolen goods into enemy territory is a recurrent issue in the development of Border law, but the pattern is fairly consistent, and fairly summarised by Nicolson and Burn:

> If any the subjects of the princes aforesaid have stolen anything, or committed any attempts within the Marches or land to which he is subject; it shall be lawful for him against whom it hath been so done and attempted freely (within six days to be accounted from the time of the said fault so committed or attempted) by authority of this ordinance without any other letter of safe conduct, to follow the same offender, and him (so following) to enter safely and surely the Marches or land into which the same evil doer is gone; so that so soon as he hath entered the said Marches or land for that cause, he go unto some honest man, being of good name and fame, inhabiting within the Marches which he hath entered, and declare unto him the cause of his entry, that is to say, to follow his goods stolen; and shall declare what goods or things he hath been spoiled or robbed of; and further shall require the same that so long as he shall make the search he go with him, that he may (when he shall be thereunto required upon the same) give testimony of truth of his behaviour in time of his search.[24]

So Dick begins his lone foray and reaches Puddingburn, about which Child quotes a comment from R. B. Armstrong:

> The place which is alluded to by Scott was pointed out to me about thirty years since. There then were the remains of a

tower which stood on a small plateau where the Dow Sike and the Blaik Grain join the Stanygillburn, a tributary of the Tinnisburn. Some remains of the building may still be traced at the northern angle of the sheepfold of which it forms part. The walls that remain are 4 feet 3 inches thick, and measured on the inside about 6 feet high. They extend about 18 feet 6 inches in one direction and 14 feet in another, forming portions of two sides with the angle of the tower . . . There must have been a considerable building of a rude kind . . . This place, as the crow flies, is quite two miles and a quarter from Kershope-foot, and by the burn two miles and a half . . . The Laird's Jock's residence [Plate 9] is marked on a sketch map of Liddesdale by Lord Burleigh, drawn when Simon was laird of Mangerton. (Simon, son of Thomas, was laird in 1578-9.) It is also marked at the mouth of the Tinnisburn on a 'platt' of the country, of 1590.[25]

Here Dick runs into thirty-three Armstrongs, is understandably daunted, but nevertheless makes his legal complaint.

> 'I'm come to plain o' your man, fair Johnie Armstrang,
> And syne o' his billie Willie,' quo' he;
> 'How they've been in my house last night,
> And they hae ta'en my three kye frae me.'

So far, Dick has acted with reasonable formality, but as one might expect the Armstrongs show a violent disregard for protocol:

> 'Ha!' quo' fair Johnie Armstrang, 'we will him hang'.
> 'Na', quo' Willie, 'we'll him slae.'
> Then up and spak another young Armstrang,
> 'We'll gie him his batts, and let him gae'.

The Armstrong name is guarantee enough that these are not empty threats, and Dick's life is worth little, when 'the gude Laird's Jock' takes the heat out of the situation:

> 'Sit down thy ways a little while, Dickie,
> And a piece o' thy ain cow's hough I'll gie thee'.

Again, though the pace has slackened, a blend of violence and humour carries the narrative forward on a temporarily different level, and induces a partisan view of Dick's troubles. The ballad throws in an interesting verse here on the domestic arrangements of the Mangerton and Puddingburn *ménages*:

> It was then the use of Puddingburn House,
>   And the house of Mangerton, all hail,
> Them that came na at the first ca',
>   Gat nae mair meat till the neist meal.

Dick escapes after cruelly hamstringing thirty of the thirty-three horses; of the remainder, he rides one, leads another, and leaves the third, which belongs to the Laird's Jock. It is on this that Johnie Armstrong chases him. They fight, and though Dick is no swordsman (he is referred to throughout in such terms as 'the innocent', 'a merry fule', 'ae innocent fule') he unheroically and clumsily stuns Johnie with the hilt of his sword, and takes the third horse.

The episode follows a couple of stanzas in which Dick moralises most improbably:

> 'There is a preacher in our chapell,
>   And a' the live lang day teaches he:
> When day is gane and night is come,
>   There's ne'er ae word I mark but three.

> 'The first and second is—Faith and Conscience;
>   The third—Ne'er let a traitour free:
> But, Johnie, what faith and conscience was thine,
>   When thou took awa my three kye frae me?'

The abstractions here, and the statement in a later stanza that Dick was saved by 'the powers above' strike an alien note of literary primness. Well into the seventeenth century, as I have indicated, religion in the Border marches had at best a tickle existence.

When he returns to his master with three stolen horses, Dick is threatened with summary execution, not only for having taken the animals, but because one of them belonged to the Laird's Jock whom Scroope here sees as an honest man:

> 'But what garr'd thee steal the Laird's Jock's horse?
>   And, limmer, what garr'd ye steal him?' quo' he;

'For lang thou mightst in Cumberland dwelt,
  Ere the Laird's Jock had stown frae thee.'

But when Dick announces that he has won the third horse in
fair combat with Johnie Armstrong, Scroope is mollified to the
extent of offering him fifteen pounds for it (twenty, in one
version). Dick bargains for twenty pounds (thirty in the other)
and Scroope pays on the nail, throwing in a milch cow for good
measure. On his way home, Dick meets Scroope's brother,
Bailiff Glozenburrie, and again after bargaining ('Trow ye aye to
make a fule o' me!') he gets twenty pounds from him for
Johnie's horse, as well as a milch cow. (The stanzas of the two
negotiations are almost exact repetitions, in the essentials.)
Then Dick does a little dance for joy, because he has kept the
best beast for himself.

In all, we have here the old tale of the clever fool outwitting
both his foes and his master, keeping just inside the law himself;
an unheroic hero. As often happens in Border Ballads, however, there is a qualified ending to the tale, a sad contrast to
Dick's delight at the conclusion of the two deals when 'Dickie
lap a loup fu' hie, / And I wat a loud laugh laughed he'.
Knowing that he will not be safe in Cumberland, because the
feud would be pursued and 'The Armstrongs they would hang
me hie', he retires to Burgh under Stanmuir. According to extra-
poetic tradition he was eventually seized by the Armstrongs;
one source has it that 'out of revenge they tore his flesh from his
bones with red-hot pincers' (Caw's *Museum*), while in another 'he
was plunged into a large boiling pot and so put to death'
(Chambers, *Scottish Ballads*). Both are quoted by Child, who
adds with petulant irrelevance, 'No well-wisher of Dick has the
least occasion to be troubled by these puerile supplements of the
singers'.[26] *The Lochmaben Harper* is another tale in which a
simple man outwits authority. The harper (in some versions
blind) goes to England to steal the Lord Warden's mare,
Wanton Brown (in some versions, King Henry's mare), and
succeeds; but there is about it, as Gummere says, 'a calculated
jocosity which leaves it far behind *Dick o' the Cow*'.

The essentials of the tale of *Johnie Armstrong* are soon told; in
the year 1530 he was treacherously taken by the King and

hanged, with many of his men, without trial. According to one commentator, there is not a shred of documentary evidence to support the incident: 'It is just the sort of story that would gain currency and credence in a district where half the inhabitants were mosstroopers, and half of the rest in league with them.'[27] Pitcairn remarks, however, 'It is somewhat singular that the circumstances as they are detailed in the popular ballad or song are substantially correct; and there cannot now be a doubt that Armstrong was not basely betrayed and put to death, even without the mockery of a form of trial.'[28] The ascertainable facts are few, but the circumstantial evidence is strong. James V, determined to pacify the Borders, took the business into his own hands. He first removed from the scene those very lords and barons in whose charge the Border marches lay. On 19 May 1530, he called a meeting of the council, which by that time included no Border lord except the provost of Lincluden, and here it was decided that the King himself should lead an expedition into the Borders, and that those lords and barons who had been placed in ward should remain there during the King's pleasure, at their own expense, under pain of forfeiture of life, lands and goods. On 5 July James and his retinue were in 'Carlanrig', Johnie Armstrong is known to have died before 8 July. Buchanan suggests that Maxwell, afraid of Armstrong's power, engineered his destruction. Lindsay of Pitscottie gives an interesting account:

> After this hunting he hanged John Armstrong laird of Kilknocky, and his complices, to the number of thirty six persons: for the which many Scottish-men heavily lamented; for he was the most redoubted chiftain that had been, for a long time, on the Borders, either of Scotland or England. He rode ever with twenty four able gentlemen, well horsed; yet he never molested any Scottish-man. But it is said, that, from the borders to Newcastle, every man, of whatsomever estate, paid him tribute to be free of his trouble. He came before the king, with his foresaid number richly apparelled, trusting that, in respect of his free offer of his person, he should obtain the king's favour. But the king, seeing him and his men so gorgeous in their apparel, with so many brave men under a

tyrant's commandment, frowardly turning him about, he
bade take the tyrant out of his sight, saying What wants that
knave, that a king should have? But John Armstrong made
great offers to the king, that he should sustain himself with
forty gentelmen, ever ready at his service, on their own cost,
without wronging any Scottish-man. Secondly. That there
was not a subject in England, duke, earl or baron, but, within
a certain day, he should bring him to his majesty, either quick
or dead. At length, he feeling no hope of favour, said, very
proudly, It is folly to seek grace at a graceless face: But,
(said he) had I known this, I should have lived on the borders,
in despite of King Hary and you both; for I know King Hary
would downweigh my best horse with gold, to know that I
were condemned to die this day.[29]

In addition to such accounts as this, and broadside elabora-
tions, some slight literary allusions have survived: 'Ihonne
Ermistrangis dance' is mentioned in *The Complaynt of Scotland*
(1549) and Sir David Lindsay of the Mount has a pardoner in
The Satyre of the Thrie Estaitis who, in presenting his goods,
offers

> 'The cordis baith grit and lang,
> Quhilt hangit Johnie Armstrang,
> Of gude hempt, soft and sound.
> Gude haly pepill, I stand ford,
> Wha' evir beis hangit in this cord
> Neidis never to be drowned!'

R. B. Armstrong refers to a 'copy of the nootes of the interluyde'
mentioned in a letter from Eure to Cromwell of 26 January 1539-
40. A poor man complains of the state to which he and many
others are reduced, declaring there is no remedy,

for thoughe he wolde suyte the king's grace, he was naither
acquaynted with conciouller nor treasourer, and withoute
thaim myght noe man gote noe goodenes of the king. And
after he spered for the king. And whene he was shewed to the
man that was king in the playe, he aunsuered and said he was
noe king, for ther is but one king, whiche made all and
gouerne the all, whoe is eternall, to whom he and all erthely

kings ar but officers, of the whiche thay muste make recknynge, and soe furthe muche moor to that effecte. And thene he loked to the king, and saide he was not the king of Scotlande, for ther was an other king in Scotlande that hanged John Armestrang with his fellowes, and Sym the Larde and many others moo, which had pacified the countrey and stanched thifte.[30]

John Armstrong was a brother of Thomas Armstrong, Laird of Mangerton, and lived in the tower of Gilnockie, on the Esk near Langholm (Plate 10). The site of the real Gilnockie has been disputed, since what remains of Hollows Tower, commonly called Gilnockie, though a strong pele, is poorly situated for defence.[31]

Three versions of the ballad have survived, two of them English, in which Armstrong appears as a Westmorland man. The third, which I refer to here, is from Allan Ramsay's *The Evergreen*, and is substantially that printed by Scott. As ever, authenticity is far to seek. Motherwell comments:

Ramsay mentions that this is the true old ballad of the famous John Armstrong of Gilnockhall in Liddisdale, and which he copies from a Gentleman's mouth of the name of Armstrong, who was the sixth generation from this John, and who told him that it was ever esteemed the genuine ballad—the common one false. This noted Border-pricker was gibbeted by James V in 1529. The common ballad alluded to by Ramsay is the one, however, which is in the mouths of the people. His set I never heard sung or recited; but the other frequently. The common set is printed in *Wit Restored London* 1658, under the title of *A Northern Ballet*, and in the London collection of old ballads, 1723, as 'Johney Armstrong's last Goodnight'. That collection has another ballad on the subject of Armstrong, entitled 'Armstrong and Musgrave's Contention'. In J. Stevenson's Catalogue, Edinburgh, 1827, is a copy on a broadside with this title, 'John Armstrong's last Farewell, declaring how he and eight score men fought a bloody battell at Edinburgh, to the tune of Fare thou well, bonny Gilt Knock Hall', an edition still adhered to in the stall copies of the ballad.[32]

The 'common set' to which Motherwell refers is the English version, and it is in this that the fight occurs in which so many men are slain. Ramsay's version has no fight.

There is no question in the ballad of whose side we are supposed to be on. The old theme recurs, of the dashing free-booter betrayed to the gallows, but this time most shamefully by a deceitful king, and most grossly with fifty of his followers. The tale has about it an air of pathetic splendour:

> Sum speiks of lords, sum speiks of lairds,
>   And siclike men of hie degrie;
> Of a gentleman I sing a sang,
>   Sumtyme calld Laird of Gilnockie.
>
> The king he wrytes a luving letter,
>   With his ain hand sae tenderly:
> And he hath sent it to Johny Armstrang,
>   To cum and speik with him speedily.

Thus far the prologue, with the proleptic irony of a reconciliation between king and mosstrooper. Yet one is taken by the innocence of Johnie, the excitement, the bucolic generosity of the preparations for a state occasion:

> The Eliots and Armstrangs did convene,
>   They were a gallant company:
> 'We 'ill ryde and meit our lawful king,
>   And bring him safe to Gilnockie.
>
> 'Make kinnen and capon ready, then,
>   And venison in great plenty;
> We 'ill welcome hame our royal king;
>   I hope he 'ill dyne at Gilnockie!'
>
> They ran their horse on the Langum howm,
>   And brake their speirs with mekle main;
> The ladys lukit frae their loft-windows,
>   'God bring our men weil back again!'

From this point, the ballad shows for a time a more formal structure in the dialogue between Armstrong and the king, prefaced by an antagonism of display:

When Johny came before the king,
  With all his men sae brave to see,
The king he movit his bonnet to him;
  He weind he was a king as well as he.

The episode echoes closely Pitscottie's: 'But the king, seeing
him and his men so gorgeous in their apparel, with so many
brave men under a tyrant's commandment, frowardly turning
him about, he bade take the tyrant out of his sight, saying,
"What wants that knave, that a king should have?" ' The
dialogue is a series of offers on Armstrong's part, alternating
with a pattern of rejections by the king. Horses, mills, wheat,
henchmen are all refused with contempt, but perhaps the offer
most clearly illustrative of Armstrong's power is this:

'Grant me my life, my liege, my king,
  And a brave gift I'll gie to thee;
All between heir and Newcastle town
  Sall pay thair yeirly rent to thee.'

'Away, away, thou traytor strang!
  Out of my sicht thou mayst sune be!
I grantit never a traytors lyfe,
  And now I'll not begin with thee.'

This interchange takes up almost one-third of the ballad, and
after it the tone changes; Armstrong's betrayal is now clear to
him, and honesty no more than a regal equivocation:

'Ye lied, ye lied, now king,' he says,
  'Althocht a king and prince ye be,
For I luid naithing in all my lyfe,
  I dare well say it but honesty;

But a fat horse, and a fair woman,
  Twa bonny dogs to kill a deir:
But Ingland suld haif found me meil and malt,
  Gif I had livd this hundred yeir!'

It could well be argued that Armstrong's record has done little
to recommend his honesty, and that his moralising when his life
is at stake comes a little late in the day. The context of Johnie's

attitude, however, is the context of Border 'honesty' or good faith; R. B. Armstrong quotes one, Constable, a spy in the pay of Sir Ralph Sadler: 'they would not care [i.e. scruple] to steal, and yet they would not bewray any man that trust in them for all the gold in Scotland and France.'[33] There are many examples of this kind; it is not a mere ballad convention. Hence the bitterness of:

> 'I haif asked grace at a graceless face,
> But there is nane for my men and me'.

For a moment we return from the dispute to the splendour, but now this too is tarnished with recrimination:

> Ther hang nine targats at Johnies hat,
> And ilk an worth three hundred pound:
> 'What wants that knave that a king suld haif,
> But the sword of honour and the crown!
>
> 'O whair gat thou these targats, Johnie,
> That blink sae brawly abune thy brie?'
> 'I gate them in the field fechting,
> Where, cruel king, thou durst not be'.

So Johnie is condemned and, like Hobbie Noble, Parcy Reed and Hughie the Graeme, utters his last 'goodnight'; the ballad closes in pathos:

> John murdred was at Carlinrigg,
> And all his galant companie:
> But Scotlands heart was never sae wae,
> To see sae mony brave men die.
>
> Because they savd their country deir
> Frae Englishmen; nane were sae bauld,
> Whyle Johnie livd on the border-side,
> Nane of them durst cum neir his hald.

'The music of Mattei', wrote Goldsmith, 'is dissonance to what I felt when our old dairymaid sung me into tears with Johnny Armstrong's Last Good Night, or the Cruelty of Barbara Allen.'

The tradition that the trees on which the men were hanged withered away is remembered sentimentally by Leyden in his 'Scenes of Infancy':

Where rising Teviot joins the Frostylee,
Stands the huge trunk of many a leafless tree.
No verdant wood-bine wreaths their age adorn;
Bare are the boughs, the gnarled roots uptorn.
Here shone no sun-beam, fell no summer-dew,
Nor ever grass beneath the branches grew,
Since the bold chief who Henry's power defied,
True to his country, as a traitor died.

The popularity of the story has been unaffected by time, though some of its metamorphoses show an irrelevant indulgence in romantic fantasy, well represented by the following title page from a broadsheet now in the Robert White Collection of the University of Newcastle:

The Pleasant and delightful HISTORY of JOHNY ARMSTRONG. SHEWING His noble deeds in his youth in divers countries, in arms against the Turks and Saracens in the Holy Land; His dwelling at Guiltnock-hall in Westmoreland, and by his industry, without any estate in lands or rents, kept eightscore men to attend him richly apparell'd, well mounted and armed: How he married a fair lady, a poor knight's daughter, and of the grand entertainment he made at his wedding: His lady brought him a son, and great rejoicings were made: Also an account of his many victories over the Scots: and of his going to Edinburgh, upon a friendly invitation of that king; How he and his valiant men were all slain, and how his death was revenged by his Son; with many other matters of note.

Perhaps, however, one may let Walter Scott of Satchells have the last word before we leave the Armstrong exploits, in lines which endeavour not only to excuse the predatory habits of the Borderers, but to make a subtle distinction between freebooters and thieves:

On the border was the Armstrangs, able men;
Somewhat unruly, and very ill to tame;
I would have none think that I call them thieves,
For if I did it would be arrant lies;
For all frontiers and borders, I observe,
Wherever they lie, are freebooters.

And does the enemy much more harms,
Than five thousand marshal-men in arms;
The freebooter ventures both life and limb,
Good wife, and bairn, and every other thing;
He must do so, or else must starve and die;
For all his lively-hood comes of the enemie:
His substance, being, and his house most tight,
Yet he may chance to lose all in a night;
Being driven to poverty, he must needs a freebooter be,
Yet for vulgar calumnies there is no remedie:
An arrant liar calls a freebooter a thief,
A freebooter may be many a man's relief:
A freebooter will offer no man wrong,
Nor will take none at any hand;
He spoils more enemies now and then,
Than many hundreds of your marshal men:
Near to a border frontier in time of war:
There ne'er a man but he's a freebooter;
Where fainting fazard dare not show their face;
And calls their offspring thieves to their disgrace;

* * *

Yet with the freebooter I have not done,
I must have another fling at hime,
Because to all men it may appear,
The freebooter he is a volunteer;
In the muster-rolls he has no desire to stay;
He lives by purchase, he gets no pay.

* * *

It's most clear a freebooter doth live in hazard's train,
A freebooter's a cavalier that ventures life for gain:
But since king James the sixth to England went,
There has been no cause of grief,
And he that has transgress'd since then
Is no freebooter, but a thief.[34]

Once we leave the heroic villainy of the Armstrongs, we are really on much less sure ground as far as the location of ballads and personalities goes in the West Marches. Consequently, the attribution to the West March of a number of the ballads which follow is a matter of critical convenience rather than of territorial accuracy since, in any case, variant versions use different names.

Hughie the Graeme, of which Child gives five separate versions and a few odd stanzas, tells the story of a Hugh Graeme (historically untraceable, in spite of the notorious surname) whose wife has become the mistress of the Bishop of Carlisle. In revenge, Graeme steals the Bishop's mare, is pursued and arrested by the Warden, Scroope, and, in spite of weighty intercessions, is hanged. Child rejects the 'tradition' as absurd, and patently derived from the ballad, pointing out the absurdity of making Graeme steal a mare in revenge for his wife's faithlessness. He quotes Allan Cunningham: 'tradition, in all the varieties of her legends, never invented such an unnecessary and superfluous reason as this. By habit and by nature thieves, the Graemes never waited for anything like a pretence to steal.'[35] Perhaps, however, this takes the revenge too literally and leaves unremarked the sharp irony, possibly more obvious to a modern reader, of the exchange of one mare for another. We have already seen in other ballads how sombre situations are often relieved, if only briefly, by wit or horseplay; it seems ungracious to deny Graeme's exploit a similar interpretation.

Like Armstrong, Graeme was a name to be feared in the Borders; though they were apparently of Scottish descent, and lived in the Debatable Land, their political allegiance appears to have been to the English crown rather than the Scottish. In a letter to Scroope of 19 September 1600, a body of Graeme signatories protest their innocence of charges made against them by certain Gentlemen of the West March, writing:

> We her majesty's tenants and faithful subjects . . . will stand bound unto your good lordship, every man particularly for himself, his children, servants and tenants . . . [and] if any offence be committed within your lordship's Marche by any of Scotland, we shall be ready to serve your good lordship truly in seeking revenge.

The lengthy letter was dismissed energetically as disingenuous and fulsome by their gentlemen accusers, who conclude their reply to Scroope on 25 September:

As often before, so now we humbly beseech your Honour to be the means that the *Grames* and the residue of our Borderers may be drawn in obedience to your lordship's authority, and may be compelled to answer her highness's laws from time to time in some reasonable manner for their offences, the better to stay their common robberies and spoils of our country, whereof the *Grames* are not blameless.[36]

I have here used the *Minstrelsy* version 'Procured for me', writes Scott, 'by my friend Mr. W. Laidlaw, in Blackhouse, and has been long current in Selkirkshire. Mr. Ritson's copy has occasionally been resorted to for better readings'. The vigour and economy of the opening stanza are sustained throughout:

> Gude Lord Scroope's to the hunting gane,
>   He has ridden o'er moss and muir;
> And he has grippit Hughie the Graeme,
>   For stealing o' the Bishop's mare.

The action and urgency of 'gane', 'ridden', 'grippit', and 'stealing', are carried swiftly on in the dialogue which immediately follows for three stanzas, culminating in a duel which is interrupted by the arrival of Scroope's posse:

> Then they hae grippit Hughie the Graeme,
>   And brought him up through Carlisle town;
> The lasses and lads stood on the walls,
>   Crying, 'Hughie the Graeme, thou'se ne'er gae down!'

and we are reminded somewhat of the adulatory welcome of the defeated hero, Hobbie Noble.

The pattern that follows is now a familiar one; like the dialogue between Johnie Armstrong and the King, we have a series of four alternating verses, representing the offers made for Graeme's life after the jury has cried 'Hughie the Graeme, thou must gae down!'

> Then up bespak him gude Lord Hume,
>   As he sat by the judge's knee,—
> 'Twenty white owsen, my gude lord,
>   If you'll grant Hughie the Graeme to me'.

> 'O no, O no, my gude Lord Hume!
>   Forsooth and sae it mauna be;
> For, were there but three Graemes of the name,
>   They suld be hanged a' for me'.

Lady Hume is equally unsuccessful. (In Child A the equivalent
of Hume is 'Boles', possibly Sir Robert Bowes, Warden of the
East March of England in 1550. Hume was Warden of the East
March of Scotland from about 1550 to 1564.) Seeing there is no
help, Hughie then performs a most spectacular and pointless
'loup' of 'fifteen feet and three', dismisses his father, and bids a
farewell to his wife:

> ' 'Twas thou bereft me of my life,
>   And wi' the Bishop thou play'd the whore'.

to which Scott adds the note: 'Of the morality of Robert
Aldridge, Bishop of Carlisle, we know but little, but his political
and religious faith were of a stretching and accommodating
texture. Anthony à Wood observes that there were many
changes in his time, both in church and state, but the worthy
prelate retained his offices and preferments during them all'.
Like the revenge, this farewell or 'goodnight' is in ballad terms
ironical, especially if we think of Armstrong, Maxwell, or Parcy
Reed, but like a true folk hero, Hughie dies hopefully, handing
on the torch:

> 'Here Johnie Armstrong, take thou my sword,
>   That is made o' the metal sae fine;
> And when thou comest to the English side,
>   Remember the death of Hughie the Graeme'.

Again we have the hero betrayed, and judicially murdered, but
this time with a sexual motive not uncommon in the literature,
life and thought of the Border.

The Graemes appear again in the ballad of *Bewick and Graham*
one of those which Gummere categorises as 'ballads of Kinship'.
The tragedy here arises from quite different sources from those
I have discussed hitherto. In the Riding Ballads our sympathies
are engaged on behalf of the hero/villain usually because he is
popular, isolated and betrayed; there is no question here of a
classical tragic pattern, whereas in *Bewick and Graham* we have

a moral dilemma where young Graham, the hero, is destroyed by
a conflict of loyalties in which he is required to kill either his
father or his brother-in-arms. 'The ballad is remarkable', says
Scott, 'as containing probably the very latest allusion to the
institution of brotherhood-in-arms, which was held so sacred in
the days of chivalry . . . The quarrel of the two old chieftains
over their wine, is highly in character. Two generations have not
elapsed since the custom of drinking deep and taking deadly
revenge for slight offences produced very tragical events on the
Border, to which the custom of going armed to festive meetings
contributed not a little.'[37] Child records eight versions, or part-
versions, but prints only one, with variant notes, commenting,
'No copy of this ballad earlier than the last century is known to
me . . . I am persuaded that there was an older and better copy
of this ballad than those which are extant. The story is so well
composed, proportion is so well kept, on the whole, that it is
reasonable to suppose that certain passages (as stanzas 3, 4, 50)
may have suffered some injury. There are also phrases which are
not up to the mark of the general style, but it is a fine-spirited
ballad as it stands, and very infectious'.[38] It is Child's version I
refer to in what follows. Old Graham and old Bewick meet in
Carlisle:

> In arms to the wine they are gone,
>   And drank till they were both merry.

Their conviviality leads to a discussion of their sons, and by the
end of the fourth stanza the tragic potential is complete, and
beginning to act:

> Old Grahame he took up the cup,
>   And said, 'Brother Bewick, here's to thee;
> And here's to our two sons at home,
>   For they live best in our country'.

> 'Nay, were thy son as good as mine,
>   And of some books could he but read
> With sword and buckler by his side,
>   To see how he could save his head,

> 'They might have been calld two bold brethren
>   Where ever they did go or ride;

> They might [have] been calld two bold brethren,
>   They might have crackd the Border-side.

> 'Thy son is bad and is but a lad,
>   And bully to my son cannot be;
> For my son Bewick can both write and read,
>   And sure I am that cannot he'.

Not the best stanzas in the ballad as literature, but surely astonishing, indeed unique, in invoking literacy, or lack of it, as pretext for a family feud. One wonders if in fact this was the original cause of the difference, though it would appear likely, since images of teaching and scholarship run throughout the ballad and, before the final duel, Bewick flings his psalm-book out of his hand. The combination of piety, loyalty and literacy is altogether unusual and in its consistency unparalleled in any other Border Ballad.

Graham returns home and upbraids his unscholarly offspring:

> 'I put thee to school, but thou would not learn,
>   I bought thee books, but thou would not read;
> But my blessing thou's never have
>   Till I see with Bewick thou can save thy head.'

So physical prowess is still for old Graham to decide the issue, and so insistent is he against his son's protestation of love for young Bewick, 'a man that's faith and troth to me', that he offers his own challenge:

> 'What's that thou sayst, thou limmer loon?
>   Or how dare thou stand to speak to me?
> If thou do not end this quarrel soon,
>   Here is my glove thou shalt fight me'.

Bewildered by this dilemma, the illiterate young Graham retires, and the ironic overtones are neatly placed in stanza 18:

> Christy Grahame is to his chamber gone,
>   And for to study, as well might be,
> Whether to fight with his father dear,
>   Or with his bully Bewick he.

He decides that he must fight his friend, arms himself, and leaves to offer his challenge, with great misgiving, not the least element in which is his knowledge that to kill his 'bully' is a deadly sin. While he is on his way, the scene shifts to young Bewick who, with another neat irony, is engaged in teaching 'his scholars five'. He is teaching them to fence, not to read. So the young men meet, reluctantly challenge, and as reluctantly fight. In the stanzas which follow one sees the tragic proportion of this ballad; the very movement of the lines is retarded, and the conflict in both men between love and duty is seen through a tormented delaying dialogue during stanzas 28-41, for example:

> 'Now if it be my fortune thee, Grahame, to kill,
>   As God's will's, man, it all must be;
> But if it be my fortune thee, Grahame, to kill,
>   'Tis home again I'll never gae'.

> 'Thou art of my mind then, bully Bewick,
>   And sworn-brethren will we be;
> If thou be a man, as I trow thou art,
>   Come over this ditch and fight with me'.

They fight for two hours, until, by 'an ackward stroke', Graham mortally wounds Bewick, after which he dies a Roman death on the point of his own sword. Bewick's father arrives in time to hear the bitter regret of his son's last words:

> '[Father, co]uld ye not drunk your wine at home,
> [And le]tten me and my brother be?
> 'Nay, dig a grave both low and wide,

>   And in it us two pray bury;
> But bury my bully Grahame on the sun-side,
>   For I'm sure he's won the victory'.

The tale ends with the self-recrimination and the deep sense of loss experienced by the old men, and a concluding superfluous verse in which the singer places the blame on the fathers.

The theme of *Bewick and Graham* has many features in common with the group Scott listed as romantic in the *Minstrelsy* (which is where he places it); in particular the central characters bound by their own love, sundered by family feud, and buried in the same grave. To these we shall come shortly; for the moment there remain two more songs of raid and violence before we move to these of love and violence. *Rookhope Ryde*, says Scott, 'is a bishoprick Border song, composed in 1569; taken down from the chanting of George Collingwood, the elder, late of Boltsburn in the neighbourhood of Ryhope, who was interred at Stanhope the 16th December 1785'.[39] The event can be dated with fair certainty to 6 December (i.e. St Nicholas Day) 1569, when during the rebellion of the Northern Earls (Scott inexplicably gives the year as 1572) the marauders know they have the advantage:

> 'For Weardale men is a journey ta'en;
>   They are so far out-oer yon fell
> That some of them's with the two earls,
>   And others fast in Barnard castell'.

They come from Thirwall in Northumberland and Willeva in Cumberland, to Rookhope at the head of Weardale in Durham. The ballad begins not unlike *Parcy Reed*, with a complaint against thieves:

> Rookhope stands in a pleasant place,
>   If the false thieves wad let it be;
> But away they steal our goods apace,
>   And ever an ill death may they die!

They seize in four hours six hundred sheep and some horses, but the warning has gone out, and the men of Weardale assemble to fight. They acquit themselves nobly, in the face of an insolent band of reivers:

> Thir limmer thieves, they have good hearts,
>   They nevir think to be oerthrown;
> Three banners against Weardale men they bare,
>   As if the world had been all their own.

> Thir Weardale men, they have good hearts,
>   They are as stif as any tree;
> For, if they'd every one been slain,
>   Never a foot back man would flee.

It is a simple, fairly crudely assembled tale, without any of the irony or subtlety, or humour we have seen in some of the others; historically interesting, but otherwise somewhat barren.

The Lads of Wamphray celebrates a skirmish between the Johnstons and the Crichtons which took place in 1593. William Johnston of Wamphray, known as the Galiard, with a band of companions attacks the Crichtons in Nithsdale. He steals a horse, but it turns out to be blind, so he is overtaken and hanged. Will o' Kirkhill witnesses the killing and swears revenge. He raises a band again in Wamphray:

> Saying, My lads if ye'll be true,
> Ye's a' be clad in the noble blue.

> Back to Nidsdale they are gane,
> And away the Crichtons' nout they hae taen.

They are pursued and stand to fight when they reach the Biddess-law:

> And through the Crichtons Willy he ran,
> And dang them down both horse and man.

> O but these lads were wondrous rude,
> When the Biddess-burn ran three days blood!

They return, interestingly, with clear consciences:

> 'Sin we've done na hurt, nor we'll take na wrang,
> But back to Wamphray we will gang

> *   *   *

> Drive on my lads, it will be late;
> We'll have a pint at Wamphray Gate'.

Again, apart from some historical interest, the scope and treatment are limited; the ballad lacks the depth of, say, *Hobbie Noble*, and the pace and violence of *Kinmont Willie*, though its two-line form is unusual. Gummere considers that 'It differs . . . from the mass of the ballads which were founded on deeds of the border, on feud, murder, burnings, in its fresh and immediate tone. It seems to spring straight from the fact; and one is tempted here, if anywhere, to apply Bishop Leslie's *ipsi confingunt*, and to charge the making of the ballad to the very doers of its deed of revenge. It is certainly not made at long range'.[40] We need not pursue such speculation. The ballad is what it is.

Ballads of the West Marches

Probably the most unusual ballad in the entire Border is *The Fray of Suport*. Though this appeared in the *Minstrelsy*, it was left out of Child after the first edition. Hart comments on this: 'A number of tales which employ a highly artificial stanza, such as *The Fray of Suport*, *The Raid of the Reidswire*, or *The Flemish Insurrection*, do not find their way into the later collection.[41] This ballad is ignored by critics such as Gummere, Henderson, Gerould and Fowler; and though W. H. Auden included it in *The Poet's Tongue* it is not frequently found in anthologies. Its authenticity is established from Robert Shortreed's account of his 'raids' into Liddesdale with Scott, when the latter was first collecting pieces for the projected *Minstrelsy*. The only ballad which he is said by Shortreed to have got direct from the recitation of a countryman on these excursions was *The Fray of Suport*, supplied by Jonathan Graham, 'the lang quaker' (see the Introduction). Scott writes:

Of all the Border ditties which have fallen into the Editor's hands this is by far the most uncouth and savage. It is usually chaunted in a sort of wild recitative, except the burden, which swells into a long and varied howl, not unlike to a view hollo. The words, and the very great irregularity of the stanza (if it deserves the name), sufficiently point out its intention and origin. An English woman, residing in Suport, near the foot of the Kershope, having been plundered in the night by a band of the Scottish moss-troopers, is supposed to convoke her servants and friends for the pursuit, or *Hot Trod*.[42]

Sleep'ry Sim of the Lamb-hill,
And snoring Jock of Suport-mill,
Ye are baith right het and fou';—
But my wae wakens na you.
Last night I saw a sorry sight—
Nought left me, o' four-and-twenty gude ousen and ky,
My weel-ridden gelding, and a white quey,
But a toom byre and a wide,
And the twelve nogs on ilka side.
     Fy lads! shout a' a' a' a' a',
     My gear's a' gane.

Weel may ye ken,
Last night I was right scarce o' men:
But Toppet Hob o' the Mains had guesten'd in my house by
    chance;
I set him to wear the fore-door wi' the speir, while I kept the
    back door wi' the lance;
But they hae run him thro' the thick o' the thie, and broke
    his knee-pan,
And the mergh o' his shin bane has run down on his spur
    leather whang:
He's lame while he lives, and where'er he may gang.
       Fy lads! shout a' a' a' a' a',
       My gear's a' gane.

But Peenye, my gude son, is out at the Hagbut-head,
His e'en glittering for anger like a fiery gleed;
Crying—'Mak sure the nooks
Of Maky's-muir crooks;
For the wily Scot takes by nooks, hooks, and crooks,
Gin we meet a' together in a head the morn,
We'll be merry men.'
       Fy lads! shout a' a' a' a' a',
       My gear's a' gane.

There's doughty Cuddy in the Heugh-head,
Thou was aye gude at a' need:
With thy brock-skin bag at thy belt,
Ay ready to mak a puir man help.
Thou maun awa' out to the Cauf-craigs
(Where anes ye lost your ain twa naigs),
And there toom thy brock-skin bag.
       Fy lads! shout a' a' a' a' a',
       My gear's a' ta'en.

Doughty Dan o' the Houlet Hirst,
Thou was aye gude at a birst:
Gude wi' a bow, and better wi' a speir,
The bauldest march-man that e'er followed gear;
Come thou here.
       Fy lads! shout a' a' a' a' a',
       My gear's a' gane.

Rise, ye carle coopers, frae making o' kirns and tubs,
In the Nicol forest woods.
Your craft has na left the value of an oak rod,
But if you had had ony fear o' God,
Last night ye had na slept sae sound,
And let my gear be a' ta'en.
>> Fy lads! shout a' a' a' a' a',
>> My gear's a' ta'en.

Ah! lads, we'll fang them a' in a net!
For I hae a' the fords o' Liddel set;
The Dunkin, and the Door-loup,
The Willie-ford, and the Water-slack,
The Black-rack and the Trout-dub of Liddel;
There stands John Forster wi' five men at his back,
Wi' buft coat and cap of steil:
Boo! ca' at them e'en, Jock;
That ford's sicker, I wat weil.
>> Fy lads! shout a' a' a' a' a',
>> My gear's a' ta'en.

Hoo! hoo! gar raise the Reid Souter, and Ringan's Wat,
Wi' a broad elshin and a wicker;
I wat weil they'll mak a ford sicker.
Sae whether they be Elliots or Armstrangs,
Or rough riding Scots, or rude Johnstones,
Or whether they be frae the Tarras or Ewsdale,
They maun turn and fight, or try the deeps o' Liddel.
>> Fy lads! shout a' a' a' a' a',
>> My gear's a' ta'en.

'Ah! but they will play ye another jigg,
For they will out at the big rig,
And thro' at Fargy Grame's gap.'
But I hae another wile for that:
For I hae little Will, and stalwart Wat,
And lang Aicky, in the Souter moor,
Wi' his sleuth dog sits in his watch right sure;
Shou'd the dog gie a bark,
He'll be out in his sark,
And die or won.

> Fy lads! shout a' a' a' a' a',
> My gear's a' ta'en.

Ha! boys—I see a party appearing—wha's yon!
Methinks it's the captain of Bewcastle, and Jephtha's
    John,
Coming down by the foul steps of Catlowdie's loan:
They'll make a sicker, come which way they will.
> > Ha lads! shout a' a' a' a' a',
> > My gear's a' ta'en.

Captain Musgrave, and a' his band,
And coming down by the siller strand,
And the muckle toun-bell o' Carlisle is rung:
My gear was a' weel won,
And before it's carried o'er the Border, mony a man's gae
    down.
> > Fy lads! shout a' a' a' a' a',
> > My gear's a' gane.

What appears to be an interesting counterpart to this is referred to in Sir Walter Scott's Journal: 'The Duke [of Northumberland] tells me his people in Keeldar were all quite wild the first time his father went up to shoot there. The women had no other dress than a bedgown and petticoat. The men were savage and could hardly be brought to rise from the heath either from sullenness or fear. They sung a wild tune, the burden of which was *Ourina Ourina Ourina*. The females sung, the men danced round and at a certain part of the tune Ourina they drew their dirks which they always wore.'[43]

In such contexts 'ballad' and 'Border ditty' alike are mis-nomers; the words of *Suport* make up a cry for vengeance in the face of whose desolate and savage vigour literary criticism would be a mere genteel impertinence.

When we look at *Adam Bell, Clym of the Clough, and William of Cloudesly*, we have a different kind of problem; although the action centres on Carlisle, the whole tone of the tale is alien to the Border, and certainly strikes a different note from any ballad I have discussed hitherto. It is much more in the vein of the Robin Hood ballads, as the first stanzas show:

> Merry it was in grene forest,
>   Amonge the leves grene,
> Where that men walke both east and west,
>   Wyth bowes and arrowes kene . . .

An exceptionally long ballad of 170 stanzas, it even has a second
part ('a pure manufacture', says Child) of 111 stanzas. Neither
Scott nor Motherwell print it, and on the whole I believe it to be
foreign to the theme of this volume.

This leaves then only three further ballads of the West March
to consider, and in doing so to introduce topics I shall explore
much more fully in a later chapter: romance and folklore. Of
Johnie Cock Hodgart remarks that it is vaguer in setting and
richer in folklore than the Riding Ballads and 'is based on the
blood-feud, perhaps of an earlier period'.[44] Child calls it a
'precious specimen of the unspoiled traditional ballad', and
prints eight complete versions as well as five fragmentary ones.
The hero is variously called 'Johnie Cock', 'Johnie of Cockerslee',
'Johnie o' Cocklesmuir', 'Johnie of Breadislee', 'Johnie Brad',
'Johnie of Braidisbank', but all versions agree on the essentials. I
include it as belonging to the West March on the strength of
Scott's *Johnie of Breadislee*, 'an ancient Nithsdale ballad' which
he compiled by selecting 'the stanzas of greatest merit' from
each of several different copies (Child F). Breadislee and Durris-
deer are in Dumfriesshire but in this type of ballad, the locality
is less significant than the romance of the tale.

'Johnie rose up in a May morning' and goes off with his
hounds to poach deer, in spite of the anxiety of his mother:

> 'O Johnie, for my bennison,
>   To the grenewood dinna gang!
>
> Eneugh ye hae o the gude wheat-bread,
>   And eneugh o the blude-red wine,
> And therefore for nae vennison, Johnie,
>   I pray ye, stir frae hame'.

His hunting is successful, and with his hounds he sits down to
enjoy their prey:

> And Johnie has bryttled the deer sae weel
>   That he's had out her liver and lungs,

> And wi these he has feasted his bludey hounds
>   As if they had been erl's sons.

> They eat sae much o the vennison,
>   And drank sae much of the blude,
> That Johnie and a' his bludey hounds
>   Fell asleep as they had been dead.

The blood drinking is presumably an echo of the ancient northern belief that by drinking the blood of the animal you have killed, you acquire its qualities. A 'silly auld carle' sees him sleeping and betrays him to the Seven Foresters; they attack him:

> Johnie's set his back against an aik,
>   His fute against a stane,
> And he has slain the Seven Foresters,
>   He has slain them a' but ane.

> He has broke three ribs in that ane's side,
>   But and his collar bane;
> He's laid him twa-fald ower his steed,
>   Bade him carry the tidings hame.

It is here that traditional lore enters the tale, with marked effect; the talking bird appears:

> 'O is there na a bonny bird
>   Can sing as I can say,
> Could flee away to my mother's bower,
>   And tell to fetch Johnie away?'

> The starling flew to his mother's window-stane,
>   It whistled and it sang,
> And aye the ower-word to the tune
>   Was Johnie tarries lang!

It is most tempting to insert between these verses a single, haunting, isolated stanza from Finlay's *Scottish Ballads*:

> 'There's no a bird in a' this foreste
>   Will do as meikle for me
> As dip its wing in the wan water
>   And straik it on my ee-bree'.

particularly as it matches so beautifully the melancholy, the
dying fall of the concluding stanza:

> Now Johnie's gude bend bow is broke,
> And his gude graie dogs are slain,
> And his bodie lies dead in Durrisdeer,
> And his hunting it is done.

The location of *Annan Water* is equally vague, in spite of the
apparent precision of the title. Child prints Scott's version of
this as an appendix to *Rare Willie Drowned in Yarrow*, and
dismisses it in the words of Allan Ramsay as one of the 'Scots
poems wrote by the ingenious before 1800'.[45] Scott's comment is
that 'The following verses are the original words of the tune of
"Allan Water", by which name the song is mentioned in
Ramsay's *Tea-Table Miscellany*. The ballad is given from tradition' (for which, Child retorts, 'a more precise expression would
be "oral repetition" ') and tells the sad tale of a lover drowned
on his way to meet his mistress:

> 'Gar saddle me the bonny black,
> Gar saddle sune and make him ready,
> For I will down the Gatehope-Slack,
> And all to see my bonny ladye'.

After a gruelling journey over rough country on a weary horse,
he reaches the river in flood; the boatsman refuses to face the
crossing, the lover dares it alone and is drowned. It is a
melancholy theme, not at all unfamiliar in ballad literature, but
it lacks the compelling pathos and involvement of *Willie's rare*,
which I shall consider in a later chapter. The last verse, indeed,
has more about it of prudence than of wild tragedy, and one
cannot but agree with Child in his strictures.

One would like to know, however, why he bothered to print
and comment on this piece, and yet ignore utterly *Fair Helen
of Kirconnel*; though a good company of critics follow him in
silence. As Scott prints it, the ballad falls into two parts, the
first of which he rejects as spurious, and indeed anthologists
ever since have tended to print only the second part, beginning
'I wish I were where Helen lies'. Kirconnel is in Dumfriesshire,
and this is the only identifiable feature of the narrative, but it is

none the less moving for that. Helen, beloved of two men, returns the love of the one least favoured by her family, and the pair must of necessity meet in secret. The rejected lover attempts to shoot his rival, but succeeds only in killing Helen, who throws her body in the path of the bullet. The two men fight and the murderer is hacked to pieces.

Such a bald account fails entirely to convey the quality of the poem, whose brevity, simplicity and unpretentious melancholy produce an unusually acute sense of isolation, grief and resignation:

> As I went down the water side,
> None but my foe to be my guide,
> None but my foe to be my guide
>   On fair Kirconnel Lee.
>
> I lighted down, my sword did draw,
> I hacked him in pieces sma';
> I hacked him in pieces sma',
>   For her sake that died for me.
>
> O Helen fair beyond compare!
> I'll make a garland of thy hair,
> Shall bind my heart for evermair,
>   Until the day I die.

It is instructive to compare such stanzas, and the quiet eloquence of their lament, with the version of the same tale by William Wordsworth, *Ellen Irwin: or, The Braes of Kirtle*, of which the following verses are representative:

> Proud Gordon, maddened by the thoughts
> That through his brain are travelling,
> Rushed forth, and at the heart of Bruce
> He launched a deadly javelin!
> Fair Ellen saw it as it came,
> And, starting up to meet the same,
> Did with her body cover
> The youth, her chosen lover.
>
> And, falling into Bruce's arms,
> Thus died the beauteous Ellen,

Thus, from the heart of her True-love,
The mortal spear repelling.
And Bruce, as soon as he had slain
The Gordon, sailed away to Spain;
And fought with rage incessant
Against the Moorish crescent.

Border violence, however, was the prerogative neither of the Armstrongs nor of the West Marches. If we move now north-east up the valley of the Liddel, through the territory of the Keeper of Liddesdale, we shall enter the Middle March at Kershopefoot, from where the ballads lead us along Teviotdale into the shires of Selkirk and Roxburgh, and into Northumbrian Redesdale and Tynedale.

CHAPTER 3

THE MIDDLE MARCHES (1)

The West March borders the Middle March at Kershopefoot in Liddesdale, and here, by the Liddel water lies Stonegarthside Hall, from where the Captain of Bewcastle rode into Teviotdale to plunder Jamie Telfer of the Fair Dodhead. Child prints two versions of this tale, one from Scott, whose authenticity he suspects, another given to him by his correspondent Macmath in which the Elliots replace the Scotts but which varies in no significant narrative feature. Scott is non-committal about the source of his version in his introductory remarks:

> There is another ballad, under the same title as the following, in which nearly the same incidents are narrated, with little difference, except that the honour of rescuing the cattle is attributed to the Liddesdale Elliots, headed by a chief there called Martin Elliot, of the Preakin Tower, whose son Simon is said to have fallen in the action. It is very possible that both the Teviotdale Scotts and the Elliots were engaged in the affair, and that each claimed the honour of the victory.
>
> The editor presumes that the Willie Scott here mentioned must have been a natural son of the Laird of Buccleuch.

Dobie comments:

> The true version of *Jamie Telfer*, as Col. the Hon. Fitzwilliam Elliot has shown (*The Trustworthiness of Border Ballads*, etc. 1906) seems to be that in which the Elliots are the heroes and the Scotts the villains. But it would be wrong to accuse Scott of felony in inverting the rôles. His grandmother's version presumably favoured the Scotts, and even if he remembered the merest snatches of this, and was given the Elliot version entire in Liddesdale, he would feel justified in grafting the former on to the latter, which he doubtless numbered among the variations due to 'the prejudices of clans and districts' which had to be corrected.'[1]

The ballad opens energetically with a series of stanzas which succinctly localise the time, the place and the action:

> It fell about the Martinmas tyde,
>> When our border steeds get corn and hay,
> The captain of Bewcastle hath bound him to ryde,
>> And he's ower to Tividale to drive a prey.

> The first ae guide that they met wi',
>> It was high up in Hardhaughswire;
> The second guide that we met wi',
>> It was laigh down in Borthwick water.

> 'What tidings, what tidings, my trusty guide?'
>> 'Nae tidings, nae tidings I hae to thee;
> But gin ye'll gae to the fair Dodhead,
>> Mony a cow's cauf I'll let thee see.'

> And when they came to the fair Dodhead,
>> Right hastily they clam the peel;
> They loosed the kye out, ane and a',
>> And ranshakled the house right weel.

The significance of Martinmas (November 11) here (as of Lammas in *The Battle of Otterburn*) is revealed if one recalls the passage from 'Replies to the King of Scots' Proposals' in the *Calendar of Border Papers* for August 1597 (see above p. 28). The invaders are guided to Dodhead (the site of this is doubtful, in spite of Scott's location, but the general development of the other place-names is feasible) and here the narrative is carried through by dialogue which, in a single stanza, varies the narrative tone, personalises the action, and renders more immediate the complexity of Border loyalties and allegiances, since here the English band seems to be picking up its information on the northern side of the border. (This international allegiance in feud is clearly demonstrated in *The Death of Parcy Reed*.) The sudden assault and ransacking of the tower house is met at first, perhaps unexpectedly, not by battle, but by a distressed Jamie Telfer pleading with the raiders:

> Now Jamie Telfer's heart was sair,
>> The tear aye rowing in his e'e;

He pled wi' the captain to hae his gear
Or else revenged he wad be.

He is answered with contempt, and then sets off on foot to seek
help from those to whom he has paid black mail (see p. 50).
There now follows a series of exchanges as Jamie runs from
tower to tower trying to gather men. His first request is refused
with disdain by Gibby Elliott of Stobs' Ha':

'Gae seek your succour at Branksome Ha',
For succour ye'se get nane frae me!
Gae seek your succour where ye paid black-mail,
For, man! ye ne'er paid money to me.'

He runs on to Coultart Cleugh where Jock Grieve, his brother-
in-law, lends him a horse to ride on to Catslockhill. Here
William's Wat remembers the hospitality he has always received
at Dodhead:

'I never cam by the fair Dodhead,
That ever I fand thy basket bare'

so he rides with his two sons alongside Jamie towards Branksome Hall. Slowly the band is gathering, knit by bonds of blood
and neighbourliness, but the climax comes when they reach
Branksome and Jamie repeats the pattern of his appeal which
we have now heard three times:

And whan they came to Branksome Ha'
They shouted a' baith loud and hie,
Till up and spak him auld Buccleuch,
Said—'Whae's this brings the fray to me?'

'It's I, Jamie Telfer o' the fair Dodhead,
And a harried man I think I be!
There's nought left in the fair Dodhead,
But a greeting wife and bairnies three.'

'Alack for wae!' quoth the gude auld lord,
'And ever my heart is wae for thee!
But fye gar cry on Willie my son,
And see that he comes to me speedilie!

'Gar warn the water braid and wide,
  Gar warn it sune and hastily!
They that winna ride for Telfer's kye,
  Let them never look on the face o' me!

'Warn Wat o' Harden and his sons,
  Wi' them will Borthwick water ride;
Warn Gaudilands, and Allanhaugh,
  And Gilmanscleugh, and Commonside.

'Ride by the gates at Priesthaughswire,
  And warn the Currors o' the Lee;
As ye cum down the Hermitage Slack,
  Warn doughty Willie o' Gorrinberry.'

The Scotts they rade, the Scotts they ran,
  Sae starkly and sae steadilie!
And aye the ower-word o' the thrang
  Was—'Rise for Branksome readilie!'

'Raising the water' to follow the fray is never so clearly seen
in ballad literature as here though, as I have suggested earlier,
in the case of *Kinmont Willie*, the pattern of both ballad and the
action described are explicit enough to make one suspect the
organising hand of Scott. Nevertheless, the pace of these stanzas
is compelling and the urgency of the occasion intensified not
only by the long time it has taken Jamie to gather his supporters,
but by the varied sweep of the sequence of place-names:

'Warn Gaudilands and Allanhaugh,
  And Gilmanscleugh and Commonside.

'Ride by the gates at Priesthaughswire . . .'

Meanwhile the English marauders are driving their spoil up
the Frostylee, a burn in Teviothead which flows hard by
Carlinrigg, where Johnie Armstrong was hanged. They are
intercepted by Telfer's men, possibly as they come from their
final appeal to Gorrinberry over the tops from the Hermitage
water and down the Frostylee burn, and challenged by Willie
Scott:

'O will ye let Telfer's kye gae back?
  Or will ye do aught for regard o me?

Or, by the faith o my body,' quo Willie Scott,
'I'se ware my dame's cauf's skin on thee.'

'I winna let the kye gae back,
   Neither for thy love nor yet thy fear;
But I will drive Jamie Telfer's kye
   In spite of every Scott that's here.'

The mild equivocation of this interchange again suggests that to
Willie Scott and to the Captain of Bewcastle there is some hope,
however faint, of a truce based on a former allegiance not on
mere force of numbers; the defiance in this instance is as much
one of personality as of nationality, especially if one accepts the
reading of 'Scott' rather than of 'Scot' in the last line. The
fighting begins, and once more one senses the elegance of the
poet rather than that of the singer:

And mony a horse ran masterless,
   And mony a comely cheek was pale.

But the loyal and enthusiastic Willie is slain (at which 'Harden
grat for very rage').

The battle now develops into a matter of revenging his death,
and

. . . or they wan to the Kershope ford,
   The Scotts had gotten the victory.

However the leader of the English band suffers more than
defeat,

The Captain was run through the thick of the thigh
   And broken was his right leg bane;
If he had lived this hundred years,
   He had never been loved by woman again.

'Hae back the kye!' the Captain said;
   'Dear kye, I trow, to some they be;
For gin I suld live a hundred years
   There will nee fair lady smile on me.'

'The Editor has used some freedom', notes Scott, 'with the
original—the account of the Captain's disaster (teste laeva

vulnerata) is rather too naïve for literal publication.' Macmath's version is less squeamish:

> The Captain was shot through the head,
>   And also through the left ba-stane . . .

But the tale would be incomplete without due personal redress. The Captain is led into captivity, to the distress of his wife who would rather he had died than been so disgraced over the border, and Watty Wudspurs rides on to Stanegarthside with some followers to complete their revenge. (See map of 1590. Curwen maintains that the point here marked 'Staingarthsyde' is what is now Stonehaugh Tower, while 'Ro-forsters' a little further up the Liddel is Stanegarthside Hall. Pevsner describes this as 'an unusual and forbidding-looking three-storeyed house on an H plan, with four-stepped gables'. It carries a date 1682.)

> When they came to the Stanegirthside,
>   They dang wi trees and burst the door;
> They loosed out a' the Captains kye
>   And set them forth our lads before.

So Telfer is saved by his friends, and with interest:

> For instead of his ain ten milk-kye
>   Jamie Telfer has gotten thirty and three.

But the tale ends in pathos rather than in celebration, for one of the boldest of them all is missing, and cannot be rewarded with the gold and silver which Jamie dispenses:

> And he has paid the rescue-shot,
>   Baith wi gowd and white monie,
> And at the burial o Willie Scott
>   I wat was mony a weeping ee.

a concluding stanza missing from Macmath's version. Jamie's liberality, however, may be a generous fiction, since coin of any kind was scarce in the Borders in the sixteenth century.

Apart from its intrinsic narrative excitement, this tale is especially interesting, and unusual, for the way in which that excitement is developed in terms of human relationships, where unspoken loyalties are tested and formal agreements of black mail carry little moral obligation.

The Outlaw Murray derives from the same region, though whether Murray's tower was the now vast ruin of Newark Castle, or the more modest and neighbouring Hangingshaw, is dubious; but the ballad itself is of hazy provenance, and Child prints it (No. 305) with clear misgiving: 'The original manuscript, unfortunately and inexplicably, is no longer in the Philiphaugh archives, and has not come to light after search.' It first appeared in Scott's *Minstrelsy* of 1802.

The ballad is the story of an outlaw who defies the king over the ownership of land, and eventually, after protesting his independence, vows allegiance if the king will make him sheriff, and all ends happily:

> The keys of the castell he gave the king,
>   With the blessing of his fair ladye;
> He was made sheryff of Etrick forest,
>   Surely while upward grows the trie.

In spite of some pleasing pastoralisms which frame the familiar theme of the individual defying authority, the ballad remains trivial and improbable, representing little of importance in either history, song or literature. South of the border, however, we return from the greenwood to the bitterness of internecine feud in the upper reaches of Redesdale.

An act of the Merchant Adventurers of Newcastle, passed in 1554, declaims vigorously against the general wildness of apprentices, the extravagance of their dress and behaviour, and sternly forbids them to 'daunse, dyse, carde, or mum, or use any gytternes; to wear any cut hose, cut shoes, or pounced jerkens, or any berds'. But the merchants are particularly wary of apprentices born in Tynedale or Redesdale. It is 'assented, accordide, and agreyd . . . that no fre brother of this Fellysshype shall, from hensfourthe, take none apprentice, to serve in this Fellysshype of non suche as is or shal be borne or brought up in Tyndall, Ryddisdall, or anye other suche lycke places; in payne of XX^{li}' because, as was explained when the act was revised and amplified, 'the parties there brought up ar knowen, either by educatyon or nature, not to be of honest conversatyon.'[2] Master Richard Crompton, 'un apprentice de le common ley', in a work he wrote in 1584 on the responsibilities of a justice of the peace, laid it down as a maxim that the country in which a man is born generally declares his natural inclination—for instance, if he were born or brought up in Tynedale or Redesdale he ought to be the more suspected.[3]

The people of Redesdale, wrote Sir Ralph Sadler, Warden of the East and Middle Marches in 1559, are 'naughty, evil, unruly and misdemeaned'. They had already been described in Bowes' Survey of 1542 as

living in sheds during the summer months, and pasturing their cattle in the grains and hopes of the country on the south side of the Coquet, about Wilkwood and Ridlees, or in the waste grounds, which sweep along the eastern marches of North Tindale. At this time they not only joined with their neighbours of Tindale in acts of rapine and spoil, but often went as guides to the thieves of Scotland, in expeditions to harry and to burn the towns and villages, which were separated from them by the broad tracts of waste land, which stretched from the sources of the Wansbeck, about Fallowlees, towards Birtley and Bootland; so that these districts suffered as grievously from them, as the places to the north of the Coquet did from their natural enemy, the Scotch.[4]

Scott also comments on the area: 'The men of Tynedale and Reedsdale, in particular, appear to have been more frequently tempted by the rich vales of the Bishoprick of Durham, and other districts which lay to the southward, than by the rude desolation of the Scottish hills.'[5] This is a fair indication of the kind of supra- or contra-national alliances that existed for so long in the Borders, and in the Northumbrian ballad of *The Death of Parcy Reed* we find an example of a Redesdale family, the Halls, entering a league with the Scots Crosiers of Liddesdale, against another Redesdale family, the Reeds.

Three versions exist of this ballad: one among Robert White's papers, marked 'Woodburn, December 1, 1829, Thomas Hedley, Bridge End, Corsonside Parish' (Corsenside is in Redesdale between Otterburn and Bellingham). Another (Child B) was first published in *The Borderer's Table Book* of 1846, 'An old ballad, taken down by James Telfer from recitation, with an introduction by Robert White'; White points out that it was

chanted to Telfer by an old woman, named Kitty Hall, who
resided at Fairloans in the head of Kale water, Roxburghshire.
'She was a native of Northumberland, and observed she never
liked to sing the verses, as she knew them to be perfectly true,
and consequently couldn't bear to think there had been, of her
own surname, such wretches as the betrayers of Parcy Reed.'[6]
White then mentions a transcript of this which Telfer gave to
Scott, who placed it at the end of his copy of Roxby's 'Lay of
the Reedwater Minstrel'. Child gives it in an appendix: ' "Parcy
Reed, exactly as it is sung by an old woman of the name of
Cathrine Hall, living at Fairloans, in the remotest corner of
Oxnam parish." James Telfer, Browndeanlows, May 18, 1824.'
For the purpose of this commentary, I have used the second of
these. The 'original' is, typically, impossible to arrive at. Of the
first version, White wrote to J. H. Dixon, 'Parcy Reed, as you
suspect, is not genuine, for it bears the marks of our friend's
improvements. I have a copy of the original somewhere, but
may not be able to find it.' Telfer himself in a letter to the
Northumbrian poet Robert Story said of it, 'I will send Mr.
Dixon the real verses, but it is but a droll of a ballad'.[7] White
mentions none of this in his introduction to the second version,
but adds a footnote that the word 'hard' in line 4 of stanza 38 is
'black', in the original; Child prints this as 'black', but it is also
'black' in his Cathrine Hall version.

The ballad begins with stanzas which recall the spirit of
Maitland's *Complaynt*

> God send the land deliverance
>   Frae every reaving, riding Scot:
> We'll sune hae neither cow nor ewe,
>   We'll sure hae neither staig nor stot.
>
> The outlaws come frae Liddesdale,
>   They herry Redesdale far and near;
> The rich man's gelding it maun gang,
>   They canna pass the puir man's mear.
>
> Sure it were weel had ilka thief
>   Around his neck a halter strang;
> And curses heavy may they light
>   On traitors vile oursel's amang.

and have about them a self-conscious detachment which leads
one to suspect Telfer's own hand and indeed to see in it a skill
almost equal to Scott's. These opening lines are, moreover,
absent from the other two versions.

With the fourth stanza (the theme of which forms the opening
of the other two accounts) we are given the cause of the
impending conflict which is to be the burden of the rest of the
ballad:

> Now Parcy Reed has Crosier ta'en,
>   He has delivered him to the law;
> But Crosier says he'll do waur than that,
>   He'll make the tower o' Troughend fa'.

> And Crosier says he will do waur—
>   He will do waur if waur can be;
> He'll make the bairns a' fatherless.
>   And then, the land it may lie lee.

It is interesting to see how these verses, and the story which
follows, point the irrelevance of the opening lines. This ballad is
not about cattle stealing, but about treachery and feud, though
it may be true that the Crosiers' original offence was reiving.
The surname occurs frequently in the records of Border affrays,
and, particularly, in the sixteenth century, is linked with
English families.

14 Sept. 1544

The Crosyers, Ollyvers, Halls and Trombles, which are entred
bond with England, have gotten a castle in Tevedaill, called
Egerton, by pollicie, and in wynning thereof slew 2 Scotts
stonding in the defence thereof, and they have left in the
same 20 of their company, and keepeth the same, 2 Scotts
slain.

17 Sept. 1544

Threscore of Ryddesdall, with the Halls, Ollyvers, Trombles,
Ruddeforths, and Crosyers aforesaid, dyd an exploit in
Scotland thre myles beyond Mewres, and there toke up a
town named Beamontsyde, and hath taken 20 prisoners, 120
nolt, and hurt divers Scottishmen.[8]

The Reeds had long inhabited Troughend (pronounced Trowhen), a tower no longer traceable near Troughend Hall about two miles west of Otterburn. Hodgson's account of the family includes the following comment: 'They were reckoned the second clan in the dale in power and reputation, in 1542. In the reign of queen Elizabeth, John Reed, "one laird of Troughen, the chief of the name of Reed," kept up the celebrity of his house by adhering to the habits, and cultivating the martial spirit for which the thanes of Redesdale had been immemorially celebrated'[9] and adds the footnote: 'The laird of Troughwen, the chief of the name of Reed, and divers of his followers—a ruder and a more lawless crew there needs not be; yet if well tutored, they might do her maj[ie] good service; but their practices are not to be defended.'[10]

A number of raids on Troughend are recorded, like the following:

1584 May 3-19 Complaints of Forster and others
By Percevall Reade the young larde of Trochen, against Arche Ellott called Hobbes Archie, Edie Ellott of the Shawe, Gawens Archie Ellot, Arche Ellot of the Hill, Clemy Crosier called nebles Cleymey, Hobby Ellot of the Ramsgill, and other 200 men, for running an open foray on the 19th May, 1584, at Burduppe in the Middle March, stealing 200 kye and oxen, 80 horses and meires, insight worth 200 l., and taking 80 prisoners 'in horse and geire.'

1590 April 13-19 Middle March Bills etc. contains the entry:
Percevall Read of Trowhen complains upon Will Ellott of Fydderton, Alexander Ellott of Fallon, Rynion Ellot of Dodborne, Robin Ellot 'the laird of Borneheades', Hob Ellett 'Hob bullie', Davye 'the Carlinge', Rynione Armestrong 'Ecktors Rynion' of the Harelawe, and 80 others for an open foray at Trowhen 'on Whitsond Mounday 1589', and reaving 51 kye and oxen, 3 horse and meares, 60 yards of 'lynne clothe' and killing 2 men, 'which is alredie agreed fyled and sworne by the sight of iiij Englishmen and iiij Scottesmen 1589'.[11]

Stanza 6 begins the narrative proper, with Reed taking the three false Halls as his companions to the hunt, and the familiar

localising features appear in the names of Rooken Edge, Ealy-
lawe and the fatal Bateinghope, a high and lonely grain which
falls away eastwards from Carter Fell (Plate 11). It is recorded
as a thieves' pass from Scotland in a record of such ways set
down in November 1597: 'Battinhop rawk, one myle from Robbs
cross in Tyndale, West Tyvidayle, from the Wharle causey in
Tyndayle to Readeswire cross.'[12] Here, late in the afternoon,
Parcy Reed took his ease after the hunting, and slept.

> There's nane may lean on a rotten staff,
>   But him that risks to get a fa';
> There's nane may in a traitor trust,
>   And traitors black were every Ha'.

> They've stown the bridle off his steed
>   And they've put water in his lang gun;
> They've fixed his sword within the sheath,
>   That out again it winna come.

> 'Awaken ye, waken ye, Parcy Reed
>   Or by your enemies be ta'en
> For yonder are the five Crosiers
>   A-coming owre the Hingin-stane'.

The proverbial wisdom of the first lines has the ring of inter-
polation, but it is interesting to find the Halls, the most powerful
family of Redesdale, here branded as traitors, and indeed shown
as such in all accounts of the tale, both prose and verse, in their
successful neutralising of the doomed Keeper of Redesdale while
the Crosiers approach for the kill. The hunting theme of the
ballad has nice irony.

When Reed wakes, he appeals like Jamie Telfer to each of the
Halls for help, in a repetitive pattern of verses, and is formally
refused by each:

> 'O turn thee, turn thee, Tommy Ha'—
>   O turn now, man, and fight wi' me;
> If ever we come to Troughend again
>   My daughter Jean I'll gie to thee.'

> 'I mayna turn, I canna turn,
>   I daurna turn and fight wi' thee;

> The Crosiers haud thee at a feud,
> And they wad kill baith thee and me.'

The Crosiers attack him, unarmed as he is:

> 'Owre lang hae we been in your debt,
> Now will we pay you as we ought.'

> They fell upon him all at once;
> They mangled him most cruellie:
> The slightest wound might caused his deid,
> And they hae gi'en him thirty-three.
> They hackit off his hands and feet
> An left him lying on the lee.

> 'Now Parcy Reed, we've paid our debt,
> Ye canna weel dispute the tale.'
> The Crosiers said, and off they rade—
> They rade the airt o' Liddesdale.

and presumably returned whence they came, though their appearance 'owre the Hingin-stane' is a puzzle. There may have been a number of Hanging Stones: the name is ambiguous. It refers probably to large rock formations on a steep hillside, or having a forward tilt, but could also be a place of execution. The Hanging Stone commonly referred to as a landmark in early Border surveys is an outcrop standing a little to the south-west of the summit of Cheviot; it indicates one point in the boundary between the Middle and East Marches, as well as between England and Scotland, and is twenty miles from Bateinghope, in the opposite direction from Liddesdale. What are now marked as Kielder Stone and Boar Stone would be possible alternatives. In the list of Scots thieves' roads made in 1597 we find: 'Hanginston from Buttrod Head one myle in Cokdayle, joynes on Chiveat on Easte Tyvidale. Aucopswire from Hangingstone half a myle from East Tyvidale', which support the surveyors' location on Cheviot.

The last ten stanzas tell how Reed, now so mutilated as to be almost unrecognisable, was found by a herdsman who brings him water from the burn, and to whom he entrusts his dying message, the 'farewell' or 'goodnight', which we have already seen in Johnie Armstrong:

'Now honest herd; ye maun do mair—
  Ye maun do mair as I you tell;
You maun bear tidings to Troughend,
  And bear likewise my last farewell.

'A farewell to my wedded wife;
  A farewell to my brother John,
Wha sits into the Troughend tower,
  With heart as black as any stone.

'A farewell to my daughter Jean;
  A farewell to my young sons five:
Had they been at their father's hand,
  I had this night been man alive.

'A farewell to my followers a',
  And a' my neighbours gude at need;
Bid them think how the treacherous Ha's,
  Betrayed the life o' Parcy Reed.

'The laird o' Clennel bears my bow;
  The laird o' Brandon bears my brand;
Whene'er they ride i' the Border side,
  They'll mind the fate o' the laird Troughend.'

Clennel tower was near Alwinton on a tributary of the Coquet
and is first mentioned in 1541 as being 'newly reparelled and
brattyshed': Brandon is on the Breamish Burn, west of Alnwick,
but no record remains of a tower there.

The tale, however, does not completely end here. In his
introduction to this version White tells of the return of Parcy
Reed's ghost to haunt the area, and of its later reappearance
'within the last century' in the form of a dove. Hodgson in his
account of the incident,[13] adds the following:

They say, too, that the spirit of Reed, ever after it was
disembodied, could find no rest; but was seen wandering far
and near, in trouble, and in various forms, till one gifted with
words to lay it to rest, summoned it to his presence and
offered it the place and form it might wish to have. It chose
the banks of the Rede, between Todlawhaugh and Pringle-
haugh, and there

('Trained forward to his bloody fall
  By Girsonfield one treacherous Hall;)
Oft by the Pringle's haunted side
  The shepherd sees his spectre glide.'—Rokeby

It had five miles of river-side scenery to range among, in which
it flitted about by night, or roosted on some stone or tree by
day. One of its favourite haunts was about the Todlaw Mill,
now in ruins, where the people, as they went to the meeting-
house at Birdhope Cragg, often saw it, uncovered their heads
as they passed, and bowed, and the courteous phantom bowed
again, till its 'certain time' was expired; on the last day of
which, as the conjuror who laid him was following his
ordinary occupation of a thatcher, at the Woollaw, he felt
something touch him like the wing of a bird whisking by,
came down the ladder, was seized with a cold trembling,
shivered, and died.

And in his letter to Scott about the ballad Telfer wrote:

There is a place in Reed Water called Deadwood Haughs,
where the country people still point out a stone where the
unshriven soul of Parcy used to frequent in the shape of a
blue hawk, and it is only a few years since he disappeared.

All this reflects the widespread superstition that the soul of the
dead may reside in a bird, one that we have already come across
in the tale of *Johnie Cock*.[14]
In spite of its doubtful origins as a ballad, there seems no
reason to doubt the authenticity of the tale itself. The ballad
does find a place in Child, something that he would not allow
The Raid of the Reidswire, which he omitted from his later
collection, according to Hart, because, like *The Fray of Suport*,
it employs 'a highly artificial stanza'[15] It remains, however, a
most interesting account of one of the last Border skirmishes
before the crowns of England and Scotland were united.
The Reidswire (Plate 12) lies just east of Carter Fell where the
road crosses the border, an open, wild watershed between
England and Scotland, from whose southern slopes the Rede
Water rises, while to the north a dozen small streams fall away
into Jed Water, Oxnam Water and Kale Water, to join Teviot

and Tweed between Jedfoot and Kelso. It is yet another thieves' passage.

One of the most striking views in the north country is that which burst on me at the Carter-gate. It is the first view that you get of Scotland after ascending out of Reedsdale to the ridge of the Carter-Fell; and a strange and impressive scene it must have been to our countrymen in former ages, when they came hither as invaders and assailants. It is a region of great tawny hills, all lying silent and bare, without a living creature to be seen, but inspiring a feeling of multitudes living deep in the valleys and glens hidden from view. On all sides, mountain tops and naked ridges lying under those soft, light, transparent veils of haze and shadows of clouds that are seen only in a mountainous country. To my right was the great back of Cheviot, with the multitudinous summits of his lesser attendants; the Kurch, a chain of singular height, its green ridges running nearly in a direct line from the Cheviots towards me; far to the right the hills of Dunse; nearer, and in the direct view before me, the double rounded summits of the Eildon Hills; near to the left, the long, high, and mottled ridge of Ruberslaw; and all to the left, southwards, the Ettrick and other mountains.[16]

Allan Ramsay published the ballad first in *Evergreen*, but Scott accused him of taking too many liberties in transcribing it (from the Bannatyne MS) and presented his own version in the *Minstrelsy*, to which I refer here.

Early accounts of the fray are summarised by Scott in the *Minstrelsy*, and by Ridpath. The following is Hodgson's version of the incident which took place in July 1575:

Sir John Forster, the English warden of the middle marches, and Sir John Carmichael deputy keeper of Liddisdale, had a border meeting for redress of injuries. The Croziers of Liddisdale had some thirty years before slain a Fenwick of Northumberland and had used him with extraordinary cruelty: for which a party of their clan, about twenty-seven years after, by the guiding of one John of Stonehouse, rode into Liddisdale by night, and slew several of the Croziers in their beds. Sir George Heron, keeper of Tindal and Ridisdale, at a border meeting, had given up this John of Stonehouse to Mr. Carmichael for which he seems to have fallen into the displeasure of the English warden, and to have been dismissed from his office for a time, though he was Forster's brother-in-law. Forster, therefore, (contrary to the etiquette of the times for a warden to demean himself to set in judgment with a keeper) at a meeting at Heppithgate-head June 30, appointed to meet Mr. Carmichael at Kemmelspeth, on the 7th of July following. Carmichael, however, five days after, sent word to Forster that if he could not see him on the day appointed, at the Reedswire, instead of 'Kemmelspeth', he could not come to the meeting. Forster agreed to the proposal: on the day appointed they all assembled; and the business was conducted with temper and discretion, till one of the Croziers shot at the English warden, and wounded him in the arm; or according to another account, the broil originated in the insatiable appetite for retaliation of injuries which the individuals of each nation had one to another; but a third account makes the warden, and the keeper, after two or three hours of amicable deliberation, 'fall into comparisons', each of them asserting that he did justice better than the other; upon which the cries, comparisons! comparisons! a Tindall! a Tindall! a Jedworth! a Jedworth! and other common watch-words of provocation and plunder were reiterated. Those that had feuds fell on their enemies; the thieves upon spoil; and the day finally ended in blood, confusion and robbery. On the side of the English, Sir George Heron, and other five gentlemen were slain; Sir John Forster the warden, Sir Cuthbert Collingwood, and many others were taken prisoners; and of the Scots, a gentleman called William Symondson, and four others were killed, and many more slain. The Scots chased the English three miles over the borders, began to harry and foray, and drove off above six hundred head of cattle.[17]

The interest of the ballad lies largely in the nature of the assembly, the collection of surnames and place-names, and the way in which simple antagonisms very rapidly reach bloodshed. Scott's note on the business catches the edge which must always have been felt at such gatherings:

In the course of the day . . . a bill was fouled [i.e. was found a true bill] against one Farnstein, a notorious English freebooter. Forster alleged that he had fled from justice; Carmichael, considering this as a pretext to avoid making compensation for the felony, bade him 'play fair', to which the haughty English Warden retorted by some injurious expressions respecting Carmichael's family, and gave other open signs of resentment. His retinue, chiefly men of Reedsdale and Tynedale, the most ferocious of the English borderers, glad of any pretext for a quarrel, discharged a flight of arrows among the Scots,

> Carmichael was our warden then,
>   He caused the country to conveen;
> And the Laird's Wat, that worthie man,
>   Brought in that sirname weil beseene:
>   The Armestranges, that aye hae been
> A hardie house, but not a hail,
>   The Elliot's honours to maintaine,
> Brought down the lave o' Liddesdale.
>
> Then Tividale came to wi speed
>   The sheriffe brought the Douglas down,
> Wi Cranstane, Gladstain, good at need,
>   Baith Rewle water and Hawick town.
>   Beanjeddart bauldly made him boun,
> Wi' a' the Trumbills, stronge and stout;
>   The Rutherfoords, with grit renown,
> Convoyed the town of Jedbrugh out.

The Elliots and Armstrongs are linked again, but we find the latter here 'a hardie house, but not a hail' (i.e. whole); they are a broken clan.

The ballad is clearly seen from a Scots point of view, where Forster is despised for his pride, backed by fifteen hundred men:

> It was na wonder he was hie,
> Had Tindaill, Reedsdaill, at his hand,
>   Wi' Cukdaill, Gladsdaill on the lie
> And Hebsrime, and Northumberland

The day begins calmly, but as time wears on, and the routines
are performed, tension grows

> Yett was our meeting meek enough,
>> Begun wi' merriment and mowes,
> And at the brae, aboon the heugh,
>> The clark sate down to call the rowes.
>> And some for kyne and some for ewes,
> Called in of Dandrie, Hob, and Jock—
>> We saw, come marching ower the knows,
> Five hundred Fennicks in a flock.
>
> With jack and speir, and bows all bent,
>> And warlike weapons at their will:
> Although we were na well content,
>> Yet be my trouth, we feard no ill.
>> Some gaed to drink, and some stude still,
> And some to cards and dice them sped;
>> Till on ane Farnstein they fyled a bill,
> And he was fugitive and fled.
>
> Carmichael bade them speak out plainlie,
>> And cloke no cause for ill nor good;
> The other, answering him as vainlie,
>> Began to reckon kin and blood:
>> He raise, and raxed him where he stood,
> And bad him match him with his marrows,
>> Then Tindaill heard them reasun rude,
> And they loot off a flight of arrows.

So they set on, and at the end of all the minstrel comments:

> Who did invent that day of play,
>> We need not fear to find him soon;
> For Sir John Forster, I dare well say,
>> Made us this noisome afternoon.
>> Not that I speak preceislie out,
> That he supposed it would be perril;
>> But pride, and breaking out of feuid,
> Garr'd Tindaill lads begin the quarrel.

Child's exclusion of this on the grounds of its 'highly artificial

stanza' is hardly excusable; the rhythms are simple and orthodox
enough, and the eight-line stanza a matter more of typography
than verse structure. Perhaps he had grounds more relative than
this, but they do not appear.

The personal, family tale, often involving supernatural elements with the violence, seems to have been much more the
concern of the ballad makers than themes arising from political
events. *The Battle of Flodden* is an exception, and though
strictly it belongs to the history of the East March, this region
is so poor in ballad material that it will be convenient to mention
it here. It was first printed in *Jack of Newbury*, by Thomas
Deloney ('the ballading silk weaver of Norwich') in 1619. 'Many
Noble men of Scotland were taken prisoners at this battell, and
many more slaine: so that there never came a greater foile to
Scotland than this . . . Wherefore in disgrace of the Scots, and
in remembrance of the famous atchieved victory, the Commons
of England made this Song; which to this day is not forgotten of
many.'
It is a song, however, of little interest, among many which the
event inspired. The language is conventional and flat, and such
verses as the following stand toneless beside the evocative
fragments which Scott rescued, and which were re-worked by
Jane Elliott.

> To tell you plaine twelve thousand were slaine,
> that to the fight did stand;
> And many prisoners took that day,
> the best in all Scotland.
>
> That day made many a fatherlesse childe,
> and many a widow poore;
> And many a Scottish gay lady
> sate weeping in her bower.

'The Editor is enabled to state', wrote Scott,[18] 'that the tune of
the ballad is ancient, as well as the two following lines of the
first stanza:

> I've heard them lilting at the ewes milking,
>
> *   *   *
>
> The flowers of the forest are a' wede away.

'Some years after the song was composed, a lady, who is now dead, repeated to the author another imperfect line of the original ballad, which presents a simple and affecting image to the mind:

> I ride single on my saddle
> For the flowers of the forest are a' wede away.'

In the perspective of history the frays recorded in the ballads which follow were slighter affairs than the Battle of Flodden, but through the correcting lens of the songs we find, particularly in the account of the Battle of Otterburn, a pathetic immediacy which should prevent us from dismissing too cursorily the sufferings endured by those involved. Whether great or insignificant, all battles are one to those about to die; a point movingly and truthfully made by John Bates and Michael Williams as they chat nervously on the eve of Agincourt, manifesting in universal terms, like the ballads, what Conrad in *The Idiots* perceived as 'obscure trials endured by ignorant hearts'.

Fifteen miles south-east of the Reidswire lies the village of Otterburn, the scene of a border affray between Percy and Douglas in 1388 which is commemorated in *The Battle of Otterburn*, with the related *Chevy Chase*. These two have probably had more critical attention than any other individual ballads, and were certainly the first to receive serious literary comment. The remarks of Sidney and Addison occur almost inevitably to mind when they are mentioned. 'Certainly', wrote Sidney, in *The Apology for Poetry*:

> I must confess my own barbarousness: I never heard the old song of Percy and Douglas that I found not my heart moved more than with a trumpet; and yet it is sung but by some blind crowder, with no rougher voice than rude style; which being so evil apparelled in the dust and cobwebs of that uncivil age, what would it work, trimmed in the gorgeous eloquence of Pindar?

Addison quoted this passage in the first of his two *Spectator* essays on *Chevy Chase* (21 and 25 May 1711), having made his much-quoted remark that 'The old song of *Chevy-Chase* is the favourite Ballad of the common People of England'.

We shall probably never know the version Sidney heard, but
one hopes it was better than Addison's. Addison quotes very
fully, but for all his encomium, at its best, this is but a poor
thing compared with some of the ballads we have discussed; at
its worst, it is no more than the degenerate doggerel of a
seventeenth-century broadside. (Indeed Child B. b. c. d. e. are
broadsides.) Conscious of this weakness, Addison forbore to
quote lines which might bring into disrepute the object of his
praise, but he does refer us to *Hudibras* (1664) where the absurd
lines of stanza 50

> For Witherington needs must I wayle
>   as one in dolefull dumps,
> For when his leggs were smitten of,
>   he fought upon his stumpes.

are alluded to:

> Enraged thus, some in the rear
> Attack'd him, and some ev'ry where,
> Till down he fell; yet falling fought,
> And, being down, still laid about;
> As WIDDRINGTON, in doleful dumps,
> Is said to fight upon his stumps.

Sidney, of course, regards the ballad he heard as morally up-
lifting, encouraging as it does a courtly magnanimity; Addison,
for different reasons, views it in much the same way, in the light
of classical verse, especially the *Aeneid* and the *Iliad*: 'Earl
Piercy's Lamentation over his enemy is generous, beautiful and
passionate; I must only caution the Reader not to let the
simplicity of the Stile, which one may well pardon in so old a
Poet, prejudice him against the Greatness of the Thought.'

The ballad to which Addison refers is Child, 162 B, and
probably, for all its rhythmical ineptitude and artificiality of
diction, the most widely known. Beattie is contemptuous on
nationalistic rather than literary grounds: 'It is one of the few
English ballads to have any poetic merit, and even then what an
unimaginative performance it is, except for a few verses good
enough to excite surprise that they should be in that setting at
all! . . . the English ballads are crude and wooden, whereas the

9. TINNIS HILL AND THE REMAINS OF THE LAIRD'S JOCK'S TOWER Peeblesshire. A drawing by R. B. Armstrong. The Laird's Jock was probably nephew to Johnie Armstrong. The tower is marked 'Lards Jockes' on the 'Tinsburne' on the map of 1590.

10. GILNOCKIE TOWER On the Esk, Dumfriesshire. The home of Johnie Armstrong. The print is from Scott's *Border Antiquities*.

11. BATEINGHOPE Northumberland. Just south of the Border in upper Redesdale. The high grain on the left is the scene of the murder of Parcy Reed.

12. THE REIDSWIRE Roxburghshire. The inscription on the face of the (modern) stone reads: 'On this ridge/July 7th 1575/ was fought/ one of the last/Border frays/known as/the Raid of the Redeswire.' On one side is the slogan 'Tyndall to it' and on the other 'Jeddart's here'.

The site is on the east side of the road over Carter Bar; the photograph looks east, with Cheviot on the horizon to the right.

13. ELSDON Northumberland. This view, from Battle Hill, looks north to Cheviot. Redesdale is to the left, with Carter Bar on the horizon. The fortified tower of Elsdon is just visible beyond the church in the trees. The Mote Hills, site of a motte and bailey castle c. 1080, lie just to the right of the village.

14. ST MARY'S LOCH AND CHURCHYARD In the valley of Yarrow, Selkirkshire. (See *The Douglas Tragedy*.) The earliest legible tombstone here is dated 1699, but there are also several small uninscribed stones. The Church of St Mary of the Lowes, recorded in 1292, had decayed by the seventeenth century and was replaced by Yarrow Church in 1640.

15. DRYHOPE TOWER AND ST MARY'S LAKE Selkirkshire. An engraving by J. Heath after J. C. Schetky from Scott's *The Lay of the Last Minstrel* (1810). A sixteenth-century tower, 22×33 ft with walls averaging 4 ft 9 ins thickness. Home of Mary Scott, 'The Flower of Yarrow', who married the freebooter Walter Scott of Harden.

16. THE EILDON HILLS Roxburghshire. The Trimontium of the Romans, a centre of legend and the supernatural, it is said to have been split in three by demons at the command of the wizard Michael Scott. It is also said to be the refuge of Merlin after the battle of Arthuret in 573, and the tomb of King Arthur and his companions.

Remains of the Lands John Séver and ... at 29th July 1886 ... 3rd ... 1886

9. (*above*) Tinnis Hill

10. Gilnockie Tower

11. (*above*) Bateinghope 12. The Reidswire

13. (*above*) Elsdon   14. St Mary's Loch and Churchyard

15. (*above*) Dryhope Tower and St Mary's Lake   16. The Eildon Hills

Scottish, uncertain and commonplace though they can often be, yet rise out of that level with a poetic and dramatic intensity that remains their secret.'[19] His argument loses force, however, if we read the version of the story which he ignored (Child, 162 A) but which Sir Arthur Quiller-Couch chose to print in the *Oxford Book of Ballads*. It is clearly earlier, and though it tells the same story, and is often textually close to the later form, it suffers none of the impairment of later broadside cliché; even the Widdrington verse is realistic:

> For Wetharrington my harte was wo,
> > that ever he slayne shoulde be;
> For when both his leggis wear hewyne in to,
> > yet he knyled and fought on hys kny.

The tale, detached from either version, is simple, credible, and characteristic enough, though historically unrecorded. Northumbrian Percy decides to hunt in Douglas territory on the Scottish side of the Cheviots. (Hence the title, *Chevy* Chase. One does not need to go the length of some critics and see here a corruption of the French *chevauchée*, an incursion.) Douglas opposes him (as well he might since Percy is accompanied by fifteen hundred bowmen) with two thousand men of Tweeddale. To avoid unnecessary bloodshed he offers to settle the matter in single combat with Percy,

> Then sayd the doughte Doglas
> > unto the lord Perse:
> 'To kyll alle thes giltless men,
> > alas it wear great pitte!

> 'But, Perse, thowe art a lord of lande,
> > I am a yerle callyd within my contre;
> Let all our men uppone a parti stande,
> > and do the battell of one and of me.'

> 'Nowe Cristes cors on his crowne', sayd the lord Perse,
> > 'who-so-ever ther-to says nay!
> Be my troth, doughtte Doglas', he says,
> > 'thow shalt never se that day . . .'

But as at the Reidswire, the bow-happy English loose off a

flight of arrows, and battle begins. The two leaders meet, and
fight with chivalrous interchange, but Douglas is killed by a
stray arrow.

> The Perse leanyde on his brande,
>   and saw the Duglas de;
> He took the dede mane by the hande,
>   and sayd, Wo ys me for the!
>
> 'To have savyde thy lyffe, I wolde have partyde with
>   my lands for yeares thre,
> For a better man, of hart nare of hande,
>   was not in all the north contre.'

One of Douglas's men, Montgomery, slays Percy in revenge, but
is himself killed by an avenging Northumbrian arrow.

> The swane-fethars that his arrow bar
>   with his hart-blood the wear wete.

The battle lasts from morning to moonlight, until

> Of fifteen hondrith archers of Ynglonde
>   went away but seventi and thre;
> Of twenti hondrith spear-men of Skotlonde,
>   but even five and fifti.

and the ballad ends with a roll of the dead, the mourning of
widows and the grief of kings.

> At Otterburn begane this spurne,
>   uppone a Monnynday;
> Ther was the doughte Doglas slean,
>   The Perse never went away.
>
> Ther was never a tym on the Marche-partes
>   sen the Doglas and the Perse met,
> But yt ys mervele and the rede blude ronne not,
>   as the reane doys in the stret.
>
> Ihesue Crist our balys bete,
>   and to the blys us brynge!
> Thus was the hountynge of the Chivyat:
>   God send us alle good endyng!

The few historical references result merely in confusions and anachronisms unimportant to the narrative, but one passage is worth noting. Stanza 65 of Child A runs

> This was the hontynge off the Cheviat,
>> that tear begane this spurn;
> Old men that knowen the grownde well yenoughe
>> call it the battell of Otterburn.

The ballad which commemorates this incident of 1388, *The Battle of Otterburn*, has much in common with *Chevy Chase*, but it seems unlikely that they are no more than Scots and English accounts of the same incident.[20] The main historical source is Froissart. Beattie, in lauding *The Battle of Otterburn*, not only, as I have mentioned, ignores Child A *Chevy Chase*, but reprints Scott's *Minstrelsy* version of the former (Child C) without comment on its origins, which are complex and at many points unauthentic, being filled out by Scott and Hogg. It is, incidentally, Child A, the English version of the *Battle of Otterburn*, that is the true counterpart of the Scott version, not, as Beattie assumes, the late and impaired *Chevy Chase*. The ballad never failed to stir Scott and Lockhart writes movingly of an occasion in July 1831, when the great man was failing, and, afraid that his prodigious memory would leave him, took every opportunity to recite verses called up by conversation. During a journey in search of traditional tales in the Douglas country:

> Bodily weakness laid the delicacy of the organisation bare, over which he had prided himself in wearing a sort of half-stoical mask. High and exalted feelings, indeed, he had never been able to keep concealed, but he had shrunk from exhibiting to human eye the softer and gentler emotions which now trembled to the surface. He strove against it even now, and presently came back from the Lament of the Makers to his Douglasses, and chanted, rather than repeated, in a sort of deep and glowing, though not distinct recitative, his first favourite among the ballads . . . down to the closing stanzas, which again left him in tears.[21]

Scott took his first version (*Minstrelsy* 1802) from Herd's *Scottish Songs* of 1776 but 'corrected by a MS copy'; this consists of only fourteen stanzas. In the 1833 edition he wrote '. . . two recited copies have fortunately been obtained from the recitation of old persons residing at the head of Ettrick Forest, by which the story is brought out and completed in a manner much more correspondent to the true history.' Hogg sent twenty-nine stanzas to Scott, with this letter dated 10 September (1802?):

As for the scraps of Otterburn which I have got, they seem to have been some confused jumble, made by some person who had learned both the songs which you have, and in time had been straitened to make one out of them both. But you shall have it as I had it, saving that, as usual, I have sometimes helped the measure, without altering one original word.

[After 24] This ballad, which I have collected from two different people, a crazy old man and a woman deranged in her mind, seems hitherto considerably entire; but now, when it becomes most interesting, they have both failed me, and I have been obliged to take much of it in plain prose. However, as none of them seemed to know anything of the history save what they had learned from the song, I took it the more kindly. Any few verses which follow are to me unintelligible.

He told Sir Hugh that he was dying, and ordered him to conceal his body, and neither let his own men, nor Piercy's, know; which he did, and the battle went on headed by Sir Hugh Montgomery, and at length. [35 etc.]

[After 38] Piercy seems to have been fighting devilishly in the dark; indeed, my relaters added no more, but told me that Sir Hugh died on the field, but that. [40]

In the postscript, Hogg writes:

Not being able to get the letter away to the post, I have taken the opportunity of again pumping my old friends' memory, and have recovered some more lines and half lines of Otterburn, of which I am become somewhat enamourd. These I have been obliged to arrange somewhat myself, as you will see below; but so mixed are they with original lines and sentences that I think, if you pleased, they might pass without any acknowledgement. Sure no man will like an old song the worse of being somewhat harmonious.[22]

In the light of the foregoing, and with all respect to the compilation of Scott and Hogg, it seems opportune to consider here the English version (Child A). It is less commonly accessible than the *Minstrelsy* version, and by no means negligible, though Motherwell maintains that it 'is certainly a Scottish composition, though altered for the nonce by the English Transcriber'.[23]

The opening lines indicate, as in *Jamie Telfer*, the seasonal nature of the raid, though the topographical details in the first seven stanzas make it quite clear that we are concerned with a major military incursion, not a piece of Border insolence on the Johnie Armstrong pattern.

> Yt fell abowght the Lamasse tyde,
>   Whan husbondes wynnes ther haye.
> The dowghtye Dowglasse bowynd him to ryde
>   In Ynglond to take a praye.
>
> The yerlle of Fyffe, wythowghten stryffe,
>   He bowynd hym over Sulway;
> The grete wolde ever to-gether ryde;
>   That raysse they may rewe for aye.
>
> Over Hoppertope hyll they cam in,
>   And so down by Rodclyffe crage;
> Upon Grene Lynton they lyghted dowyn,
>   Styrande many a stage.

This puzzling last line, surprisingly ignored by Child, is given an ingenious gloss by Motherwell:

> The last line of the third stanza, Dr. Percy says, is corrupt in both MSS, being 'Many a styrande stage', and he has altered it thus, 'styrande many a stagge', a change in which subsequent editors have silently acquiesced; but the reading of the MS, is I suspect, right, and the commentator wrong; for *stage* or *staig*, in Scotland means a young horse unshorn of its masculine attributes, and the obvious intention of the poet is merely to describe that the Scottish alighted from many a prancing steed in order to prepare for action, and not to amuse themselves with hunting deer. The lines should, therefore, be—

> Upon Grene Leyton they lighted dowyn
> (Off) many a styrand stage.

It was one of the Border Laws that the Scotch array of battle should be on foot. The horses were used but for a retreat or pursuit. Various old ballads allude to this custom of debating matters of life and death on foot, see Child of Elle, Douglas Tragedy etc.[24]

This third stanza refers probably (certainly, according to Percy) to an advance over what is now Ottercops Moss, between Otterburn and Kirkwhelpington, to Rothley Crag near Hartburn, then north for a few miles to Greenleighton. The place-names are interesting, but unconfirmed in history. The opening stanzas, however, indicate an invasion of unusual ferocity and scope; the whole of Northumberland is ravaged by fire and sword, and the invaders, having looted and burnt their way through the county, move hopefully on Newcastle, and fling a haughty challenge at Sir Henry Percy:

> 'Syr Hary Perssy, and thou byste within,
> Com to the fylde, and fyght.

> 'For we have brente Northomberlonde,
> Thy erytage good and ryght.'

The injury is taken up, and Percy appoints a trysting place with the Douglas at Otterburn. Characteristically, the seven explanatory opening stanzas give way to dialogue, which in turn is followed by a few narrative stanzas describing Douglas's return to Otterburn. The battle preparations begin, and Douglas disposes his force as Percy draws near to repeat his earlier response to Douglas's challenge:

> 'For thou haste brente Northomberlonde,
> And done me grete envye;
> For thys trespasse thou hast me done,
> The tone of us schall dye.'

Douglas replies with contempt, and

> Wyth that one Perssy was grevyd sore,
> For soth as I yow saye;
> He lyghted dowyn upon his foote,
> And schoote hys horsse clene awaye.

His men followed suit, and dismounted as was customary to
fight on foot.

> Thus Syr Hary Perssye tooke the fylde,
>   For sothe as I yow saye;
> Jhesu Cryste in hevyn on hyght
>   Dyd helpe hym well that daye.
>
> But nine thowzand, ther was no moo,
>   The cronykle wyll not layne;
> Forty thousand of Skottes and fowre
>   That day fowght them agayne.

'The cronykle wyll not layne' is an interesting indication of
some kind of source material, though it could obviously be no
more than a minstrel insertion to give a spurious validity to his
anglophile statistics. A similar line occurs in 'The Rose of
England' (Child 166), a ballad about Henry Richmond's defeat
of Richard III, 'The cronickles of this will not lye'; it occurs
again exactly in 'Flodden Field' (Child 168 stanza 121).

The account of the fight begins curiously with an interruption:

> But when the batell byganne to ioyne,
>   In hast ther cam a knyght;
> The letters fayre furth hath he tayne,
>   And thus he sayd full ryght:
>
> 'My lorde your father he gretes you well,
>   Wyth many a noble knyght;
> He desyres yow to byde
>   That he may see this fyght.
>
> 'The Baron of Grastoke ys com out of the west,
>   Wyth hym a noble companye;
> All they loge at your fathers thys nyght,
>   And the batell fayne wolde they see.
>
> 'For Jhesus love,' sayd Syr Harye Perssy,
>   'That dyed for yow and me,
> Wende to my lorde my father agayne,
>   And saye thow sawe me not wyth yee.'

Percy is not to be tempted to delay by the thought of a noble audience, since it would bring him even more into contempt with Douglas. The messenger is sent away; the killing begins in earnest, and with ceremony:

'Wherfore schote, archars, for my sake,
   And let scharpe arowes flee;
Mynstrells, playe up for your waryson,
   And well quyt it schall bee.'

The battle is long, the casualties increase, and when Douglas and Percy meet hand to hand, they fight on, bleeding and sweating in their battered armour, refusing all surrender, until Percy at length kills Douglas and the slaughter stops. As in *Chevy Chase*, the account of the battle is followed by the roll of the slain, and the sad procession on the following day when, as Percy is led captive into Scotland, the widows come to fetch away their dead:

Then on the morne they mayde them beerys
   Of byrch and haysell graye;
Many a wydowe, wyth wepying teyres,
   Ther makes they fette awaye.

It is highly probable that the English dead were carried from the field to Elsdon (Plate 13), about three miles to the southeast, and there buried. In the middle ages this village, with its fourteenth-century church of St Cuthbert, its massive pele, and strange Mote Hills, was the centre of the parish of Redesdale (the present road from Newcastle north through Otterburn to Carter Bar was only made in 1777), and presumably the nearest consecrated ground to the battlefield. In 1810, writes Tomlinson in his account of the church,

during the removal of great accumulations of earth against the north wall of the nave, the bones of one hundred or more persons were discovered, in double rows, with the skulls of one row within the thigh bones of the other, packed in the smallest possible compass. These were evidently only part of a great interment which had once taken place, for in 1877 a large number of other skeletons in a similar attitude were found extending right under the north wall into the church, to all appearance the remains of young and middle-aged men. From the manner in which they were packed, it is inferred that they had been buried at one time and that shortly before the erection of the nave, since the foundations of the north wall were found to be not so deeply laid as other parts of the church, the builders evidently wishing to avoid disturbing the half-decomposed bodies.

As the church was built about 1400 and the only battle of importance that took place in the district was that of Otterburn, there seems little doubt that many of the distinguished warriors who fell on that memorable battlefield were conveyed, as the ballad says, on 'Beeres of byrch and haysell graye' to Elsdon, and interred in consecrated ground.[25]

There are few places on earth where one is more aware of the pressure of the past than in Elsdon, where the very stones breathe strange and noble consolations of old, unhappy, far-off things, and battles long ago; but one of them is the Yarrow Valley, where tragic tradition runs like blood into the Tweed, and where the place-names so familiar to Scott and Hogg awaken now the wailing echoes of a remote violence, not of theft, but of love, and a fear, not of affray, but of the strange inhuman powers which haunted the wide, quiet valleys.

CHAPTER 4

THE MIDDLE MARCHES (2)

Two miles east of St Mary's Loch in Selkirkshire, a small stream falls from Blackhouse Heights and flows into the the Yarrow Water by the Douglas Craig, passing on its way the ruined and overgrown Blackhouse Tower. This is the Douglas Burn, and at Blackhouse James Hogg herded from 1790 to 1800 in the company of his master's son, William Laidlaw, who was later to become the close friend and amanuensis of Walter Scott. Burn, tower and Heights are by local tradition the scene of a romantic ballad of European currency; the story is best known in Scott's version, *The Douglas Tragedy* (1803), which is part of a tale first fully recorded by William Motherwell in 1828 and called *Gude Earl Brand and Auld Carl Hude* (Child I, 489). Other versions of the Earl Brand story exist, varying little one from another, two of them in the former Abbotsford collection of materials for the *Border Minstrelsy* now in the National Library of Scotland. Before examining *The Douglas Tragedy*, however, it will perhaps be useful to consider *Earl Brand* (Child 7) and its Scandinavian counterparts, the Danish *Ribolt and Guldborg* and *Hildebrand and Hilde*.

The most complete versions of *Earl Brand* (= Hildebrand?) are Motherwell's (Child G) and one published by Robert Bell in 1857 (Child A) who apparently took it from the recitation of an old fiddler in Northumberland, but gives no further details; Robert White's copy is dated 1818, and was obtained from a recitation, he wrote in 1873, by James Telfer of Saughtree, Liddesdale, in some part of the neighbouring county. Child adds that 'the three are more or less "corrected" copies of the same original'. The ballad itself he describes as having 'preserved most of the incidents of a very ancient story with a faithfulness unequalled by any ballad that has been recovered from English oral tradition', though this was before he knew of Motherwell's version.

Earl Brand courts the fifteen-year-old 'King's daughter of fair England', who begs him to take her hunting, which he does on her father's horses. They meet old Carl Hood; 'He comes for ill, but never for good', and the girl asks Brand to murder him. He refuses, and Carl Hood goes free, but returns to the castle and betrays her:

> 'I saw her far beyond the moor',
>   Ay lally, o lilly lally
> 'Away to be the Earl Bran's whore',
>   All i' the night sae early.

Her father calls up fifteen men and they ride in pursuit; Brand dismounts for the fight and kills them one by one, but is mortally wounded himself. The lovers ride on to the Water o' Doune, where he washes his wounds. When they reach his home he dies, to the lamentations of his mother:

> 'O my son's slain, my son's put down'
>   Ay lally, o lilly lally
> 'And a' for the sake of an English loun'
>   All i' the night sae early.

The fate of the girl is not disclosed in the fragmentary end of this piece, though Motherwell's 1828 recitation concludes with

> She set her fit up to the wa,
>   Faldee faldee fal deediddle adee
> She's fallen down dead amang them a'
>   And the brave knights o' the valley.

The Danish *Ribolt and Guldborg* is very close to this in narrative: Ribolt tempts Guldborg to fly with him to a fairer land. She asks him how this is possible when she is so closely watched by her family, and by her husband-to-be. Ribolt tells her to dress as a man, armed and spurred in helmet and mail. With a blue cloak covering this, she sets off with him, but on their way they meet a man who suspects her identity and, in spite of her bribe, betrays the pair. They are pursued and over-taken, and then the fight occurs which is so close in detail to its Border counterparts.

'My father's horses there I see,
'And my betrothed in chase of me'.

'Guldborg to such a service deign,
'Light down and hold our horses' rein.

'Now if in fight you see me fall
'My name I pray you not to call.

'And if you see the blood run red,
'Be silent, lest you name me dead'.

Ribolt in mail was soon array'd,
For Guldborg lent her willing aid.

On the first group he dealt a blow,
Laid Truid and her father low.

He met the next and did not spare
Her brothers with the golden hair.

'Stop, stop, Ribolt, o stay thy hand,
'And sheathe I pray thy murderous brand.

'At least my youngest brother spare,
'The news let him to his mother bear;

'The mournful news that all are dead;
'Alas that she a daughter bred!'

The moment Guldborg named his name,
A fatal blow, the death blow came.

They journey together to his mother's castle, where the dying
man offers his 'goodnight':

'O God, that I one hour might live
'For time my last bequests to give!

'My father, take this faithful beast;
'O dearest mother, fetch a priest.

'Brother, for love thou bearest me,
'My dearest bride I give to thee'.

'The maid I were full fain to win,
'If free I could remain from sin.'

'Fear not; I once, I do confess,
'Enjoy'd, but only once, a kiss'.

'Nay troth to both two brothers give,
That will I never, while I live'.

Ribolt ere crow of cock was dead,
Guldborg ere morning sun was red.

Three corpses from the house they bare,
In one day three, and all so fair:

Ribolt himself, his gentle bride,
And mother, who from sorrow died.[1]

Various versions of the story exist in Danish, as in English; *Hildebrand and Hilde* is much the same as *Ribolt*, and involves the 'naming to death' incident which is almost entirely obscured in the Border accounts. The superstition that the speaking of a person's name will ensure his death is widespread, and perhaps remains in a vestigial form in *Erlinton*:

'See ye dinna change your cheer
Untill ye see my body bleed'.

and in *The Hunting of the Cheviot*:

'We will not tell the whoys men we ar', he says,
'nor whos men that we be;
But we will hount hear in this chays,
in the spyght of thyne and the.'

(Wimberly notes, however, that this refusal is a commonplace in romances where knights encountered without knowing the names of their antagonists.)[2]

The disguising of the lady occurs in a slightly different form in *The Earl o Bran*, two versions of which Child gives from the *Minstrelsy* material.[3]

That lady lookd over her left shoudder-bane:
'O guid Earl o Bran, we'll a' be taen!
For yond'r a' my father's men.

'But if ye'll take my claiths, I'll take thine,
An I'll fight a' my father's men'.

'It is no the custom in our land
For ladies to fight and knights to stand.

'If they come on me ane by ane,
I'll smash them a' down bane by bane.

'If they come on me and a'
Ye soon will see my body fa.'

Border or Danish, however, none of the versions is so clearly
localised as Scott's. He writes in the *Minstrelsy*: 'Many copies of
this ballad are current among the vulgar, but chiefly in a state
of great corruption, especially such as have been committed to
the press in the shape of penny pamphlets ... The copy
principally used in this edition was supplied by Mr. Sharpe. The
last three verses are given from the printed copy and from
tradition.'[4] In a letter of 5 August 1802, C. K. Sharpe writes:
'The Douglas Tragedy was taught me by a nursery maid, and
was so great a favourite that I committed it to paper as soon as
I was able to write.'[5] Sharpe was born in 1781.

So we come to *The Douglas Tragedy* again; and the curious
concentration of tragic song in the valley of the Yarrow Water.
It is a relatively brief tale, and begins with the Lady Douglas
rousing her husband and seven bold sons to pursue her eldest
daughter, who has eloped with the Lord William, and prevent
her wedding. The language of the opening stanzas has an
imperative vigour, a contemptuous harshness of utterance which
evokes the savagery of feud and the unrelenting pursuit of
vengeance.

'Rise up, rise up, now Lord Douglas', she says,
'And put on your armour so bright;
Let it never be said, that a daughter of thine
Was married to a lord under night.'

'Rise up, rise up, my seven bold sons,
And put on your armour so bright,
And take better care of your youngest sister,
For your eldest's awa the last night.'

The scene, traditionally, is Blackhouse Tower, a very old posses-
sion of the great house of Douglas, from which the lovers fled up

the Douglas Burn and by an old track past the Standing Stones on Bught Rig (even called the Douglas Stones) where the fight took place.

As the pursuers draw nearer, Lord William dismounts to fight on foot, while the lady holds his horse and watches the conflict, caught unbearably between two loves. She looks on in silence until, with seven brothers dead, she sees her father about to follow them, and calls out. The stanzas which describe the incident are masterpieces of economy, their sad conclusion serving only to enlarge the tragic dimension of the maid's dilemma.

> 'O hold your hand, Lord William!' she said,
>   'For your strokes they are wond'rous sair;
> True lovers I can get many a ane,
>   But a father I can never get mair.'
>
> O she's ta'en out her handkerchief,
>   It was o' the holland sae fine,
> And aye she dighted her father's bloody wounds,
>   That were redder than the wine.
>
> 'O chuse, O chuse, Lady Marg'ret', he said,
>   'O whether will ye gang or bide?'
> 'I'll gang, I'll gang, Lord William', she said,
>   'For ye have left me no other guide.'
>
> He's lifted her on a milk-white steed,
>   And himself on a dapple grey,
> With a bugelet horn hung down by his side,
>   And slowly they baith rade away.

They ride on by moonlight pausing once by 'yon wan water' to drink:

> And down the stream ran his gude heart's blood,
>   And sair she gan to fear.

They reach his home before daybreak:

> 'O mak my bed, lady mother,' he says,
>   'O mak it braid and deep!
> And lay Lady Marg'ret close at my back,
>   And the sounder I will sleep.'

> Lord William was dead lang ere midnight,
>> Lady Marg'ret lang ere day—
> And all true lovers that go thegither,
>> May they have mair luck than they!

The lovers are buried in the forgotten churchyard of St Mary's; the church itself is long gone, and the churchyard, invisible from the road, little more than pasture (Plate 14). One large tomb stands at the northern wall of the small square of consecrated ground, but most of the stones are small and raw, marking rough mounds on the quiet hill above St Mary's Loch; much, perhaps, as they might have been when the lovers were buried there:

> Lord William was buried in St. Marie's Kirk,
>> Lady Marg'ret in Mary's quire;
> Out o' the lady's grave grew a bonny red rose,
>> And out o' the knight's a brier.

> And they twa met, and they twa plat,
>> And fain they wad be near;
> And a' the world might ken right weel,
>> They were twa lovers dear.

The folklore of love-animated plants is widespread; Wimberly quotes an interesting example from a version of *Fair Margaret and Sweet William*[6] which perhaps also embodies the belief that at death the soul issues from the mouth:

> And out from her mouth there sprung a rose,
> And out of his a briar.

The quiet close of the ballad up to this point, after the violence and the grief, might recall for the visitor to the slopes of Yarrow the romantic close of *Wuthering Heights*: 'I lingered round them, under that benign sky; watched the moths fluttering among the heath and hare-bells; listened to the soft wind breathing through the grass; and wondered how any one could ever imagine unquiet slumbers for the sleepers in that quiet earth.' But in the world of the ballads no such quiet close will serve and the last stanza returns us from romance to feud, unsentimental and bitter:

But bye and rade the Black Douglas,
    And wow but he was rough!
For he pull'd up the bonny brier,
    And flang'd in St. Marie's Loch.

From St Mary's Loch the Yarrow Water flows towards the
Tweed, joining the Ettrick Water near Philiphaugh, above
Selkirk. A few miles upstream, in the Ettrick Valley, stand the
towers of Oakwood and Kirkhope, associated by Hogg with *The
Braes o Yarrow* when he sent a copy of this ballad to Scott about
1801:

> Tradition placeth the event on which this song is founded
> very early. That the song hath been written near the time of
> the transaction appears quite evident, although like others,
> by frequent singing the language is become adapted to an age
> not so far distant. The bard does not at all relate particulars
> but only mentions some striking features of a tragical event
> which everybody knew. This is observable in many of the
> productions of early times; at least the secondary bards seem
> to have regarded their songs as purely temporary.
>
> The hero of the ballad is said to have been of the name of
> Scott, and is called a knight of great bravery. He lived in
> Ettrick, some say at Oakwood, others Kirkhope; but was
> treacherously slain by his brother-in-law, as related in the
> ballad, who had him at ill will because his father had parted
> with the half of all his goods and gear to his sister on her
> marriage with such a respectable man. The name of the
> murderer is said to be Annand, a name I believe merely
> conjectural from the name of the place where they are said
> both to be buried, which at this day is called Annan's Treat,
> a low muir lying to the west of Yarrow church, where two
> huge tall stones are erected, below which the least child that
> can walk the road will tell you the two lords are buried that
> were slain in a duel.[7]

Scott himself believed that the blood was shed by John Scott of
Tushielaw who killed his brother-in-law Walter Scott of Thirle-
stane, both towers a few miles higher up the valley, near the
opening of the pass which crosses to Yarrow. Child draws on
contemporary records which lend support to Scott in this.

Many versions of the ballad have survived, though most of them are no more precise than 'Yarrow' in their placing. 'Douglas' occurs in Percy's version, but is probably spurious; Veitch, however, recorded the story from William Welsh, a Peeblesshire cottar and poet, taking great pains to authenticate it,[8] and this opens

> At Dryhope lived a lady fair,
>> The fairest flower in Yarrow;
> And she refused nine whole men
>> For a servan' lad in Gala.

The little that remains of Dryhope tower stands not far above the eastern end of St Mary's Loch, about two miles from Blackhouse (Plate 15). (In 1592, James VI issued orders that it should be demolished, but I cannot discover whether they were carried out. The tower is ruined, but not razed.)

My comments here refer to Scott's *Minstrelsy* version (Child E), called *The Dowie Dens of Yarrow*. At once, when we come to this ballad, we are aware of a change of stress; the importance here is given not to warrior courage, battle or bloodshed, but to love and grief. The ballad begins with a brief declaration of the duel:

> Late at e'en, drinking the wine,
>> And ere they paid the lawing,
> They set a combat them between,
>> To fight it in the dawing.

But for the next four stanzas we are involved only with the apprehensive clinging of his wife (whom he addresses with naïve irony as 'my ladye gaye') and the hero's sorrow:

> 'O stay at hame, my noble lord!
>> O stay at hame, my marrow!
> My cruel brother will you betray
>> On the dowie houms of Yarrow.'

> 'O fare ye weel, my ladye gaye!
>> O fare ye weel, my Sarah!
> I maun gae, though I ne'er return,
>> Frae the dowie banks o' Yarrow.'

Reluctantly the hero departs ('I wot he gaed wi' sorrow') and
meets unequal odds in the nine brothers. The fight lasts only one
stanza.

> Four has he hurt, and five has slain,
>   On the bloody braes of Yarrow,
> Till that stubborn knight came him behind,
>   And ran his bodie thorough.

As his wife Sarah foretold, he was betrayed by her brother, and
the seven stanzas which now follow to conclude the ballad are
concerned entirely with the widow and her lament. In a single
sequence of verses we find several levels of time. As the brother
leaves to bear the news to his sister, at the request of the dying
man, we shift cinematically to the wife; she is fearful; we know
she is widowed:

> 'Yestreen I dream'd a doleful dream;
>   I fear there will be sorrow!
> I dream'd I pu'd the heather green,
>   Wi' my true love, on Yarrow.

> 'O gentle wind, that bloweth south,
>   From where my love repaireth,
> Convey a kiss from his dear mouth,
>   And tell me how he fareth!

> 'But in the glen strive armed men;
>   They've wrought me dole and sorrow;
> They've slain—the comeliest knight they've slain—
>   He bleeding lies on Yarrow.'

Green is frequently a colour of ill omen in British folklore, and
often associated with death. It occurs in the same context in
most versions of this ballad, though sometimes it is applied to
other things than heather, apples (Child R) and the 'birk sae
green' (Child O). Other examples are numerous, but perhaps one
of the most interesting appears in Motherwell's copy of the
Cruel Mother where the ghosts of the murdered children appear
to their mother:

> The first o them was clad in red;
> To shew the innocence of their blood:

> The neist o them was clad in green
> To show that death they had been in.   (Child 20 H)

Sarah's journey to claim the body is described in a stanza which neatly counterpoints her lord's journey to the duel, just as her care of the corpse echoes her last goodbye:

> She kissed his cheek, she kaimed his hair,
> She searched his wounds all thorough;
> She kissed them till her lips grew red,
> On the dowie houms of Yarrow.

Comparisons are interesting here. In four versions of the ballad the lady drinks her lord's blood; one of these is from William Laidlaw, two from Hogg, and all are in the collection of materials for *Border Minstrelsy*:

> She kissed his cheek, she kaimed his hair,
> As oft she did before, O;
> She drank the red blood frae him ran
> On the dowy houms o Yarrow.   (Child 214 E)

Since so many alternatives were available, it seems clear that Scott deliberately excluded this episode. 'This is disagreeable, assuredly, and unnatural too', says Child primly. It is, however, more likely the survival of primitive practice, as in *Johny Cock* where the hunter drinks the blood of the prey to transfer its strength to his own body. In this case the drinking may well be the attempt to establish some kind of communion with the dead (*pace* Child, a natural desire) of which Wimberly quotes two parallel examples; one is from a Gaelic song, *I'd Follow Thee, Follow Thee*, where the maiden says of her dead lover: 'I could drink—though displeasing to my kindred—not of [fresh] water nor of brine, but of thy body's blood after having been drowned'; the other from the song of the widow of Gregor MacGregor of Glenstrae who was executed in 1570:

> On a block of oak they set his head,
> They shed his blood with a will;
> On the ground they spilt it, and had I a cup
> I would of it have quaffed my fill.[9]

The time levels now coincide, and we are carried past the event with the concluding dialogue between the widow and her father, with the emphasis finally on domestic faith rather than on physical prowess, family pride, or revenge.

> 'Now haud your tongue, my daughter dear!
>   For a' this breeds but sorrow;
> I'll wed ye to a better lord
>   Than him ye lost on Yarrow.'
>
> 'O haud your tongue my father dear!
>   Ye mind me but of sorrow;
> A fairer rose did never bloom
>   Than now lies cropp'd on Yarrow.'

It is a tale in which, as Gummere justly remarks, 'landscape and ballad hold together; it is superfluous to dwell on the charm of these haunting lines, which, in nearly all versions, keep the melodious name of the river sounding from verse to verse'.

Lament rather than feud is the theme too of *Rare Willie Drowned in Yarrow*, of which *The Water o Gamrie* is a northern Scots version, and *Annan Water* the dubious *Minstrelsy* equivalent (see p. 101). It has certain elements in common with *The Dowie Dens*, depending on which version one takes; I have chosen here to use Child A, reprinted in Beattie. It is a pure lament, in which narrative incident is implied, not related, and is brief enough to quote in full:

> 'Willy's rare, and Willy's fair,
>   And Willy's wondrous bony.
> And Willy heght to marry me,
>   Gin e'er he marry'd ony.
>
> 'Yestreen I made my bed fu brade,
>   The night I'll make it narrow,
> For a' the live-long winter's night
>   I lie twin'd of my marrow.
>
> 'O came you by yon water-side?
>   Pu'd you the rose or lilly?
> Or came you by yon meadow green?
>   Or saw you my sweet Willy?'

> She sought him east, she sought him west,
> She sought him brade and narrow;
> Since in the clefting of a craig,
> She found him drownd in Yarrow.

Both Veitch and Child are perhaps over-precise in seeing the first two stanzas as incompatible. 'This stanza' (2) Child comments, 'suits only a woman who has been for some time living with her husband. A woman on her wedding day could have no call to make her bed broad in her mother's house, whether yestreen or the morrow. I therefore conclude that A2 does not belong to this ballad.' The first stanza, writes Veitch, 'points distinctly to a maiden lover as the personage of the ballad, while the second stanza as clearly refers to a matron'. Such unimaginative remarks betray not only an unwillingness to think in terms of the reality of a wild society, but a deafness to the quality of the lament. The second stanza appears almost as a chorus, a cry of loneliness applicable to almost any ballad on the same theme. It falls easily between the two other verses spoken by the woman, but could equally be used as a recurrent motif. To omit it would be to remove two of the most evocative and poignant lines in Border literature, where the contrast is movingly made between the broad bed of love and the narrow bed of death, in which the lonely couch of the worthy lady deprived of her marrow, is seen to be no better than the grave.

Veitch's version of *The Braes o Yarrow* contains the consistent and logical, but unconvincing stanza:

> 'I meant to make my bed fu wide,
> But you may make it narrow;
> For now I've nane to be my guide
> But a deid man drowned in Yarrow'.

This, however, does introduce the theme of violent death which is left open in *Willy's Fair*; the idea of the man being killed in a fray and flung into the river is likely enough, and in accord with many of the romantic and supernatural ballads where the implication of violence is often more horrifying than the direct bludgeoning and bloodshed of, for instance, the Riding Ballads, possibly because in some at least one sees through the eyes of the

widow, not the warrior, and hears the pitch of a lament or a
dirge, not the cry of battle.

The two are elegantly united in Scott's *Lament of the Border
Widow*, which he prints as an independent ballad, though a
fragment, 'obtained from recitation in the Forest of Ettrick',
and concerned with 'the execution of Cockburn of Henderland, a
Border freebooter, hanged over the gate of his own tower by
James V, in the course of that memorable expedition of 1529,
which was fatal to Johnie Armstrang, Adam Scott of Tushielaw,
and many other marauders'. Child dismisses the attribution
sharply as a random invention. The *Lament* echoes the opening
stanzas of *The Famous Flower of Serving Men*, the story of a
woman whose husband is slain by thieves in the night. She
changes her name from Fair Elise to Sweet William and seeks
her fortune at court, where she becomes chamberlain to the
king. One day, when the king is out hunting, she sings her story
to an old man, who later tells all to the king who then makes her
his queen. It is a slender fairy-tale theme, written, as the
opening stanza clearly shows, in the heavy, semi-literate manner
of the broadside:

> You beauteous ladies, great and small,
> I write unto you one and all,
> Whereby that you may understand
> What I have suffered in this land.

This first appeared in Percy's *Reliques* (1765), 'from a written
copy, containing some improvements (perhaps modern ones)'.
Scott's fragment was given to him by Hogg, and 'it was printed
with no important change except in the last stanza, all of which
is the editor's but the second line. The two lines of stanza 7 are
scored through in the M.S.'[10] Whatever its origins, it is a serious,
melancholy and moving evocation of bereavement and grief,
wholly consistent in tone with the desolating first function of
widowhood, which we have seen in such ballads as *Otterburn* and
The Dowie Dens, of fetching away, or attending to the burial of
the body of her beloved.

> My love he built me a bonny bower
> And clad it a' wi' lilye flour,

> A braver bour ye ne'er did see,
> Than my true love he built for me.

Child attacks this with facetious pedantry: 'I am impelled to ask just here how a lover would go about to clothe a bower with lily-flower. Is the ballad lily a climbing plant?'[11] In its context, the notion is delicate and elegant, conceived visually, as in a medieval Book of Hours, and purely decoratively; it would be equally heavy-handed to invoke the association of the flower with Christian art, where it symbolises purity, chastity, but it is perhaps relevant to point out the medieval delight in flowers, verbal as well as visual, in such lines as the following:

> Well was her bower:
> What was her bower?
> The red rose and the—
> The red rose and the—
> Well was her bower
> What was her bower?
> The red rose and the lily flower

and in a stanza from the *Legend of Sir Owain*, quoted by Scott in a note to *Clerk Saunders*:

> Fair were her erbers with flowers
> Rose and lili divers colours,
>   Primrose and parvink;
> Mint, fever foy, and eglenterre,
> Colombim and no ther wer
>   Than ani man mai bethenke.

Her knight has been betrayed to the king, who comes and murders him at night. Deserted by her household, the widow is left alone in her sorrow to shroud the body and watch by it. Up to this point, at least she has his body, but she bears it away, digs a grave, and 'happ'd him with the sod sae green'. Now her isolation is complete, and inconsolable:

> But think na ye my heart was sair,
> When I laid the moul' on his yellow hair;
> O think na ye my heart was wae,
> When I turn'd about, away to gae?

Nae living man I'll love again,
Since that my lovely knight is slain,
Wi ae lock of his yellow hair
I'll chain my heart for evermair.

With its combination of the real and the romantic, *The Lament*
has about it an air of lonely, unpretentious dignity by which it is
deservedly distinguished.

(ii)

The pathos of such ballads is characteristic of those localised in
or near Yarrow, but not exclusively so. An Aberdeenshire ballad,
for instance, *The Trumpeter of Fyvie*, is the tragic story of a
wealthy miller's daughter beaten to death for seeking to marry
beneath her. Leyden recorded it from a girl who had heard it in
Teviotdale, and Jamieson published it in 1806, remarking that it
was 'current in the Border counties within a few years'. Others
remain, however, traditional in the Borders, but not so clearly
placed, which embody cruel themes of sexual or family vengeance, and also, by contrast, some which are simple stories of love
imperilled but happily concluded. *Long Lonkin* is a Northumbrian version of a story represented in a number of Scots ballads,
usually as Lamkin: it is incomplete, but the introduction to it in
The Borderer's Table Book is of interest. The common element in
most versions is that Lonkin or Lamkin is a stonemason whose
lord leaves him unpaid. In the absence of his employer, Lonkin
takes revenge by murdering his wife and child. Richardson
writes:

The following fragment was taken down from the recitation
of an old woman of Ovington, Co. Northumberland, several
years ago. The scene of the occurrence it describes is a ruined
tower seated on the corner of an extensive embankment, and
surrounded by a moat, on the western side of Whittle Dene,
near Ovingham. From the evidence of popular tradition (for
the ballad is so imperfect as to be of itself hardly explanatory
enough) it appears to relate the circumstances of a murder
committed by a freebooter named Long Lonkin, through the
treachery of a servant maid. A deep pool in the dene which

runs hard by is called 'Long Lonkin's hole, and is stated to have been the death place of the freebooter'.[12]

This account begins with a warning:

> The Lord said to his ladie
> As he mounted his hose,
> Beware of Long Lonkin
> That lies in the moss,

but holds no suggestion of the revenge plot of the unpaid mason. As in other forms of the tale, the marauder causes the lady to come down by making the baby cry, and then murders her. Another tale associates the crime with Nafferton Castle, between Ovingham and Whittle Dene, the site of a tower known as Lonkins Hall which was left uncompleted as it was being built without a licence to crenellate.[13] Hugill recalls a story in which Lonkin, a freebooter, murdered the wife and child of the Lord of Welton, in Welton Hall, and threw the bodies into a pool in the burn nearby which became known as 'Lang Lonkin's Hole'. Lonkin eventually hanged himself on a tree near Nafferton Castle 'and for long afterwards his skull lay within the ruined walls'.[14] In yet another version of the story, Lonkin is a gentleman who kills the lady and her child because the Lord of Nafferton had been preferred to him. 'The husband, abandoning his journey to London on account of a misgiving that all was not right at home, after finding his wife and child dead, hunts down the murderer, who drops from a tree in which he had concealed himself into a pool, thence called Long Lonkin's pool and is drowned.'[15]

Hogg provided Scott with the following version (Child X) but it did not appear in the *Minstrelsy*:

> Lamkin was as good a mason
> As ever liftit stane;
> He built to the laird o Lariston
> But payment gat he nane.
>
> Oft he came, and ay he came,
> To that good lord's yett,
> But neither at dor nor window
> Ony entrance could get.

In spite of the lord's warnings on his departure, to close up the whole house, they are betrayed by the nurse:

> Noorice steekit dor an window,
>   She steekit them to the gin;
> But she left a little wee hole
>   That Lamkin might win in.

They stab the baby so that its cries may attract the mother, who is upstairs:

> He stoggit and she rockit,
>   Till a' the floor swam,
> An a' the tors o' the cradle
>   Red wi blude ran.

Three stanzas of reciprocal dialogue follow, where the mother calls to the nurse to quieten the child, and the nurse says she cannot; the sequence ends:

> 'O still my soon, noorice,
>   O still him wi the bell;'
> 'He winna still, madam,
>   Come see him yoursel.'

The lady descends wearily, having dressed herself, significantly, in green silk; she recognises Lamkin, and begs his mercy, offering him gold, and her daughter's hand in marriage. Lamkin ignores this, and, in eleven of Child's twenty-four versions, sends for a basin in which to catch the blood of his victim. The order is given to the treacherous nurse, except in two ballads, the Tyneside one and Hogg's, where the daughter is used:

> 'Gae wash the bason, lady,
>   Gae wash't and mak it clean,
> To kep your mother's heart's blude,
>   For she's of noble kin.'

> 'To kep my mother's heart's-blude
>   I wad be right wae;
> O tak mysel, Lamkin,
>   An let my mother gae.'

The notion is possibly traceable to the blood-consciousness of a primitive past where the killer will not defile noble blood by spilling it on the ground. In Child C the line is 'That your lady's noble blood may be kepped (caught) clene', though in A the nurse bitterly refuses:

'There need nae bason, Lamkin,
   lat it run through the floor;
What better is the heart's blood
   o the rich than o the poor?'

In Hogg, Lamkin turns to the nurse, who agrees with pleasure to destroy the lady who has worked her so hard, and the ballad concludes:

But oh, what dule and sorrow
   Was about that lord's ha,
When he fond his lady lyin
   As white as driven snaw!

O what dule and sorrow
   Whan that good lord cam in,
An fond his young son murderd,
   I the chimley lyin!

In this case, the child did not live to take vengeance, but in both *Fause Foodrage* and *Jellon Grame* a survivor avenges his wronged parents. The first of these begins intriguingly with a trio of strange kings, but on the whole it is disappointing: 'While not calling in question the substantial genuineness of the ballad', writes Child, 'we must admit that the form in which we have received it is an enfeebled one, without much flavour or colour.'[16] Child prints two full versions and one fragment; all have similar opening stanzas, with evocative, meaningless names, reminiscent of the remote inventions of say W. H. Auden or Edwin Muir in the 1930s.

King Easter has courted her for her good,
   King Wester for her fee,
King Honor for her lands sae braid,
   And for her fair body.   (Child A)

The Eastmure King; and the Westmure King,
   And the King of Onorie
They have all courted a pretty maid,
   And guess wha she micht be.

The Eastmure King courted her for her gold,
   And the Westmure King for fee,
The King of Onore for womanheid,
   And for her fair beautie.   (Child B)

The third king wins the lady, after which in Child A (the *Minstrelsy* version) the nobles rebel and one of them, False Foodrage, volunteers to kill the king. He carries out his threat, but spares the queen who is with child, on cruel conditions:

'O gin it be a lass', he says,
   'Well nursed she shall be;
But gin it be a lad bairn,
   He shall be hanged hie.'

Though under heavy guard, she intoxicates the men when her time comes and eventually brings forth a son in 'the very swines' stye'. She changes the lad-bairn for the daughter of Wise William in lines which impressed Scott so much:

'And ye maun learn my gay gose-hawke
   Well how to breast a steed,
And I shall learn your turtle-dow
   As well to write and read.

'And ye maun learn my gay gose-hawke
   To wield baith bow and brand,
And I shall learn your turtle-dow
   To lay gowd wi her hand.

'At kirk or market where we meet,
   We dare nae mair avow
But, Dame how does my gay gose-hawk?
   Madame, how does my dow?'

Time goes by, and Wise William enlightens the boy about his parentage, and his right to the castle of the usurper Foodrage. The boy kills Foodrage, frees his mother, and marries Wise

William's daughter. The tale as well as the treatment smack of the broadsheet rather than the bothy.

Jellon Grame (whose opening clearly resembles that of *Child Maurice*) has a similar theme. Jellon (= Julian?) Grame sends his foot-page to seek Lillie Flower, who is to come to him in Silver Wood. She is eager, though fearful, and keeps the tryst; he has already dug her grave and, deaf to her prayers, he stabs and kills her, quick with his child:

> 'O shoud I spare your life', he says,
>   'Until that bairn be born,
> I ken fu well your stern father
>   Would hang me on the morn.'

(In *Prince Robert* a mother poisons her son at 'Sillertoun' because she disapproved of his marriage.)

> He felt nae pity for that ladie,
>   Tho she was lying dead;
> But he felt some for the bonny boy,
>   Lay weltring in her blude.

The baby unaccountably survives, and is carefully nurtured by Grame, but when he grows up he asks why his mother never invites him to visit her. Grame confesses the murder and is instantly shot with his son's bow and left to rot in the forest.

Much more interesting, and of wide European currency, is *The Twa Sisters, Binnorie* or, in the *Minstrelsy, The Cruel Sister*, which I refer to here.

> There were two sisters sat in a bour;
>   Binnorie, O Binnorie,
> There came a knight to be their wooer,
>   By the bonny milldams of Binnorie.

('Binnorie', in one version, is replaced by 'Norham', which brings the song to the Tweed. Child reproduces it from 'Mr. Thomas Lugton, of Kelso, as sung by an old cottar-woman fifty years ago; learned by her from her grandfather.') The knight courts the elder sister with gifts, but is really in love with the younger; as a result, the elder ruthlessly disposes of her:

The youngest stude upon a stane
   Binnorie, O Binnorie
The eldest came and pushed her in:
   By the bonny milldams of Binnorie.

She took her by the middle sma',
   Binnorie, O Binnorie;
And dashed her bonny back to the jaw,
   By the bonny milldams of Binnorie.

In spite of entreaties, the girl drowns, and is taken from the water at the miller's dam. A passing harper laments her death, and makes a harp out of her breast-bone, stringing it with her yellow hair. He sets it on a stone and it plays alone to the court assembled, ending with a mild curse, 'Woe ta my sister, false Helen!', though in some versions the harp (or fiddle) demands death by drowning as revenge.

Such domestic bitterness and jealousy inform a number of ballads, including *Mary Hamilton* (Scott's *The Queen's Marie*), a tale of royal infidelity, but nowhere can we find the theme of intimate bloodshed more fearfully expressed than in some of the best known of all ballads: *Edward, Lord Randal,* and *The Twa Corbies.*

Child gives two versions and a fragment of *Edward,* the earliest and best known from Percy's *Reliques,* the other from Motherwell. Both follow the same structural form of a dialogue between a mother and a son ('son Davie' in Motherwell) who has murdered his father (brother in Motherwell). The incremental interrogation begins, in the Percy version:

  'Why dois your brand sae drap wi bluid,
        Edward, Edward,
  Why dois your brand sae drap wi bluid,
    And why sae sad gang yee O?'
  'O I hae killed my hauke sae guid,
        Mither, mither,
  O I hae killed my hauke sae guid,
    And I had nae mair bot hee O.'

She disbelieves him, and presses the question until he confesses the truth, that he has killed his father:

'And whatten penance wul ye drie, for that,
                Edward, Edward?
And whatten penance will ye drie for that?
        My deir son, now tell me O.'
'Ile set my feet in yonder boat, Mither, mither,
Ile set my feet in yonder boat,
                And Ile fare ovir the sea O.'

As it appears in this version, the punishment could be a self-imposed exile; Motherwell's, however, is slightly more emphatic after Davie confesses that he has killed his brother:

'What death dost thou desire to die,
        Son Davie, son Davie?
What death dost thou desire to die?
        And the truth come tell to me.'

'I'll set my foot in a bottomless ship,
        Mother lady, mother lady:
I'll set my foot in a bottomless ship,
        And ye'll never see mair o me.'

This appears rather more closely connected with boat burial and the Northern belief that one must cross the sea in order to reach the land of the spirits, but is perhaps punishment for fratricide—exposure in an open boat[17]. The same motif appears in a version of *The Twa Brothers*, a ballad of late provenance which appears to owe a good deal to *Edward*, as does the incestuous *Lizie Wan*.

Having extracted confession and determined penance, the mother now turns to the testament:

'And what wul ye doe wi your towirs and your ha',
                Edward, Edward?

The answers to all her questions are bitter and desolate. To this, the first, he replies.

'Ile let them stand tul they doun fa,
                Mither, mither.'

The second is even grimmer; one of the most moving stanzas in English literature:

'And what wul ye leive to your bairns and your wife,
Edward, Edward?
And what wul ye leive to your bairns and your wife,
Whan ye gang ovir the sea O?'
'The warldis room, late them beg thrae life,
Mither, mither,
The warldis room, late them beg thrae life,
For thame nevir mair wul I see O.'

The stanza has an interesting counterpart in Heine's *Die Grenadiere*:

'Was schert mich Weib, was schert mich Kind,
Ich trage weit bessres Verlangen;
Lass sie betteln gehn, wenn sie hungrig sind—
Mein Kaiser, mein Kaiser gefangen!'

The Percy ballad ends bleakly with Edward implicating his mother when he concludes his last testament:

'The curse of hell frae me sall ye beir,
Mither, mither,
The curse of hell frae me sall ye beir,
Sic counsels ye gave to me O.'

a reading it has in common with some versions of *The Twa Brothers* and *Lizie Wan*.

Edward is one of those ballads which implies more than it tells, and does this successfully by simple understatement and a modest deviousness in the telling. We are haunted not by the sword dripping blood but by the fear which informs the situation: Edward afraid to confess to his mother the accomplishing of a deed in which she is an agent, and the purpose of which (though not the result) she must know. In its suspense and evasiveness the dialogue reminds one of the condition of Macbeth and his Lady after the murder of Duncan, and the intensive structure of the cumulative interrogation gives to the ballad a similar dramatic, claustrophobic quality. The effect of the words is undeniable, in spite of a dubious origin (What was Lord Hailes's source for the version he gave to Percy?) and the curious mixture of literal and antique spelling.

A similar cumulative structure occurs in *Lord Randal*, another ballad with many European versions. *Lord Randal* is Scott's title, and his version the best known, but the hero is variously named, Lord Ronald, Lord Donald, Willie Doo, 'my bonnie wee croodlin doo', 'Billy, my son', and sometimes not named at all.

Lord Randal, after hunting, dines with his true love, who poisons him; the narrative emerges from a dramatic dialogue between mother and son. Effective though the development is, however, it lacks the intensity of *Edward* where remorse and the sense of evil accompany the images of violence. Scott's version omits the concluding curse, and ends on a note of melancholy exhaustion:

> 'O yes! I am poisond; mother, make my bed soon,
> For I'm sick at the heart, and I fain wald lie down.'

The viciousness of the last words of Kinloch's version, or in Ewen MacColl's recording, is not only consistent with other ballads of the type but resists the sentimentality which is always close to such tales. The song ends with a testament, and concludes:

> 'What will ye leave your sweetheart, Lord Randal, my son?
> What will ye leave your sweetheart, my bonny young man?'
> 'The tow and the halter that hangs on yon tree,
> And there let her hang for the poisonin' o' me!'

The poisoning is effected here by the hero dining off 'eels boild in broo', and eels or fish are the poisonous ingredients in many versions, dating as far back as a Veronese broadside of 1629, though a number of copies contain the additional episode of the food being given to an animal, which immediately dies. At the end of his note on *Lord Randal*, Scott writes: 'There is a similar song in which, apparently to excite greater interest in the nursery, the handsome young hunter is exchanged for a little child, poisoned by a false step-mother.' Child gives a number of versions of this type (J-O) in which the poisoner is either stepmother or grandmother, and the child referred to as 'Willie doo' or 'croodlin doo' (i.e. cooing dove); these have neither testament nor curse, but all include the poisoning of a dog, as in the following recorded by Motherwell 'From the recitation of Miss Maxwell of Brediland':

'O whare hae ye been a' day, my bonnie wee croodlin dow?
O whare hae ye been a' day, my bonnie wee croodlin dow?'
'I've been at my step-mother's; oh mak my bed, mammie, now!
I've been at my step-mother's; oh mak my bed, mammie, now!'

'O what did ye get at your step-mother's, my bonnie wee croodlin dow?' (Twice)
I gat a wee wee fishie; oh mak my bed, mammie, now!' (Twice)

'O whare gat she the wee fishie, my bonnie wee croodlin dow?'
'In a dub before the door; oh mak my bed, mammie now!'

'What did ye wi the wee fishie, my bonnie wee croodlin dow?'
'I boild it in a wee pannie; oh mak my bed, mammie, now!'

'Wha gied ye the banes of the fishie till, my bonnie wee croodlin dow?'
I gied them till a wee doggie; oh mak my bed, mammie, now!'

'O whare is the little wee doggie, my bonnie wee croodlin dow?
O whare is the little wee doggie, my bonnie wee croodlin doo?'
'It shot out its fit and died, and sae maun I do too;
Oh mak my bed, mammie now, now, oh mak my bed, mammie, now!'

The song, especially in such nursery versions as this or Buchan's:

'Whar hae ye been a' the day, Willie doo, Willie doo?
Whar hae ye been a' the day, Willie my doo?'

is clearly parodied in the lively *Billy Boy*, including the maternal interrogation and the culinary accomplishments of the mistress. It was first printed in 1803 in Johnson's *Scots Musical Museum*, the year in which Scott published *Lord Randal* in the *Minstrelsy*.

'It is clear, at any rate', writes Bronson, 'that the records of the parody are of approximately equal age with those of the serious ballad; and that the existence of the tunes can be carried back another century in both cases.'[18] Here is the Northumbrian version:

Where hev ye been aal the day,
Billy Boy, Billy Boy?
Where hev ye been aal the day, me Billy Boy?
I've been waakin aal the day
With me charmin' Nancy Grey,
And me Nancy kittled me fancy
Oh me charmin' Billy Boy.

Is she fit to be yor wife
Billy Boy, Billy Boy?
Is she fit to be yor wife, me Billy Boy?
She's as fit to be me wife
As the fork is to the knife
And me Nancy, etc.

Can she cook a bit o' steak
Billy Boy, Billy Boy?
Can she cook a bit o 'steak, me Billy Boy?
She can cook a bit o' steak,
Aye, and myek a gairdle cake
And me Nancy, etc.

Can she myek an Irish Stew
Billy Boy, Billy Boy?
Can she myek an Irish Stew, me Billy Boy?
She can myek an Irish Stew
Aye, and 'Singin' Hinnies' too,
And me Nancy, etc.

'Such, incidentally, appears to be the destined end of too many fine old tragic ballads', Bronson concludes: 'they are not to be permitted a dignified demise, but we must madly play with our forefathers' relics and make a mock of their calamities. The high seriousness of the parents is the children's favourite joke.'[19]

We come, finally, to two ballads of love and murder, one English and one Scots. *The Three Ravens* first appeared in

Melismata. Musicall Phansies. Fitting the Court, Cittie and Countrey Humours, published at London in 1611. This is no Border Ballad but a comparison with *The Twa Corbies*, first published in the *Minstrelsy* in 1803, has proved irresistible to most editors. *The Twa Corbies*, wrote Scott, 'was communicated to me by Charles Kirkpatrick Sharpe, Esq., jun., of Hoddom, as written down from tradition by a lady. It is a singular circumstance that it should coincide so very nearly with the ancient dirge called *The Three Ravens*, published by Mr. Ritson in his *Ancient Songs*; and that, at the same time, there should exist such a difference as to make the one appear rather a counterpart than a copy of the other.'[20] Gummere describes *The Twa Corbies* as a 'cynical pendant' to *The Three Ravens*, and Hodgart finds it no more than 'a clever dramatic lyric' where hints of the supernatural which appear in the other poem have disappeared.

There were three ravens sat on a tree,
    Downe a downe, hay downe, hay downe
There were three ravens sat on a tree,
    With a downe
There were three ravens sat on a tree,
They were as blacke as they might be
    With a downe derrie, derrie, derrie, downe, downe.

The one of them said to his mate,
'Where shall we our breakfast take?'

'Downe in yonder greene field,
There lies a knight slain under his shield.

'His hounds they lie downe at his feete,
So well they can their master keepe.

'His haukes they flie so eagerly,
There's no fowle dare him come nie.'

Downe there comes a fallow doe,
As great with yong as she might goe.

She lift up his bloudy hed,
And kist his wounds that were so red.

She got him up upon her backe,
And carried him to earthen lake

– 163 –

She buried him before the prime,
She was dead herselfe ere even-song time.

God send every gentleman,
Such haukes, such hounds, and such a leman.

A narrative exists beyond these richly evocative lines which we
can perceive only intermittently like the glimpses of a rider
moving fast and distantly through a sunlit forest. We see the
dead knight first, through the eyes of the ravens, as mere
carrion, but in the sequence of stanzas 2-5 this first impression is
overlapped by the heraldic symbolism of the dead knight on the
green field protected by the hounds at his feet and the hawks
above him. The dialogue of the ravens is here a point-of-view
technique, a way into the ballad, not the theme, and the birds of
death concerned only with their own survival, are replaced by
the doe whose life, ironically, is also dependent on the knight.
She appears, heavy with young, as the metamorphosed true
love; this transformation is common in European balladry, as it
is in legend, and one repeatedly finds stanzas such as these from
Leesome Brand:

> 'Ye'll take your arrow and your bow,
> And ye will hunt the deer and roe.
>
> Be sure ye touch not the white hynde,
> For she is o the woman kind.'

In the French ballad *La Biche Blanche* the girl is maid by day
and hind by night, and Wordsworth's *White Doe of Rylstone*
takes as its theme a similar legend from Bolton Abbey in
Yorkshire. James Hogg, too, uses the theme in his story 'The
Hunt of Eildon'. Details of the change have been lost from *The
Three Ravens*, but its effect remains in its suggestion of mild and
gentle grief, where once again the bereaved woman brings away
the body of her beloved in the stillness after violence, and as
in *The Braes o Yarrow* goes through a ritualistic kissing of the
wounds.

By contrast, *The Twa Corbies* is relatively intact, evocative
without symbolism, but perhaps keener in its sinister implication of corruption and violence, and, in the superb last couplet,
in its feeling for the wide, bleak spaces of the Border fells.

As I was walking all alane,
I heard twa corbies making a mane;
The tane unto the t'other say,
'Where sall we gang and dine today?'

'In behint yon auld fail dyke,
I wot there lies a new-slain knight;
And nae body kens that he lies there,
But his hawk, his hound, and lady fair.

'His hound is to the hunting gane,
His hawk to fetch the wild-fowl hame,
His lady's ta'en another mate
So we may mak our dinner sweet.

'Ye'll sit on his white hause bane,
And I'll pike out his bonny blue een:
Wi ae lock o' his gowden hair,
We'll theek our nest when it grows bare.

'Mony a one for him makes mane,
But nane sall ken where he is gane:
O'er his white banes, when they are bare,
The wind sall blow for evermair.'

Here the events are seen entirely through the minds of the
corbies, and one feels through their deliberations the desolation
of the murdered knight, deserted by hawk and hounds, betrayed
by his mistress; an isolation summed up in the macabre indifference of the line 'So we may mak our dinner sweet'. The
ballad is perhaps a little too neat, too elegantly balanced, to
have much remaining in it of genuine tradition, and one suspects
it owes a good deal to Scott. It is interesting, however, to
compare it with Motherwell's, 'given from the singing of a
traditionary version of the ballad very popular in Scotland'.
This bears much more clearly the mark of a literary hand, but
one much less accomplished than Scott's in this genre, and in
form, doubtless owing something to the English *Three Ravens*:

There were twa corbies sat on a tree
Large and black as black might be,
And one the other gan say,

Where shall we go and dine today?
Shall we go dine by the wild salt sea?
Shall we go dine 'neath the greenwood tree?

As I sat on the deep sea sand,
I saw a fair ship nigh at hand,
I waved my wings, I bent my beak,
The ship sunk, and I heard a shriek;
There they lie, one, two, and three,
I shall dine by the wild salt sea.

Come, I will show ye a sweeter sight,
A lonesome glen and a new slain knight;
His blood yet on the grass is hot,
His sword half drawn, his shafts unshot,
And no one kens that he lies there,
But his hawk, his hound, and his lady fair.

His hound is to the hunting gane,
His hawk to fetch the wild fowl hame,
His lady's away with another mate,
So we shall make our dinner sweet;
Our dinner's sure, our feasting free,
Come, and dine by the greenwood tree.

Ye shall sit on his white hause-bane,
I will pick out his bonny blue een;
Ye'll take a tress of his yellow hair,
To theak yere nest when it grows bare;
The gowden down on his young chin
Will do to sewe my young ones in.

O cauld and bare will his bed be,
When winter storms sing in the tree;
At his head a turf, at his feet a stone,
He will sleep, nor hear the maiden's moan;
O'er his white bones the birds shall fly,
The wild deer bound and foxes cry.

'The gowden down on his young chin' is a nice touch of romantic
melancholy in its place, but one hardly needs to point out the
inferiority of this poem; basically, it is too elaborate, too

explanatory; lacking the true ballad economy, it cannot stand. Brought too immediately to our consciousness, the circumstances of profound experience and deep feeling fade into the light of common day.

(iii)

Romantic ballads, however, do not inevitably concern themselves with betrayal, revenge and murder; a number are straightforward love stories, spiced with seduction, perhaps, and emphasising the importance of virginity, but ending happily, often after a moral tale of virtue vindicated. Scott's *Cospatrick* (one of the *Gil Brenton* series in Child) is the story of a young man who brings home his bride from over the sea, and of her apprehension because she is not a virgin. Her worries are not allayed by the words of 'Sweet Willy', the boy who runs at her stirrup, and of whom she asks the custom of the country to which she is being taken:

> 'The custom thereof, my dame', he says,
> 'Will ill a gentle ladye please.
>
> 'Seven king's daughters has our lord wedded,
> And seven king's daughters has our lord bedded;
>
> 'But he's cutted their breasts frae their breast bane,
> And sent them mourning hame again.
>
> 'Yet, gin you're sure that you're a maid,
> Ye may gae safely to his bed;
>
> 'But gif o' that ye a na sure,
> Then hire some damsell o' your bour.'

The substitution is made, and the 'bour-maiden' sleeps with Cospatrick. But in an incantatory passage the bridegroom seeks reassurance from magical bedclothes:

> 'Now speak to me, blankets, and speak to me, bed,
> And speak, thou sheet, inchanted web;
>
> And speak up, my bonny brown sword, that winna lie,
> Is this a true maiden that lies by me?'

M

They answer riddlingly:

> 'It is not a maid that you hae wedded
> But it is a maid that you hae bedded.'

A similar test occurs in another version, while in Cromek[21] the household fairy, Billie Blin, betrays that the bride is already with child; in at least three versions she simply states that she is with child by another man. In all cases, the groom's mother plays a significant part: 'the auld queen she was stark and strang'. Sometimes she has a golden chair in which none but the chaste maid can sit. In one version of *Leesome Brand* we find a similar test:

> 'The morn is the day', she said,
>   I in my father's court mun stan',
> An' I'll be set in a chair o' gold,
>   To see gin I be maid or nane.'[22]

By whatever means the bride's unchasteness is discovered, her mother-in-law appears as a formidable figure:

> The carline she was stark and sture;
> She aff the hinges dang the dure.

and presents herself challengingly to the bride, who then confesses that she has been seduced in the greenwood by a young gallant, who gave her tokens. The mother recognises these as gifts she has made to her son:

> Now or a month was cum and gane,
> The ladye bore a bonny son.

> And 'twas well written on his breast bane,
> 'Cospatrick is my father's name.'

> 'O rowe my ladye in satin and silk,
> And wash my son in the morning milk.'

'This ballad', says Bronson, 'of which the non-Continental records are all Scottish, appears to have died out of tradition during the nineteenth century.'

The Fair Flower of Northumberland is another ballad which Bronson notes as having almost died out of tradition by the

opening of the twentieth century. It is first recorded by Thomas
Deloney in his *Jack of Newbury* of 1619 where it appears as 'The
Maiden's Song'. Child gives four versions of this and all have
similar refrains in the fourth line. Deloney's begins

> It was a knight in Scotland borne
> > Follow, my love, come over the strand
> Was taken prisoner, and left forlorne,
> > Even by the good Earle of Northumberland.

While Child E, a version from Robert White's papers, 'written
down from memory by Robert Hutton, Shepherd, Peel, Liddesdale', opens at a slightly later stage in the tale, but uses the same
rhythm:

> A bailiff's fair daughter, she lived by the Aln,
> > A young maid's love is easily won
> She heard a poor prisoner making his moan,
> > And she was the flower of Northumberland.

The captive Scot persuades the girl to free him and promises
marriage when they cross the border. They escape together, but
at the border he turns her back indifferently, admitting that he
is already married. She makes her way home, and the moral
tale ends with her father's forgiveness (not to mention her
mother's scolding in White's version) and a warning to maidens
whose love may be easily won, especially by the treacherous
Scots:

> Down came her step-dame, so rugged and doure,
> > O why was your love so easily won!
> 'In Scotland go back to your false paramour,
> > For you shall not stay here in Northumberland.'

> Down came her father, he saw her and smiled,
> > A young maid's love is easily won
> 'You are not the first that false Scots have beguiled,
> > And ye're aye welcome back to Northumberland.

> You shall not want houses, you shall not want land,
> > You shall not want gold for to gain a husband,
> And ye're aye welcome back to Northumberland.'

It is light stuff indeed, and the glib comfort of the father very far removed from the rejected condolence in *The Braes of Yarrow* where the sense of loss is so acute. Other ballads involving an apparent betrayal of love and ending in forgiveness or reconciliation are such as *Captin Wedderburn's Courtship*, a light, riddling song, *Sir Hugh le Blond* (*Sir Aldingar*), *Fair Annie*, *Fair Mary of Wallington* and *Brown Adam*. The only other tale of this kind with clear Border associations is the tuneful *Broom of Cowdenknowes*. In the past it was widespread in Scotland, and Child gives fourteen versions. Here we find no pretence of tragic depth, or easy moralising as in *The Fair Flower of Northumberland*, only the story of a farm girl lightly seduced by a passing horseman who eventually returns to claim her hand before their child is borne:

> 'I am the laird of the Oakland hills,
>   I hae thirty plows and three,
> And I hae gotten the bonniest lass
>   That's in a' the south country.'

CHAPTER 5

BALLADS OF THE SUPERNATURAL

It is not surprising that those ballads which involve other worlds than this are the least significantly localised of all. I propose here to discuss only two aspects of the theme: ballads concerning fairies, elves and their world, and ballads of death and revenant beings. As in the preceding chapters, my concern is only incidentally with folklore as such; we have seen, however, that two of the most immediate motifs in Border Ballads are love and death, treated in a realistic more often than in a lyrical or romantic sense; hence it is interesting to explore these themes in another dimension. In the ballads so far discussed, death is seen only this side of the grave, in violence and mourning; love appears obliquely, as in *The Dowie Dens*, or as an occasion of jealousy, feud, or a happily terminated seduction in, for example, *The Broom of Cowdenknowes*. No supernatural powers or agencies are invoked, though the presence of another world is everywhere felt: in the talking bird of *Johnie Cock*, the singing bones of *The Twa Sisters* or the speaking blankets in *Gil Brenton*.

Love in the ballads is very obviously directly sexual, as well as vague and romantic, being much concerned with maidenheads and illegitimate children. Some I have already discussed, like *Jellon Grame*, *Gil Brenton*; others, with darker themes of incest, like *The Bonny Hind*, and *Lizie Wan* are not specifically associated with the Border, though the former has stanzas very like some in *Tam Lin* and *The Broom of Cowdenknowes*. The difference in tone, however, is striking. In *The Bonny Hind*, the 'brisk young squire' demands unceremoniously

> 'Give me your green manteel, fair maid,
>   Give me your maidenhead;
> Gin ye winna gie me your green manteel,
>   Gi me your maidenhead.'

and when she discovers she has made love with her brother

> 'She's putten her hand down by her spare,
>   And out she's ta'en a knife,
> And she has putn't in her heart's bluid,
>   And taen away her life.'

Similarly, Lizie Wan, with child by her brother, tells him that she has confessed to their father. He cuts off her head, chops her body in three, and goes to his mother, when a dialogue much like that in *Edward* ensues:

> 'O what wilt thou do when they father comes hame,
>   O my son Geordy Wan?'
> 'I'll set my foot in a bottomless boat,
>   And swim to the sea-ground.'

In narratives of this kind the issues are baldly stated and starkly followed through; they are a macabre extension of the tragic/romantic songs I dealt with in Chapter 4. The other, and more rewarding love themes appear in ballads of the supernatural, where we find the tale of *Tam Lin*. Though the versions we now have of this song probably owe a good deal to the enthusiastic hands of Burns and Scott, the themes and treatment are too common in ballad literature for this one to be neglected as too literary. I refer in what follows to Child 39 A, from James Johnson's *Scots Musical Museum* (1787-1803), given to him by Burns. Scott's version is a collation of this with those of Riddell, Herd and 'several recitals from tradition'. It begins with the minstrel's warning against Tam Lin:

> O I forbid you, maidens a',
>   That wear gowd on your hair
> To come or gae by Carterhaugh,
>   For young Tam Lin is there.

but Janet goes to Carterhaugh 'as fast as she can hie', and is seduced by Tam Lin, an event which is omitted in a number of versions but provided in others, like this (39 G)

> He's taen her by the milk-white hand,
>   And by the grass-green sleeve,
> And laid her low on gude green wood,
>   At her he spierd nae leave.

> When he had got his wills of her,
>> His wills as he had taen,
> He's taen her by the middle sma,
>> Set to her feet again.

So Janet finds herself pregnant by fairy power, and refuses to acknowledge the father.

> 'If that I gae wi child, father
>> Mysel maun bear the blame;
> There's neer a laird about your ha
>> Shall get the bairn's name.

> 'If my love were an earthly knight,
>> As he's an elfin grey,
> I wad na gie my ane true-love
>> For nae lord that ye hae'.

However, neither she nor her family are happy about the business, and she returns to Carterhaugh to pluck abortive plants 'to scathe the babe away '. But again she is charmed by Tam Lin, who wishes her to keep the child, and tells her how he was captured by the Queen o' Fairies, after a fall from his horse, and taken away 'in yon green hill to dwell'. Now he is afraid that he will be offered as the tithe which must be paid to hell every seven years and beseeches Janet's help.

> 'But the night is Halloween, lady,
>> The morn is Hallowday;
> Then win me, win me, an ye will,
>> For weel I weet ye may.'

It is clear from this, as from most other ballads of the supernatural, that the ballad fairy is not a diminutive creature, but one of mortal dimensions. The Wee Wee Man, whose legs 'were skant a shathmont lang', is exceptional. Janet seeks reassurance, however, in Christian terms, attempting to find out whether Tam Lin is 'a spirit of health, or goblin damn'd'. The whole context is seen in contemporary terms if we turn to King James the First's *Daemonologie* of 1597. In the third book, chapter five, he writes:

– 173 –

Epi. That fourth kinde of spirites, which by the Gentiles was called *Diana*, and her wandring court, and amongst us was called the Phairie . . . or our good neighboures, was one of the sortes of illusiones that was rifest in time of *Papistrie*: for although it was holden odious to Prophesie by the devill, yet whome these kind of Spirites carryed awaie, and informed, they were thought to be sonsiest and of best life. To speake of the many vaine trattles founded upon that illusion: How there was a King and Queene of *Phairie*, of such a jolly court and train as they had, how they had a teynd, and dutie, as it were, of all goods; how they naturallie rode and went, eate and drank, and did all other actions like naturall men and women: . . . the devil illuded the senses of sundry simple creatures, in making them beleeve that they saw and harde such thinges as were nothing so indeed.

Phi. But how can it be then, that sundrie Witches have gone to death with that confession, that they have ben transported with the *Phairie* to such a hill, which opening, they went in, and there saw a faire Queene . . .

Janet, however, is convinced by Tam's response: she asks how she may recognise him and he describes in detail the process by which he may be disenchanted.

'They'll turn me in your arms, lady,
Into an esk and adder;
But hold me fast and fear me not,
I am your bairn's father.

'They'll turn me to a bear sae grim,
And then a lion bold,
But hold me fast and fear me not,
As ye shall love your child.

'Again they'll turn me in your arms
To a red het gaud of airn;
But hold me fast and fear me not,
I'll do to you nae harm.

'And last they'll turn me in your arms
Into the burning gleed;

> Then throw me into well water,
> O throw me in wi speed
>
> 'And then I'll be your ain true-love,
> I'll turn a naked knight;
> Then cover me wi your green mantle
> And cover me out o' sight!'

After a scholarly and allusive analysis of these stanzas, Wimberly concludes: 'the "primitive" rationale of Tam Lin's turning into a "red het gaud of airn" in escaping from the elves is somewhat puzzling in view of the well-known effect of iron upon fairies, demons and spirits generally'; but in lines of such obviously sexual overtone there seems nothing puzzling at all. The sequence which disturbs Wimberly is clearly logical here in a sexual context: snake, animal strength, red hot bar, burning followed by quenching in the 'well'.

A similar series of sexual transformations occurs in *The Twa Magicians* (Child 44). This song opens with a neat socio-sexual interchange between a blacksmith and a lady:

> The lady stands in her bower door,
> As straight as willow wand;
> The blacksmith stood a little forbye,
> Wi hammer in his hand.
>
> 'Well may ye dress ye, lady fair,
> Into your robes o red;
> Before the morn at this same time,
> I'll gain your maidenhead.'

She replies disdainfully and at length, but the smith is undeterred: 'the rusty smith your leman shall be, / For a' your muckle pride.' The transformations follow: dove and dove, eel and trout, duck and drake, hare and hound:

> Then she became a gay grey mare,
> And stood in yonder slack,
> And he became a gilt saddle,
> And sat upon her back.

Was she wae, he held her sae,
  And still he bade her bide;
The rusty smith her leman was,
  For a' her muckle pride.

Then she became a het girdle,
  And he became a cake
And a' the ways she turnd hersell,
  The blacksmith was her make.

     Was she wae, etc.

She turnd hersell into a ship
  To sail out ower the flood;
He ca'ed a nail intill her tail
  And syne the ship she stood.

     Was she wae, etc.

Then she became a silken plaid,
  And stretched upon a bed,
And he became a green covering,
  And gaind her maidenhead.

     Was she wae, etc.

The sexual overtone here requires no comment.

Kemp Owyne, with its Northumbrian but mainly manu-
factured counterpart *The Laidly Worm of Spindlestoneheugh* is
another transformation ballad, but of a much simpler nature.
Kemp frees his 'dove Isabel' from 'Craigy's sea' where she lies,
monstrously bewitched by her stepmother. He kisses her repul-
sive form, and after some intermediate parrying she emerges 'As
fair a woman as fair could be'.

The ballad of *Tam Lin* I can only call sexually positive in that
a strong vein of realism informs it. Janet *seeks* Tam Lin, accepts
his child in spite of the implied stigma, and ultimately restores
Tam to human shape; the tale ends, not with wedding bells but
with the chagrin of the outwitted fairy queen. Maidenhead less
lightly forfeited we find in *The Broomfield Hill*, where the
heroine's dilemma is relieved by witchcraft. Scott's version
(Child 43) begins:

There was a knight and a lady bright,
　Had a true tryste at the broom;
The ane gaed early in the morning,
　The other in the afternoon.

And ay she sat in her mother's bower door,
　And ay she made her mane:
'O whether should I gang to the Broomfield Hill,
　Or should I stay at hame?

For if I gang to the Broomfield Hill
　My maidenhead is gone;
And if I chance to stay at hame,
　My love will call me mansworn.'

'Then up and spake a witch-woman', recommending the scatter-
ing of broom blossom about her true-love's head and feet so that,
having clearly fallen asleep before she arrives, he will continue
to slumber and so be deprived of his desire. She does, and he is.
When he wakes he reviles his horse and his hawk for failing to
warn him (they had been faithful, but he was bewitched) and the
girl is now out of reach,

　　　　'Ye need na burst your good white steed
　　　　　Wi racing oer the howm;
　　　　Nae bird flies faster through the wood
　　　　　Than she fled through the broom.'

It is a pretty but inconclusive piece, hinting throughout at
some plot between the lovers which the maiden could not carry
out when the moment came; at least this appears in Scott's
version. In Child C, however, the story begins not with a 'true
tryste' but with a bet; the first stanza is like Scott's, then

　　　　'I'll wager a wager wi you', he said,
　　　　　'An hundred merks and ten,
　　　　That she shall not go to Broomfield Hills,
　　　　　Return a maiden again.'

The sequence of events is much the same until the end, which
is cynical. Even the knight's animals are worldly wise about his
behaviour:

'Ye'll sleep mair on the night, master,
 And wake mair on the day;
Gae sooner down to Broomfield Hills
 When ye've sic pranks to play.'

but the knight himself is vicious:

'O had I waked when she was nigh,
 And o' her got my will,
I shouldna cared upon the morn
 Tho sma birds o' her were fill.'

Similarly in Child D, where Lord John addresses his horse:

'Then be it sae, my wager gane,
 Twill skaith frae meikle ill,
For gif I had found her in bonnie broomfields,
 O her heart's blood ye'd drunken your fill.'

The wager and the callousness are, in fact, the burden of five of
the six versions in Child, though the last, a late broadsheet
version, concludes merrily, presumably to suit public taste,
with the 'young squire' disconsolate and the young lady
triumphant:

'Be chearful, be chearful, and do not repine,
 For now 'tis as clear as the sun,
The money, the money, the money is mine,
 The wager I fairly have won.'

In this ballad the girl preserves her chastity (with dubious zeal
in some cases) by using the broom as a sleeping charm, and in C
by circle magic ('But when we gang to Broomfield Hills / Walk
nine times round and round').

 Marriage longing or some kind of sex fantasy is common. In
The Elfin Knight the young girl dreams of her hero, who
abruptly appears and says she is too young. In most forms (Child
has eleven) it is a riddling song, but the sexual theme is pre-
dominant, as in Child A:

The elphin knight sits on yon hill
 Ba, ba, ba, lilli ba

> He blows his horn both lowd and shril
> The wind hath blown my plaid awa

> He blowes it east, he blowes it west,
> He blowes it where he lyketh best.

> 'I wish that horn were in my kist,
> Yea, and the knight in my armes two.'

> She had no sooner these words said,
> When that one knight came to her bed.

> 'Thou art over young a maid', quoth he,
> Married with me thou il wouldst be.'

> 'I have a sister younger than I,
> And she was married yesterday.'

If she is to be a fit wife for him, the knight challenges, she must perform certain 'courtesies':

> 'For thou must shape a sark to me,
> Withouten any cut or heme,' quoth he.

The desire and fear of her sexual envy emerge in her counter-challenge:

> 'I have an aiker of good ley-land,
> Which lyeth low by yon sea-strand.

> 'For thou must eare it with thy horn,
> So thou must sow it with thy corn.'

but the knight refuses, so no one is hurt. He returns to his wife and seven bairns, while the girl concludes:

> 'My maidenhead I'l then keep still,
> Let the elphin knight do what he will'.
> The wind's not blown my plaid awa.

Unwanted babies are not uncommon in ballad literature. In the disordered *Bonnie Annie*, the gay seduction of an only child ends at sea when the sailors 'threw her ower shipboard, baith her and her babie'; but in *Willie's Lady* the desire to be rid of an unborn child by witchcraft brings us into a world of darkness and evil far from that of romantic tragedy.

In ballads such as *Edward*, *Lord Randal*, and *Gil Brenton* we have already seen strong hints of matriarchal power. *Willie's Lady* gives us a harsh version of the tension existing between the young wife and her mother-in-law who in this case attempts by witchcraft to prevent the birth of her daughter-in-law's baby. The man comes to his mother pleading and with gifts but the witch is adamant:

> 'Of her young bairn she'll ne'er be lighter
> Nor in her bower to shine the brighter
>
> 'But she shall die and turn to clay,
> And you shall wed another may.'

The girl pleads wearily, despairingly, and fruitlessly, meeting with the same reply. However 'Belly Blind', the benevolent household demon whom we met as 'Billie Blin' in *Gil Brenton*, saves the day with a very interesting device:

> 'Ye doe ye to the market place,
> And there ye buy a loaf o' wax.
>
> 'Ye shape it bairn and bairnly like,
> And in twa glassen een ye pit;
>
> And bid her come to your boy's christening
> Then notice weel what she shall do'.

Billy's further detailed instructions have been dropped from the ballad, but we see them indirectly in the description of what has been done, and the happy birth,

> And now he's gotten a bonny young son,
> And mickle grace be him upon.

Commerce with the fairy world, however, was sometimes direct. Tam Lin entered it, and his love Janet witnessed it on Halloween. Other ballads record similar traffic in this shadowy region, with more or less of sexual overtones. One of the most popular is *Thomas the Rhymer*.

The identity of True Thomas has a romantic obscurity: there is sufficient evidence of his existence to excite speculation, but

not enough to dispel wild conjecture. Documents indicate that
Thomas of Erceldoune lived in the thirteenth century, his name
probably deriving from the village of Ercheldun/Erceldoune/
Ercyltoun on the banks of the Leader (the present Earlston, not
far west of Smailholm). The name Rymour could refer to his
vocation, but it was common in medieval Berwickshire. A
Thomas Rimour de Erceldoune is witness to a late thirteenth-
century deed of Melrose Abbey, but there are other possible
claimants to the gifts of prophecy and poetry which attach to
the name, as well as possible victims of the forgeries which have
been foisted upon it. Some of these have considerable power:

> 'At three-burn Grange in after day
> There shall be long and bloody fray:
> When a three-thumbed wight by the reins shall hald
> Three kings' horses baith stout and bald;
> And the three burns three days will rin
> Wi' the blude o' the slain that fa' therein.'[1]

The story of True Thomas first appears as *Tomas Off Ersseldoune*
in a fifteenth-century manuscript, edited by J. A. H. Murray
in 1875. Its opening is similar to two of the three versions in
Child:

> Als j me wente þis Endres daye,
> ffull faste in mynd makand my mone,
> In a merry mornynge of Maye,
> By huntle bankkes my selfe allone,
> I herde þe jaye, and þe throstyll cokke,
> The Mawys menyde hir of hir songe,
> Þe wodewale beryde als a belte,
> That alle þe wode a-bowte me ronge.

Child B and C localise it further by having True Thomas not only
on Huntly Bank but seeing a lady bright 'Come riding down by
the Eildon Tree'. The site, marked as Rhymer's Glen on the map
and lying between Abbotsford and the Eildon Hills, was planted
and christened by Scott (Plate 16). 'The locality', writes Murray,
'in fact possesses no view, and is not even in sight of the Eildon
Tree, distant more than two miles on the other side of the
mountain mass of the Eildons, and it may be more than

suspected that the desire of bringing some of the romance of the old story to his own estate, was Sir Walter Scott's reason for naming it "the Rhymer's Glen".'

The fifteenth-century romance is the story of True Thomas's enchantment by 'a lady gaye', and of his seven-year sojourn in fair Elfland. The lady is queen of a realm not in heaven, paradise, hell, purgatory or in 'middle-earth', but 'another cuntre'. The enchantment, however, is not entirely one-sided.

> 'If þou be parelde moste of pryse,
> And here rydis thus in thy folye,
> Of lufe, lady, als þou erte wysse,
> Þou gyffe me leue to lye the bye!'
> Scho sayde, 'þou mane, þat ware folye,
> I praye þe, Thomas, þou late me bee;
> ffor j saye þe full sekirlye,
> Þat synne will for doo all my beaute.'
> Now, lufly ladye, rewe one mee,
> And j will euer more with the duelle;
> Here my trouthe j will the plyghte,
> Whethir þou will in heuene or helle.'
> 'Mane of Molde! þou will me marre,
> Bot ȝitt sall hafe all thy will;
> And trowe it wele, þou chewys þe werre,
> ffor alle my beaute will þou spylle.'
> Downe þane lyghte þat lady bryghte,
> Vndir-nethe þat grenewode spray;
> And, als the storye tellis full ryghte,
> Seuene sythis by hir he laye.
> Scho sayd, 'mane, the lykes thy playe:
> Whate byrde in boure maye delle with the?
> Thou merrys me all þis longe daye,
> I praye the, Thomas, late me bee!'

'Als the storye tellis full ryghte', like some other lines in the poem, appears to indicate a source version. But the interesting feature about this passage is the suggestion of sexual guilt. The lady tells him that his activities will mar her beauty, but they indulge regardless, and Thomas is afterwards ashamed at what he has done, since her beauty is changed.

Þan said Thomas, 'allas! allas!
In faythe þis es a dulfull syghte;
How arte þou fadyde þus in þe face,
Þat schane by-fore als þe sonne so bryghte!'

He recognises that in some way he must atone for what he has
done, and when the lady bids him accompany her, to leave
'medill erthe' for a twelvemonth,

'Allas!' he sayd, 'and wae is mee!
I trowe my dedis wyll wirke me care;
My saulle, jhesu, by-teche j the,
Whedir-some þat euer my banes sall fare.'

She transports him to her own country, and we have a series of
stanzas mingling Christian and pagan, sexual and religious ideas
in the fantasy geography of the other world. He is tempted to
pull forbidden fruit, but the lady warns him

'Thomas, þou late þame stande,
Or ells þe fende the will atteynt.'

If he plucks the fruit his 'saule gose to the fyre of helle', so she
consoles him by asking him to lay his head on her knee

'And þou sall se þe fayrest syghte
Þat euer sawe mane of thi contree'.

She describes the fair landscape and the way to paradise with
similar ambiguity. Eventually, the devil's tithe is due, and she
guides him back to his own land. This is the end of Fytt I,
though they do not part until she has prophesied at length in
Fytt II about the future of Scotland.

I have dwelt somewhat on the romance, not only for its
intrinsic interest, but partly because it indicates a remoter
source for at least some of the story, and because in Scott's
version the sexual theme of their first lying together is curiously
and ambiguously obscured. (Scott knew the romance from the
Cottonian MS which he printed as an appendix to his version.)

'Harp and carp, Thomas,' she said,
'Harp and carp along wi me,
And if ye dare to kiss my lips,
Sure of your bodie I will be.'

The theme is omitted entirely in Child A and B. Otherwise, the ballad story is the same as that in the romance, but tidier and, ironically, less realistic. Perhaps the romance, whatever the vicissitudes of its composition, was not subjected to the refining mind in the way the following passage suggests. In a letter to Bishop Percy, Anderson, editor of *British Poets*, wrote:

> Mr. Jamieson visited Mrs. Brown on his return here from Aberdeen, and obtained from her recollection five or six ballads and a fragment . . . the greatest part of them is unknown to the oldest persons in this country. I accompanied Mr. Jamieson to my friend (Walter) Scott's house in the country, for the sake of bringing the collectors to a good understanding. I then took on me to hint my suspicion of modern manufacture, *in which Scott had secretly anticipated me.* Mrs. Brown is fond of ballad poetry, writes verses, and reads everything in the marvellous way. Yet her character places her above the suspicion of literary imposture; but it is wonderful how she should happen to be the depository of so many curious and valuable ballads . . . It is remarkable that Mrs. Brown never saw any of the ballads she has transmitted here, either in print or manuscript, but learned them all when a child by hearing them sung by her mother and an old maidservant who had been long in the family, and does not recollect to have heard any of them either sung or said by anyone but herself since she was about ten years of age. She kept them as a little hoard of solitary entertainment, till, a few years ago, she wrote down as many as she could recollect, to oblige the late Mr. W. Tytler, and again very lately wrote down nine more to oblige his son, the professor.[2]

Scott's tale 'is given from a copy, obtained from a lady residing not far from Ercildoune, corrected and enlarged by one in Mrs. Brown's MSS'. How far the ballad is based on the romance is impossible to tell, but the resemblance is much too close for it to be accidental.

The Wee Wee Man also has a fourteenth-century counterpart in eight-line stanzas, followed, like *Thomas of Erceldoune*, by a series of prophecies to which it is not linked. It begins:

Als y yod on ay Mounday
  Bytwene Wyltinden and Walle,
Me ane aftere brade waye
  Ay litel man y mette withalle;
The leste that ever I sathe, to say,
  Oithere in boure, oither in halle;
His robe was noithere grene na gray,
  Bot alle yt was of riche palle.

Scott characteristically locates his version 'by Carterhaugh', but all versions carry the same story of a meeting with a wee man, a journey with him to fairyland where, after a diminutive pageant, 'in the twinkling o an eye, / They sainted clean awa'. As Child says, it is an 'extremely airy and sparkling little ballad', and, one feels, not to be served by egregious comment.

The otherworld landscape is a significant feature of *The Daemon Lover*, though its provenance as a Border Ballad proper rests with Scott, who first published it in the fifth edition of the *Minstrelsy* (1812): 'This ballad, which contains some verses of merit, was taken down from recitation by Mr. William Laidlaw, tenant in Traquair-Knowe. It contains a legend, which, in various shapes is current in Scotland. I remember to have heard a ballad in which a friend is introduced paying his addresses to a beautiful maiden, but, disconcerted by the holy herbs which she wore in her bosom, makes the following lines the burden of his courtship:

    Gin ye wish to be leman mine
    Lay aside the St. John's wort and the vervain.

The heroine of the following tale was unfortunately without any similar protection.'

The earliest printed copy of the tale is a broadside called *James Harris*: 'A Warning for Married Women, being an example of Mrs Jane Reynolds (a West-country woman), born near Plymouth, who, having plighted her troth to a Seaman, was afterwards married to a Carpenter, and at last carried away by a Spirit'. It was sung to a West-country tune called 'The Fair Maid of Bristol', 'Bateman', or 'John True'. One Scott version, taken down from the recitation of Walter Grieve by William Laidlaw,

is unsatisfactory in many respects, certainly 'improved' by
Laidlaw, and erratic with a kind of inconsistency uncharacter-
istic of Border Ballads, which, though often contradictory in
fact or evidence, are rarely so in tone. Here, the revenant devil
seeks to take away the lady, but when she refuses him he
responds quite undiabolically:

> He turned him right and round about,
>   And the tear blinded his ee:
> 'I wad never hae trodden on Irish ground,
>   If it had not been for thee.'

He carries her off to sea, she weeps to see his cloven hoof, and
again he speaks out of character, asking her to cease her weeping
and he will show her 'how the liles grow / on the banks of Italy'.
Both narrative and atmosphere in this version are thinner than
in the broadside, since the devil carrying off a woman to hell
is less poignant a theme than that of the spirit of an earlier
husband, lost at sea, returning to claim his widow, now re-
married.

The revenant theme in other Border Ballads, however, is
powerful. In most cases the return of the dead is presented as
merely factual, neither spooky nor spiritualistic, and their
return is usually a manifestation of love, or guilt. In *The Cruel
Mother*, for example, we return to the motif of illegitimate birth,
though this time infanticide brings its retributive visitation.
The ballad, also known as *Fine Flowers in the Valley*, exists in
many versions. This one is given in Johnson's *Museum* and
Scott's *Minstrelsy*. The earliest printed copies are late eighteenth-
century.

> She sat down below a thorn,
>   Fine flowers in the valley,
> And there she has her sweet babe born,
>   And the green leaves they grow rarely.

> 'Smile na sae sweet, my bonie babe,
> And ye smile sae sweet, ye'll smile me dead.'

> She's ta'en out her little pen-knife
> And twinnd the sweet babe o' its life.

> She's howket a grave by the light o' the moon,
> And there she's buried her sweet babe in.
>
> As she was going to the church
> She saw a sweet babe in the porch.
>
> 'O sweet babe, and thou were mine,
> I wad cleed thee in the silk so fine.'
>
> 'O mother dear when I was thine
> You did na prove to me sae kind.'

This is simple, economical, melancholy, and probably the most frequently reprinted. Some versions, however, are more intensely circumstantial. A number describe the birth, like Motherwell's:

> She leaned her back unto a thorn,
> Three, three, and three by three
> And there she has her two babes born
> Three, three and thirty-three

or Kinloch's

> She's set her back untill an oak
> First it bowed and then it broke.
>
> She's set her back untill a tree,
> Bonny were the twa boys she did bear.

The frequency of this suggests it may be connected with some old tree cult. Wimberly quotes the Swedish practice of women twining their arms about the 'guardian tree' in order to ensure an easy birth. Other versions are more explicit about the burial, sometimes with moving simplicity. The babes speak:

> 'Ye howkit a hole aneath the moon,
> And there ye laid our bodies down.
>
> 'Ye happit the whole wi mossy stanes,
> And there ye left our wee bit banes.'

Sometimes we find transformation themes:

> 'Ye sall be seven years eel i the pule
> An ye sall be seven years doon into hell'.

But undoubtedly one of the most interesting features of this ballad is its survival. A song clearly related to it is quoted by Iona and Peter Opie in their *Lore and Language of School-children*, 'recited in a dead-pan manner by a boy, aged about 11, Waterloo, London'.

> There was an old girl called Old Muvver Lee,
>   Old Muvver Lee, Old Muvver Lee,
> There was an old girl called Old Muvver Lee,
>   Under the walnut tree.
>
> She 'ad 'er baiby on 'er knee, on 'er knee,
>   on 'er knee,
> She 'ad 'er baiby on 'er knee,
>   Under the walnut tree.
>
> A carvin' knife was in 'er 'and,
>   in 'er 'and, in 'er 'and
> A carvin' knife was in 'er 'and,
>   Under the walnut tree.
>
> She ran it through the baiby's 'art, baiby's 'art,
>   baiby's 'art,
> She ran it through the baiby's 'art,
>   Under the walnut tree.
>
> The rich red blood went runnin' dahn, runnin' dahn,
>   runnin' dahn,
> The rich red blood went runnin' dahn,
>   Under the walnut tree.
>
> The corny cops came runnin' dahn, runnin' dahn,
>   runnin' dahn,
> The corny cops came runnin' dahn,
>   Under the walnut tree.
>
> They strung 'er up and 'ung 'er 'igh, 'ung 'er 'igh,
>   'ung 'er 'igh,
> They strung 'er up and 'ung 'er 'igh,
>   Under the walnut tree.

A far cry, indeed, from Smith's *Scottish Minstrel*:

> A lady lookd out at a castle wa . . .

but a reminder that one is never so very far away from the acute distress of real people, and that one must guard against the easy romantic melancholy which may be induced by the (false) distancing effect of the ballad. Unwanted pregnancy and infanticide are by no means the prerogative of medieval Borderers, but few have turned them into songs of such quality.

Proud Lady Margaret we first see 'Looking o'er her castle wall', opening another ballad in which the revenant brings guilt and retribution. Lady Margaret (Janet in some versions) is visited by a knight who courts her. She gives him a riddle test, in which he succeeds, and thereby, unlike his predecessors, escapes death. She acknowledges his victory, and boasts of her inheritance, which he denies. Then

> 'I am your brother Willie', he said,
>   'I trow ye ken na me;
> I came to humble your haughty heart,
>   Has gard sae mony die.'

Scott's version of this, obtained from 'Mr. Hamilton, music-seller, Edinburgh, with whose mother it had been a favourite', is erratic and inconclusive, though in its own way effective. Why does the ghostly knight wish to humble his sister? How does he propose to achieve it? From this version it would appear by implanting in the lady a desire for purification which is denied:

> 'If ye be my brother Willie', she said,
>   'As I trow weel ye be,
> This night I'll neither eat nor drink,
>   But gae along wi thee.'

> 'O hold your tongue, Lady Margaret', he said,
>   'Again I hear you lie;
> For ye've unwashen hands and ye've unwashen feet
>   To gae to clay wi me.

> 'For the wee worms are my bedfellows
>   And cauld clay is my sheets,
> And when the stormy winds do blow,
>   My body lies and sleeps'.

This tale ends, in fact, in a series of ironies; that she, who has

apparently lived a proud life, should be denied her wish for a
humble death; that having driven many men to death, she
now drives a dead man to life. (The calm security of the grave is
not an unusual ballad motif nor is the dialogue between its
tenant and a prospective sharer, movingly developed in *The
Unquiet Grave*, though this is not a Border song.) Motherwell's
version is altogether more explicit in its conclusion, where the
revenant brother warns:

> 'Leave aff your pride, jelly Janet,' he says,
>   'Use it not ony mair;
> Or when ye come where I hae been
>   You will repent it sair.
>
> 'Cast aff, cast aff, sister,' he says,
>   'The gowd lace frae your crown;
> For if ye gang where I hae been,
>   Ye'll wear it laigher down.
>
> 'When ye're in the gude church set,
>   The gowd pins in your hair,
> Ye take mair delight in your feckless dress
>   Than ye do in your morning prayer.
>
> 'And when ye walk in the church-yard,
>   And in your dress are seen,
> There is nae lady that sees your face
>   But wishes your grave were green.
>
> 'You're straight and tall, handsome withall,
>   But your pride owergoes your wit,
> But if ye do not your ways refrain,
>   In Pirie's chair ye'll sit.
>
> 'In Pirie's chair you'll sit, I say,
>   The lowest seat o' hell;
> If ye do not amend your ways,
>   It's there that ye must dwell.'
>
> Wi that he vanished frae her sight,
>   Wi the twinkling o' an eye;
> Naething mair the lady saw
>   But the gloomy clouds and sky.

The stanzas seem to indicate a dire enforcement of sumptuary laws, though the nature of 'Pirie's chair' remains to me, as to Motherwell, obscure. Could it conceivably have anything to do with the Henderland freebooter? 'In a deserted burial place attached to what was the chapel, and near the Tower of Henderland, there is a large stone broken in three parts. On this there are carved a cross, sword, and shield, with the brief inscription —"Here lyis Perys of Cokburne and hys wife Marjory"'.[3] Whatever the truth, one feels that the ballad is more than Fowler's mere 'gothic reconstruction of the memento mori'. Sir Richard Maitland of Lethington, author of *Aganis the Theivis of Liddisdaill*, wrote with equal feeling a poem of sixteen stanzas about the costly vanity of women. His terms are much like those of the ballad:

> Thair schone of velwot and thair muillis
> In kirk ar not content with stuillis
> the sermon quhen thay sit to heir
> bot caryis cuschingis lyik vaine fuillis
> And all for newfangilnes of geir.

> *   *   *

> And sum will spend mair I heir say
> In spyice and droggis on ane day
> Nor wald thair motheris in ane ʒeir
> quhilk will gar monye pak decay
> quhen thay sa vainlie waist thair geir.

> *   *   *

> Thair Collaris carcattis and hals beiddis
> With veluot hattis heicht on thair heidis
> Coirdit with gold lyik ane ʒounkeir
> Broudrit about with goldin threiddis
> And all for newfangilnes of geir.

In *The Wife of Usher's Well* the revenants appear without purpose: they come neither to chide, punish nor warn. Nor do they appear to be made restless in their graves by the grief of the living, though in a nineteenth-century Shropshire version the wife calls on Jesus to resurrect her three sons 'that their mother may take some rest'. He does so, but after being given nine days in which to repent her sins, she follows them to heaven. In the

Border version, the three 'stout and stalwart sons' appear to be the mourning dream of a bereaved mother.

Young Benjie, on the other hand, is a ballad of vengeance, and one in which we are soon aware of an underlying realism:

> Of a' the maids of fair Scotland
>   The fairest was Marjorie,
> And young Benjie was her ae true-love,
>   And a dear true-love was he.
>
> And wow! but they were lovers dear,
>   And loved fu constantlie;
> But ay the mair, when they fell out,
>   The sairer was their plea.

After a quarrel, Marjorie rejects young Benjie and takes another love. He visits her, and ironically she comes down to him, since she fears he may be killed by her brothers. He drowns her in the river, whence she is brought by her brothers for the wake.

> 'The night it is her low lyke wake,
>   The morn her burial day,
> And we maun watch at mirk midnight
>   And hear what she will say'.
>
> Wi door ajar, and candlelight,
>   And torches burning clear,
> The streikit corpse, till still midnight,
>   They waked, but naething hear.

Scott sheds some light on these verses: 'In the interval betwixt death and interment the disembodied spirit is supposed to hover around its mortal habitation, and, if invoked by certain rites, retains the power of communicating, through its organs, the cause of its dissolution. Such inquiries, however, are always dangerous, and never to be resorted to unless the deceased is suspected to have suffered *foul play*, as it is called . . . One of the most potent ceremonies in the charm for causing the dead bodies to speak is setting the door ajar.' In the case of Marjorie, the wake was successful. Her body begins to twist about, and she tells how she was killed. The vengeance follows, with a brutal deliberation at first:

'Sall we Young Benjie head, sister?
Sall we Young Benjie hang?
Or sall we pike out his twa grey een,
And punish him ere he gang?'

The macabre violence here, at midnight, by candlelight, with the
cocks crowing, raises a remote echo of a similar deliberation,
when *Dick o' the Cow* lay in Armstrong hands at Puddingburn:

'Ha! quo' fair Johnie Armstrang, 'we will him hang'.
'Na', quo' Willie, 'we'll him slae.'
Then up and spak another young Armstrang,
'We'll gie him his batts, and let him gae.'

Marjorie's body dictates the vengeance—blinding, then the life-
time of sightless servitude and penance:

'Tie a green gravat round his neck,
And lead him out and in,
And the best ae servant about your house
To wait Young Benjie on.

'And ay, at every seven year's end,
Ye'll tak him to the linn;
For that's the penance he maun drie,
To scug his deadly sin.'

One is inevitably reminded here of the famous *Lyke Wake
Dirge*, an inescapable experience in school anthology, memorable
in the music of Benjamin Britten, powerfully dramatic in *Chips
With Everything*. Its claim to inclusion as a Border song is
dubious, since it was discovered by Ritson in a late sixteenth-
century account of Cleveland, Yorkshire. However, my authority
(or excuse) here must be Scott, who included it in the *Minstrelsy*
as 'a sort of charm sung by the lower ranks of Roman Catholics
in some parts of the north of England'. Child ignores it. It is a
haunting dirge, depicting the journey of the soul from this
world to the next, a progress whose ease or pain depends on the
quality of the spirit in life:

If meate or drinke thou never gavest nane,
Every night and alle;

> The fire will burn thee to the bare bane;
> And Christe receive thye saule.

In passing from this world to the next, the soul must cross the
narrow 'Brig o Dread'. The ordeal is widespread in folklore, but
the bridge is described in unusual detail in the *Legend of Sir
Owain*, which Scott quotes:

> And Owain seigh ther ouer ligge
> A swithe strong naru brigge:
>   The fendes seyd tho;
> 'Lo! Sir Knight, sestow this?
> This is the brigge of paradis,
> Here ouer thou must go.'
>
>   *   *   *
>
> The brigge was as heigh as a tour,
> And as scharpe as a rasour,
>   And naru it was also;
> And the water that ther ran under,
> Brend o' lightning and of thonder,
> That thocht him michel wo.

Traffic between the two worlds is given almost a physical
existence here, with its very concrete imagery, but such a landscape is rare in Border Ballads. The dead, it is frequently
suggested, need to cross water, as when Son Davie swears to 'set
my foot in a bottomless ship', or when Sweet William's 'bones
are buried in yon kirk-yard, afar beyond the sea' (Child 77A);
but in many cases, the revenant, like *Clerk Saunders* is of the
earth, earthy.

This ballad was first published by Scott in 1802, printed from
Herd's manuscript 'with several corrections from a shorter and
more imperfect copy in the same volume, and one or two
conjectural emendations in the arrangement of the stanzas'.
Herd is generally recognised as the most reliable of collectors,
constitutionally incapable of elaborating on recited versions
(though he left no record of how he came by these), and here I
take as my text his longer version, a combination of Child 69 A
and Child 77 B, *Sweet William's Ghost*. Beattie prints it as one
poem, but uses Scott's *Minstrelsy* version in which, as Child

says, 'his account of his dealing with Herd's copies is far from
precisely accurate'. Scott, indeed, tidies up too smoothly. Herd's
lines,

> 'For in it will come my seven brothers,
>   And a' their torches burning bright;
> They'll say, We hae but ae sister,
>   And here her lying wi a knight.'

become, in Scott

> 'For in may come my seven bauld brothers,
>   Wi torches burning bright,
> They'll say—"We hae but ae sister,
>   And behold she's wi a knight!" '

In both sections, the ballad has Scandinavian analogues and is
the basis of Bürger's *Lenore*, from which the youthful Scott
drew inspiration in 1796 for *William and Helen*, an absurdly
written gothic tale, as worthy of the original as Wordsworth's
Ellen Irwin is of *Helen of Kirconnel*.

Clerk Saunders opens with all the vigour and violence of a
Riding Ballad. Though in the first few lines the lovers are
respectably melancholy, we soon know where we are:

> 'A bed, a bed,' Clark Sanders said,
>   'A bed, a bed for you and I;'
> 'Fye no, fye no,' the lady said,
>   'Until the day we married be.
>
> 'For in it will come my seven brothers,
>   And a' their torches burning bright;
> They'll say, We hae but ae sister,
>   And here her lying wi a knight.'

The lively interchange continues as they devise means to avoid
perjury should the maid Margaret be interrogated by her
brothers:

> 'Ye'l take the sourde fray my scabbord,
>   And lowly, lowly lift the gin,
> And you may say, your oth to save,
>   You never let Clark Sanders in.

'Yele take a napken in your hand,
    And ye'l ty up baith your een,
And ye may say, your oth to save,
    That ye saw na Sandy sen late yestreen.

'Yele take me in your armes twa,
    Yele carrey me ben into your bed,
And ye may say, your oth to save,
    In your bower-floor I never tread.'

After this prologue events take a rasher turn. The braw
Margaret carries out her lover's instructions, including carrying
him to bed, but the seven brothers arrive at midnight, with 'all
their torches burning bright', and see the lovers asleep together.
The discussion that follows is not unfamiliar, as they try to
decide what to do. Six of them are sympathetic and wish no
harm to the pair, but the seventh acts impulsively:

Out he has taen a bright long brand,
    And he has striped it throw the straw,
And throw and throw Clark Sanders' body
    A wat he has gard cold iron gae.

Soundly asleep, they embrace in death, and Margaret wakes in a
stanza of horrifying realism, where the language unites violence
and love.

She thought it had been a loathsome sweat,
    A wat it had fallen this twa between;
But it was the blood of his fair body,
    A wat his life days wair na lang.

She swears seven years mourning, promising to go shoeless,
unkempt and dressed in black; despite her father's entreaties,
she remains inconsolable:

'Comfort well your seven sons,
    For comforted will I never bee;
For it was neither lord nor loune
    That was in bower last night wi mee.'

With this stanza (26), the first part of the narrative ends, and is
taken up in *Sweet William's Ghost*, with the spirit of the murdered
man returning after the funeral to Margaret's window. Here lies

the true interest of the supernatural in the poem, centred again once more on an exchange between the living and the dead. This is informed throughout with ritual significance. The revenant returns to claim the 'faith and trouth' he has given to the maid. She refuses to pledge her troth unless he will come in and kiss her, but

> 'My mouth it is full cold, Margret.
> It has the smell now of the ground:
> And if I kiss thy comely mouth,
> Thy life days will not be long.'

Words which emphasise very clearly the commonplace of such occasions, that the revenant is no disembodied spirit, but an incarnate soul, such as we find, for example, in the still popular, evocative, but not Border, ballad, *The Unquiet Grave.*

> 'You crave one kiss of my clay-cold lips;
> But my breath smells earthy strong;
> If you have one kiss of my clay-cold lips,
> Your time will not be long.'

Margaret seeks to know of him what becomes of women who die in childbirth, if she is to give him back his faith and troth; he tells her, but the urgency to return is upon him, since the 'cocks are crowing a merry midd-larf'. This is generally understood to refer to 'middle-earth' or the mortal world, and may indeed be evidence of the integrity of Herd's version, since his scribe has faithfully copied what he heard, or thought he heard, without attempting to rationalise or improve.

Now satisfied, Margaret performs a ritual upon the dead man,

> Up she has tain a bright long wand,
> And she has straked her trouth thereon;
> She has given [it] him out at the shot window,
> Wi many a sad sigh and heavy groan.

In other versions, the action is slightly different:

> She took up her white, white hand,
> And she struck him in the breast,
> Saying, Have there again your faith and troth,
> And I wish your soul good rest.   (Child 77 C)

Then she has taen a silver key,
  Gien him three times in the breast;
Says, There's your faith and troth, Willie,
  I hope your soul will rest.   (Child 77 D)

Then Margret took her milk-white hand,
  And smoothd it on his breast,
'Tak your faith and troth, William,
  God send your soul good rest!'   (Child 77 E)

Of this last version, Gummere conjectures that 'we are dealing with a confused survival of the common method by which savages and even European peasants get rid of a disease by rubbing the affected part upon a stick, a tree or what not'.⁴ The answer can be found, however, much more simply.

The faith and troth for which Clerk Saunders has returned, is presumably a love token, like a ring, which she places on a stick to avoid touching his body; the fatal effects of touching the dead are made clear in the verses quoted above from this ballad and *The Unquiet Grave*. The handing it out through the 'shot window' also suggests her dwelling as a Border pele, as well as emphasising with ironic melancholy the distance both physical and spiritual which separates those who so recently had shared one bed. He leaves, but she follows, aching to share his grave with him, as she had willingly shared his bed. But the end of the ballad is realistic enough in its evocation of the long loneliness of young widowhood which is about to begin, and it is fitting that this account should close with stanzas in which we find so typical a Border theme: violence and love culminating, not without humour, in yearning, separation, a longing for peace in the chill mould of the grave.

'Is there any room at your head, Sanders?
  Is there any room at your feet?
Or any room at your twa sides?
  Whare fain, fain would I sleep.'

'Their is na room at my head, Margret,
  Their is na room at my feet;
There is room at my twa sides,
  For ladys for to sleep.

'Cold meale is my covering owre,
  But an my winding sheet;
My bed it is full low, I say,
  Down among the hongerey worms I sleep.

'Cold meal is my covering owre,
  But an my winding sheet;
The dew it falls na sooner down
  Then ay it is full weet.'

*   *   *

And what, after all, remains? In R. L. Stevenson's words

Grey recumbent tombs of the dead in desert places,
  Standing stones on the vacant wine-red moor,
Hills of sheep, and the homes of the silent vanquished races,
  And winds, austere and pure.

The families; names ringing with steel—Armstrong, Maxwell Crosier, Rutherford, Davison—peacefully span the windows of grocer, chemist, ironmonger and butcher from Langholm to the Merse.

Crumbling peles, most primitive and stark of medieval refuges, where trees spill out from the fallen bartizans, and where all that is left of the murderous newel staircases are hollow, craggy cylinders of stone, slowly falling inward from dungeon to sky.

Their names too linger: Goldielands, where Buccleuch sought help for Jamie Telfer, square and high above Teviot, whose glaring bale-fires blaze no more; Gilnockie on the Esk, where Johnie Armstrong kept his hold. Dryhope, home of Mary Scott, the Flower of Yarrow, looks yet in defiant isolation over the tragic valley, its walls softened against the sky by a rampart of wild roses. Blackhouse, Tushielaw, Mangerton, have almost vanished, though some towers, like Askerton, from where the land-sergeant hunted down Hobbie Noble, live on as farms, or as vicarages, like Elsdon pele standing very near the last resting place of the dead of the Battle of Otterburn.

The list is long and evocative, yet perhaps most moving of all are those forgotten towers lying remote, anonymous, unsung on broad stretches of the Border fells. Their story is lost, yet in the mute eloquence of their stones the ancient prophecies endure:

> Apone A brode mure þar sall a batell be,
> Be-syde a stob crose of stane þat standis on A mure:
> It sall be coueret wyght corsis all of a kynth,
> That þe craw sall not ken whar þe cross standis.

And the Ballads. In spite of our commentaries, they remain richly elusive; but they remain.

> Though long on time's dark whirlpool toss'd,
> The song is saved, the bard is lost.

SELECT BIBLIOGRAPHY

The main texts used for this volume have been Scott's *Minstrelsy* (page numbers are given for Henderson's 1931 editon in one volume), Child's *The English and Scottish Popular Ballads* (Dover Publications five-volume reprint of 1965) and Dr William Beattie's *Border Ballads* (Penguin Books, 1952, now out of print). At present, no collection of Border Ballads is available in this country. General ballad collections are not listed here.

C.B.P.	*Calendar of Border Papers*
C.S.P.D.	*Calendar of State Papers, Domestic*
C.S.P.S.	*Calendar of State Papers, Scotland*
C.W.A.S.	Cumberland and Westmorland Antiquarian Society, *Transactions*
E.B.S.	Edinburgh Bibliographical Society, *Transactions*
E.E.T.S.	Early English Text Society
H.A.S.	*Proceedings of the Hawick Archaeological Society*
P.M.L.A.	Publications of the Modern Languages Association
S.H.R.	*Scottish Historical Review*
S.T.S.	Scottish Text Society

I. DOCUMENTARY SOURCES

Acts of Parliament of Scotland (London 1814)

BAIN, J. (ed.) *Calendar of Border Papers* (Edinburgh 1894-6), 2 vols.

Calendar of State Papers Scotland (Edinburgh), 13 vols.

DONALDSON, G. *Scottish Historical Documents* (Edinburgh 1970)

GREEN, M. A. E. (ed.). *Calendar of State Papers, Domestic (1595-1597)* (London 1868)

POLLARD, A. F. *Tudor Tracts, 1532-1588* in E. Arber, *An English Garner* (London 1903)

Publications of the Surtees Society, xciii (London 1895)

RYMER, T. *Foedera*, etc. (2nd edn., London 1728)

State Papers of King Henry VIII (London 1830-52), vols. iv and v

II. BORDER HISTORY

ARMSTRONG, R. B. *History of Liddesdale* (Edinburgh 1883)

ARMSTRONG, W. A. *The Armstrong Borderland* (Galashiels 1960)

BATES, C. J. *History of Northumberland* (Newcastle 1895)

BRENAN, G. *A History of the House of Percy* (London 1902)

Select Bibliography

BROWN, T. CRAIG. *History of Selkirkshire* (Edinburgh 1886)

CAMDEN, W. *Britannia* (2nd edn., London 1806)

CAREY, R. *The Memoirs of Robert Carey* (ed. F. H. Mares) (Oxford 1972)

DIXON, D. D. *Upper Coquetdale* (Newcastle 1903)

DIXON, D. D. *Whittingham Vale* (Newcastle 1895)

DOUGLAS, G. B. S. *History of the Border Counties* (Edinburgh 1899)

FERGUSON, R. S. *A History of Cumberland* (London 1890)

FORDUN, J. *Scotichronicon* (ed. Thos. Hearne) (Oxford 1722)

FRASER, G. M. *The Steel Bonnets* (London 1971)

HODGKIN, T. *The Wardens of the Marches* (London 1908)

HODGSON, J. *History of Northumberland* (Newcastle 1820-58), 7 vols.

HYSLOP, J. and R. *Langholm* (London 1912)

LESLIE, J. *The Historie of Scotland* (ed. E. G. Cody) (S.T.S. Edinburgh 1888)

LINDSAY, R. OF PITSCOTTIE. *The History of Scotland* (Edinburgh 1728)

MACK, J. L. *The Border Line* (2nd edn., London 1926)

MACKENZIE, W. M. 'The Debatable Land' in *S.H.R.* xxx (1951)

NEILSON, G. 'The March Laws', ed. T. I. Rae, in *Stair Miscellany* I (Edinburgh 1971)

NICOLSON, J. and BURN, R. *The History and Antiquities of the Counties of Cumberland and Westmoreland* (London 1777), 2 vols.

Northumberland County History (Newcastle 1893-1940), 15 vols.

OLIVER, J. R. *Upper Teviotdale and the Scotts of Buccleuch* (Hawick 1887)

PEASE, H. *The Lord Wardens of the Marches of England and Scotland* (London 1913)

RAE, T. I. 'Some Aspects of Border Administration in the Sixteenth Century' in H.A.S. (1958)

RAE, T. I. 'Feud and the Jurisdiction of the Wardens of the Marches' in H.A.S. (1961)

RAE, T. I. *The Administration of the Scottish Frontier 1513-1603* (Edinburgh 1966)

RICHARDSON, M. A. (ed.). *Newcastle Reprints* (Newcastle 1849), 20 vols.

RIDPATH, G. *The Border History of England and Scotland* (London 1776)

SCOTT, SIR W. *The Border Antiquities of England and Scotland* (1st edn., London 1814) (London 1889)

SITWELL, W. *The Border* (Newcastle 1927)

SPOTTISWOODE, J. *The History of the Church and State of Scotland* (4th edn., London 1777)

SURTEES, R. *The History and Antiquities of Durham* (London 1816-40), 4 vols.

TATE, G. *A History of Alnwick* (Alnwick 1866-9), 2 vols.

TOMLINSON, W. W. *Life in Northumberland during the Sixteenth Century* (London n.d.)

TOUGH, D. L. W. *The Last Years of a Frontier* (Oxford 1928)

WHITE, R. *A History of the Battle of Otterburn* (London 1857)

WILLIAMS, P. 'The Northern Borderland under the Early Stuarts' in *Historical Essays 1600-1750, presented to David Ogg*, ed. H. F. Bell and R. L. Ollard (London 1963)

III. LITERATURE AND MUSIC

BEATTIE, W. *Border Ballads* (London 1952)

BEWICK, T. *A Memoir* (1862) (London 1961)

BLAND, D. S. *Chapbooks and Garlands* (Newcastle 1956)

BLAND, D. S. 'The Evolution of "Chevy Chase" and "the Battle of Otterburn" ' in *Notes and Queries*, XCX, vi (1951), pp. 160 f

BRONSON, B. H. *The Traditional Tunes of the Child Ballads* (Princeton 1959-   ), 3 vols. to be completed in 6 vols.

BROWN, J. W. *Kinmont Willie in Ballad and History* (Carlisle 1922)

BROWN, J. W. *Carlisle in Ballad and Story* (Carlisle 1912)

BUCHAN, J. *Sir Walter Scott* (London 1932)

CHAMBERS, E. K. *English Literature at the Close of the Middle Ages* (Oxford 1945)

CHILD, F. J. *The English and Scottish Popular Ballads* (1882-98) (Reprinted New York 1965), 5 vols.

CHRISTOPHERSON, P. *The Ballad of Sir Aldingar* (Oxford 1952)

CORSON, J. C. *A Bibliography of Sir Walter Scott* (New York 1968)

CREMER, R. W. KETTON, *The Early Life and Diaries of William Windham* (London 1930)

DOBIE, M. R. 'The Development of Scott's *Minstrelsy*' in E.B.S., ii (1946)

ENTWISTLE, W. J. *European Balladry* (Oxford 1939)

FARRER, J. A. *Literary Forgeries* (London 1907)

FOWLER, D. C. *A Literary History of the Popular Ballads* (Durham N. C. 1968)

GEROULD, G. H. *The Ballad of Tradition* (Oxford 1932)

GREIG, G. *Last Leaves of Traditional Ballads and Ballad Airs* collected in Aberdeenshire by the late Gavin Greig (ed. A. Keith, Aberdeen 1925)

GUMMERE, F. B. *Old English Ballads* (Boston 1894)

GUMMERE, F. B. *The Popular Ballad* (1907) (Reprinted New York 1959)

HART, W. M. 'Professor Child and the Ballad' in P.M.L.A. N.S. xiv No. 4 (1906), (Reprinted in vol. 5 of *English and Scottish Popular Ballads*)

HENDERSON, T. F. *Scottish Vernacular Literature* (London 1898)

HENDERSON, W. *Folk Lore of the Northern Counties of England and the Borders* (London 1879)

HODGART, M. J. C. *The Ballads* (London 1950)

HODGART, M. J. C. 'Medieval Lyrics and the Ballads' in *The Pelican Guide to English Literature* (ed. Boris Ford), vol. i (London 1954)

HUSTVEDT, S. B. *Ballad Books and Ballad Men* (Harvard 1930)

JAMES VI and I *Daemonologie* (1597) (Reprinted Edinburgh 1966)

Select Bibliography

JOHNSON, E. *Sir Walter Scott* (London 1970), 2 vols.

KER, W. P. *English Literature—Medieval* (Oxford 1912)

KITTREDGE, G. L. *The English and Scottish Popular Ballads* (an abridged edition of Child) (London 1904)

LANG, A. *Sir Walter Scott and the Border Minstrelsy* (1910)

LANG, A. 'Border History *v.* Border Ballads' in *Cornhill Magazine* (1907)

LEYDEN, J. *Poems and Ballads* (Kelso 1858)

LOCKHART, J. *The Life of Sir Walter Scott* (London 1906)

LUMBY, J. R. (ed.). *Bernardus de cura rei famuliaris with some early Scottish Prophecies*, E.E.T.S. O.S.42 (1870)

MAITLAND, R. *The Maitland Folio Manuscript* (ed. W. A. Craigie), S.T.S. (1919, 1927), 2 vols.

MAITLAND, R. *The Maitland Quarto Manuscript* (ed. W. A. Craigie), S.T.S. (1920)

MOTHERWELL, W. *Minstrelsy Ancient and Modern* (1827) (Paisley 1873)

MUIR, E. *Scott and Scotland* (London 1936)

MUIR, W. *Living with Ballads* (London 1965)

MURRAY, J. A. H. (ed.). *Thomas of Erceldoune*, E.E.T.S. O.S.61 (1875)

MURRAY, J. A. H. (ed.). *The Complaynt of Scotland* (1549), E.E.T.S. E.S.17, 18 (1872)

NICHOLS, J. *Illustrations of the Literary History of the 18th Century* (London 1817), 8 vols.

POWER, W. *Literature and Oatmeal* (London 1935)

PRIOR, R. C. A. *Ancient Danish Ballads Translated from the Originals* (London 1860), 3 vols.

RICHARDSON, M. A. (ed.) *The Borderer's Table Book* (London 1846), 8 vols.

SCOTT, SIR W. *Minstrelsy of the Scottish Border* (1802-3) (ed. T. Henderson) (London 1931)

SCOTT, SIR W. *The Journal of Sir Walter Scott* (ed. W. E. K. Anderson) (Oxford 1972)

SPEIRS, J. *The Scots Literary Tradition* (London 1940)

TAYLOR, G. 'Memoir of Robert Surtees' in R. Surtees' *History and Antiquities of Durham* (London 1840)

TREVELYAN, G. M. 'The Border Ballads' in *A Layman's Love of Letters* (London 1954)

VEITCH, J. *The History and Poetry of the Scottish Border* (Edinburgh 1893)

VEITCH, J. *Border Essays* (Edinburgh 1893)

WIMBERLY, L. C. *Folklore in the English and Scottish Ballads* (Cambridge 1938)

ZUG, C. E. 'Sir Walter Scott and the Ballad Forgery' in *Studies in Scottish Literature*, viii (1970)

Select Bibliography

IV. ARCHITECTURE

BATES, C. J. *The Border Holds of Northumberland* (Newcastle 1891) (Reprinted in *Archeologia Aeliana* (2) XIV)

CLARK, G. T. *Medieval Military Architecture in England* (London 1884), 2 vols.

CRUDEN, S. *The Scottish Castle* (Edinburgh 1963)

DUNBAR, J. G. *The Historic Architecture of Scotland* (London 1966)

HUGILL, R. *Castles and Peles of the English Border* (Newcastle 1970)

LONG, B. *Castles of Northumberland* (Newcastle 1967)

MACGIBBON, D. and ROSS, T. *The Castellated and Domestic Architecture of Scotland* (1896-7) (Reprinted Edinburgh 1971), 5 vols.

MACKENZIE, W. M. *The Medieval Castle in Scotland* (London 1927)

NEILSON, G. *Peel: its meaning and derivation* (Edinburgh 1894)

PEVSNER, N. *The Buildings of England—Northumberland* (London 1957)

PEVSNER, N. *The Buildings of England—Cumberland and Westmorland* (London 1967)

RAMM, H. G., MCDOWALL, R. W., MERCER, E. *Shielings and Bastles* (London and Edinburgh 1970)

SIMPSON, W. D. *Scottish Castles* (London and Edinburgh 1959)

TOY, S. *The Castles of Great Britain* (London 1953)

Note: The reader who is interested in more detailed information about specific buildings should consult the Royal Commission on Ancient Monuments, Scotland, Inventories, particularly those for Peeblesshire, Roxburghshire and the County of Selkirk.

V. TOPOGRAPHY

(Some of the books in this section are heavily derivative, especially from Scott, and are unreliable in terms of scholarship. They are nevertheless of special interest to the student of literature and environment.)

BOGG, E. *The Border Country* (Leeds 1898)

BORLAND, R. *Border Raids and Reivers* (Dalbeattie 1898)

BRADLEY, H. G. *The Romance of Northumberland* (London 1908)

EYRE-TODD, G. *Byways of the Scottish Border* (Selkirk n.d.)

GOULD, H. D. *Brave Borderland* (Edinburgh n.d.)

GRAHAM, P. A. *Highways and Byways in Northumbria* (London 1920)

HOWITT, W. *Visits to Remarkable Places* (London 1842)

LANG, A. and J. *Highways and Byways in the Border* (London 1914)

MAXWELL, SIR HERBERT E. *Memories of the Months*, 6th series (London 1897-1907)

ROBSON, J. *Border Battles and Battlefields* (Kelso 1897)

RUSSELL, J. *Reminiscences of Yarrow* (Selkirk 1894)

RUTHERFORD, J. *Border Handbook* (Kelso 1849)

Select Bibliography

TOMLINSON, W. W. *Comprehensive Guide to Northumberland* (London n.d.)

TREVELYAN, G. M. *The Middle Marches* (Newcastle 1935)

WHITE, W. *Northumberland and the Border* (London 1859)

VI. DISCOGRAPHY

The following discs are suggested as useful recordings of many of the Ballads discussed in this book. It has not been thought necessary to attempt a complete listing of the many other records of folk song in which some Border Ballads find a place.

The Child Ballads I	Topic 12T160
The Child Ballads II	Topic 12T161
English and Scottish Folk Ballads	
A. L. Lloyd and Ewen MacColl	Topic 12T103
The Long Harvest	
Peggy Seeger and Ewen MacColl	Decca DA66-69
The Shepherd's Song	
Willie Scott	Topic 12T183

NOTES

INTRODUCTION

1. *Edinburgh Review*, April 1805.
2. J. Nichols, *Literary Illustrations*, ii, 28.
3. Quoted by William Windham, 1784; see R. W. K. Cremer, *The Early Life and Diaries of William Windham*, p. 264.
4. J. Lockhart, *Life of Sir Walter Scott*, Everyman edn., p. 30.
5. T. F. Henderson, *Scottish Vernacular Literature*, p. 338.
6. Ritson, *The Gentleman's Magazine*, November 1784.
7. *Minstrelsy of the Scottish Border*, p. 524.
8. *Life*, p. 103.
9. *Minstrelsy*, p. 70.
10. See W. E. Wilson, H.A.S. 18 November 1932 and *Cornhill Magazine*, September 1932.
11. Motherwell, *Minstrelsy Ancient and Modern*, p. iv.

CHAPTER 1. THE BORDERS AND THE BALLADS

1. Thomas Musgrave to Lord Burghley at the end of 1583. *C.B.P.* i, 120.
2. *Scott and Scotland*, p. 89.
3. W. Camden, *Britannia*, p. 65.
4. *The Description of Tweeddale*, 1715.
5. *A Memoir*, p. 10.
6. Ibid., pp. 67-9.
7. G. M. Trevelyan, *The Middle Marches*, p. 25.
8. G. Ridpath, *The Border History of England and Scotland*, p. 706.
9. *C.B.P.* i, 30.
10. *C.B.P.* ii, 256.
11. *C.B.P.* i, 98.
12. *C.B.P.* i, 30.
13. *C.S.P.S.* xiii, 682.
14. See T. I. Rae, *The Administration of the Scottish Border*, pp. 226-32.
15. *C.B.P.* i, 126.
16. *C.B.P.* ii, 163.
17. *Chorographia* or *Survey of Newcastle*, 1649; M. A. Richardson (ed.), *Newcastle Reprints*, ix, 47.
18. J. Leslie, *Historie of Scotland*.
19. M. A. Richardson (ed.), *Newcastle Reprints*, iv, 29.
20. *C.B.P.* i, 82.
21. *C.B.P.* i, 89.
22. *C.B.P.* i, 109.
23. See Rae, *Administration*, pp. 147-8.
24. *C.S.P.D.*, p. 420.
25. R. White, *A History of the Battle of Otterburn*, p. 119.

26. J. G. Dunbar, *Historic Architecture of Scotland*, p. 253.
27. *C.B.P.* ii, 311.
28. *C.B.P.* ii, 391.
29. See Scott, *Border Antiquities*, i, 148.
30. See R. B. Armstrong, *A History of Liddesdale*, p. 77.
31. *Life in Northumberland during the Sixteenth Century*, p. 31.
32. William Patten in A. F. Pollard, *Tudor Tracts*, pp. 87-9.
33. *State Papers, Henry VIII*, v, 515.
34. *C.B.P.* ii, 80.
35. *C.B.P.* ii, 125.
36. *C.B.P.* ii, 208.
37. *State Papers, Henry VIII*, iv, 416.
38. *Minstrelsy*, p. 50.
39. See J. L. Mack, *The Border Line*, p. 88.
40. *C.B.P.* ii, 51.
41. See H. Pease, *Lord Wardens of the Marches*, p. 75.
42. Richardson (ed.), *Newcastle Reprints*, iv, 18.
43. T. Rymer, *Foedera*, xv, 633.
44. *C.B.P.* ii, 567.
45. *History and Antiquities of the Counties of Cumberland and Westmoreland*, p. xcviii.
46. See Pease, *Lord Wardens*, p. 166.
47. *C.B.P.* ii, 99.
48. *C.B.P.* i, 42.
49. *C.B.P.* ii, 198-9.
50. *C.B.P.* i, 111.
51. J. A. H. Murray, *Thomas of Erceldoune*, E.E.T.S. 1875. Introduction.

CHAPTER 2. BALLADS OF THE WEST MARCHES

1. *Scottish Vernacular Literature*, p. 262.
2. *The Scots Literary Tradition*, p. 93.
3. For a detailed and spirited defence of the Armstrongs, see W. A. Armstrong, *The Armstrong Borderland*.
4. *C.B.P.* i, 127.
5. *History and Poetry of the Scottish Border*, ii, 157.
6. *Liddesdale*, App. LXV, LXVI.
7. *Minstrelsy*, p. 199.
8. Nicolson and Burn, *History of Cumberland*, p. xxxiii.
9. Publications of the Bannatyne Club, No. 13. Edinburgh, 1825.
10. *C.B.P.* ii, 120-1.
11. 'The Development of Scott's *Minstrelsy*', p. 76.
12. *Ballad Books and Ballad Men*, p. 53.
13. *C.B.P.* ii, 129.
14. J. W. Brown, *Kinmont Willie in Ballad and History*, p. 13. See also *C.B.P.* ii, 290.
15. Nicolson and Burn, *Cumberland*, p. xxxi.
16. *C.B.P.* ii, 736-7.
17. 'The Development of Scott's *Minstrelsy*', p. 68.
18. *The Border Country*, Part II, p. 46.
19. Scrope to Walsingham, January 1583-4. *C.B.P.* i, 128.
20. See Mack, *The Border Line*, p. 38.

21. Nicolson and Burn, *Cumberland*, pp. lxxxiii-iv. 'Cryssop' = Kershope.
22. See H. G. Ramm, R. W. McDowell and E. Mercer, *Shielings and Bastles*, pp. 14, 16, 53.
23. *Minstrelsy*, p. 206.
24. Nicolson and Burn, *Cumberland*, p. xviii.
25. See Child, *English and Scottish Popular Ballads*, iii, 463.
26. Child, iii, 462.
27. Sir Herbert Maxwell, *Memories of the Months*, 6th ser., p. 225.
28. R. Pitcairn, *Ancient Criminal Trials in Scotland* (Bannatyne Club, 1829-33), i, 153.
29. *History of Scotland*, p. 145.
30. *State Papers, Henry VIII*, v, 170.
31. See Mack, *The Border Line*, pp. 108-9.
32. *Minstrelsy Ancient and Modern*, p. lxii.
33. *Liddesdale*, p. 83.
34. Scot of Satchells, *History of the Name of Scott*, see R. B. Armstrong, *Liddesdale*, pp. 67-8.
35. Child, iv, 9.
36. Nicolson and Burn, *Cumberland*, pp. cvi-cx.
37. *Minstrelsy*, p. 367.
38. Child, iv, 145.
39. The word 'Bishopric' refers to the county of Durham. Scott takes the term from Ritson's *The Bishopric Garland or Durham Minstrel*, Stockton, 1784.
40. *The Popular Ballad*, p. 249.
41. Child, v, 794.
42. *Minstrelsy*, p. 223.
43. *Journal*, 7 Oct. 1827.
44. *The Ballads*, p. 134.
45. Child, iv, 184.

CHAPTER 3. THE MIDDLE MARCHES (1)

1. 'The Development of Scott's *Minstrelsy*', p. 84.
2. Publications of the Surtees Society, vol. xciii, p. 27. Durham, 1895, 'Extracts from the Records of the Merchant Adventurers of Newcastle upon Tyne', F. W. Denby.
3. See W. W. Tomlinson, *Life in Northumberland during the Sixteenth Century*, p. 131.
4. J. Hodgson, *History of Northumberland*, pt. 2, i, 68.
5. *Border Antiquities*, i, lxxiii.
6. M. A. Richardson (ed.), *Borderer's Table Book*, vii, 363.
7. See Child, iv, 24.
8. Lord Eure's letters. See R. B. Armstrong, *Liddesdale*, App. xxxvi.
9. *Northumberland*, pt. 2, i, 136.
10. Surtees, *Durham*, i, 166.
11. *C.B.P.* i, 138, 346-52.
12. *C.B.P.* ii, 470.
13. *Northumberland*, pt. 2, ii, 110 n.
14. See L. C. Wimberly, *Folklore in the English and Scottish Ballads*, pp. 44 ff.
15. Child, v, 794.
16. W. Howitt, *Visits to Remarkable Places*, p. 543.
17. *Northumberland*, pt. 2, i, 155.

18. *Minstrelsy*, p. 493.
19. *Border Ballads*, p. 16.
20. Child discusses the relationships fully, but for more recent speculation the reader is referred to D. S. Bland's article in *Notes and Queries*, 14 April 1951, 'The Evolution of Chevy Chase and the Battle of Otterburn'.
21. Lockhart, *Life of Scott*, p. 609.
22. Child, iv, 501.
23. *Minstrelsy Ancient and Modern*, p. lxxi.
24. Ibid.
25. *Comprehensive Guide to Northumberland*, p. 304.

CHAPTER 4. THE MIDDLE MARCHES (2)

1. R. C. A. Prior, *Ancient Danish Ballads*, pp. 403 f.
2. *Folklore*, p. 86.
3. Child, iv, 443 ff.
4. *Minstrelsy*, p. 339.
5. Child, iii, 497.
6. *Folklore*, p. 39 from a text recorded in the *Journal of the Folk-Song Society*, iii, 64 f.
7. Child, iv, 163.
8. *History and Poetry of the Scottish Border*, ii, 194-207; *Border Essays*, p. 55.
9. *Folklore*, pp. 73-4.
10. Child, iv, 492.
11. Child, ii, 429.
12. M. A. Richardson, *Borderer's Table Book*, viii, 410.
13. B. Long, *Castles of Northumberland*, p. 136.
14. *Castles and Peles of the English Border*, p. 164.
15. Child, v, 295.
16. Child, ii, 296.
17. See Wimberly, *Folklore*, p. 108, and Hodgart, *Ballads*, p. 87.
18. *Traditional Tunes of the Child Ballads*, i, 226.
19. Ibid., i, 191.
20. *Minstrelsy*, p. 337.
21. As quoted in Child, i, 72.
22. G. Greig, *Last Leaves of Traditional Ballads*, ix.

CHAPTER 5. BALLADS OF THE SUPERNATURAL

1. T. F. Henderson, *Scottish Vernacular Literature*, p. 24.
2. Murray, *Thomas of Erceldoune*, p. liii.
3. J. Russell, *Reminiscences of Yarrow*, p. 267.
4. *Old English Ballads*, p. 349.

GLOSSARY

ackward: backward, backhanded
aggrege: aggravate, increase
aik: oak
ain: own
airns: irons, shackles
airt: direction
aller: alder
alluterlie: altogether
amaist: almost
ark: chest
ba: ball
baith: both
bale: faggot, blaze
bane: bone
barnikin: barmkin, walled
  enclosure
be: by
bewis: boughs
bigged: built
bill: see below
billy, bully: brother, friend
black mail: protection money
bower, bour: house, chamber
braid: broad, wide
brand: sword
brattice: a temporary breastwork
  or parapet, used during a siege
bree, brie: brow, eyebrow
brent: burnt
bryttle: to cut up (a deer)
bucht, bught: a sheep or cattle fold
caill: cold
carl(e): old man
carline: old woman
carp: sing (of a minstrel)
cauf: calf
chaipe: escape
clam: climbed
clene bill: see below
cleugh: narrow valley

clock: limper, hobbler
contemne: neglect
crag, craig: neck, throat
craig: crag, cliff
crakit his creddence: broke his faith
curch: kerchief, woman's head
  covering
debate: champion, support
den, dean: glen, dene
dight: wipe; prepare; clad
dike, dyke: in Scotland, a wall of
  stone or turf; in England, a
  ditch
ding: smash
dow, doo: dove
dowie: mournful, melancholy
dree: endure, suffer
dreire: harm
duelland: dwelling
ee: eye
eiket: added
elskin: shoemakers awl
esk: newt
fail: turf
fang: catch
fause: false
fazard: coward
foirbearis: forebears
foranen(s)t: opposite to
forfoughen: exhausted
fou: full, drunk
foul bill: see below
fra(e): from
fray: alarm
fyle a bill: see below
gad: lance
gae: go, walk
gae doon: be executed
gait: influence
gait(t): way, road

Glossary

gang: go, walk,
gar: cause, make, compel
gavlock: crowbar, iron rod
gif: if
gin: if
gleed: glowing ember
gob: mouth
gowd: gold
grain: a high narrow declivity or watercourse
grayne: family group
greeting: crying
gytternes: guitars
hackbut: gun
hail: whole, wholly
Hairibee: the place of execution at Carlisle
haugh: low, level ground beside a stream
herreit: harried
herschip, heirschippis: plundering
het: hot
hie: high
houm, holm: level ground by a river
howk: dig
ilk ane: every one
innymeis: enemies
insyght gear: household goods
ja(c)k: leather or stout canvas jacket, sometimes quilted and strengthened with steel plates
Jeddart: Jedburgh
jelly: merry, agreeable
kaim: comb
kinnen: rabbits
kist: chest
knapscap: steel cap
kye: cows
laigh: low
lake: pit
lap: leaped
lave: rest, remainder
law: hill
layne: to tell a lie
lear: lore, information
leiuesum: permissible

limmer: rogue
linn: stream
loan(ing): lane, milking place
loun: rogue
loup: leap
luges: huts, lodges
lukit: looked
mail(l): rent, levy
mains: home farm on an estate
make: mate, spouse
malisoun: curse
mansworn: perjured
marrow: companion, mate
maun: must
maut: malt, ale
mavis (mawys): thrush
meikle, mickle: much, great
mergh: marrow
mind: remember
moss: boggy moorland
mosstrooper: Border freebooter
mowes: jokes
muckle: big
neist: next
nog: notch, stake
nolt, nout: cattle
nychtbouris: neighbours
onsett: attack
or: ere, before
orgmount: barley
ourgang: oppress
owerword: refrain
owre: over
owsen: oxen
pa': a slight movement
pakis: packs
pall: fine cloth
parson: person
pick: pitch
pled: pleaded
pricker: rider
quey: heifer
quhilk: which
quhill: till
ranshackle: ransack
raxed: stretched
reif: robbery

Glossary

remuffit: removed
resett: receive stolen goods, harbour
rich(t) nocht: nothing at all
rig: ridge
rive, reve: tear
rok: distaff
row-footed: rough-shod
rowe: roll, wind
rug(g): tear
rype: rob
saiffing: securing
sair: sore
sark: shirt
schene: bright, beautiful
schill: shrill
scug: to shelter; expiate
s(c)haw: wood
shot: reckoning
sic, sik: such
sicker: safe, sure
skraugh: scream
slack: a pass in the hills; a morass
sloknyt (sloken): quenched
solist: solicitous
sowch: moaning of the wind
spare: slit in a gown
speir: ask
spoil: despoil
spulzeis: despoiling
sta': stole
stark: strong, violent
steek: shut
stoire: goods, stock
stot: young ox
stour, sture: stern
stouth: stealing
stown: stolen
suld: should
sun-side: the good side, used of the heart
swarf: faint

swire, swyre: a high hill-slope
syke: a marshy hollow, ditch, trench
syne: ago, since, after
tane: taken
teind: tithe
thainself: themselves
thanen: them
theek: thatch
thocht: though
thrang: throng, party
throw: through
tile: till
toom: empty
tor: ornamental knob on cradle etc.
tow: rope
trod: pursuit
turses: carry
upweir: defend
wame: belly, womb
war: aware
waresoun: curse
waryit: cursed
wawis: walls
wear: guard
wede: faded, removed by death
weir: war
wele: well
whang: thong
whiles: sometimes, now and then
wicker: twig, pliant rod
wiete: know, be assured
win: make one's way, get there
wob: web of cloth
wodewale: golden oriole
wood: mad, excited
wyllis: tricks
yett: gate. In Scottish peles and tower houses often in the form of an iron grille, with bars about 8 in. apart, sometimes of ingenious construction.

Bill: a formal complaint making specific accusations against specified persons; it was 'enrolled' before the warden clerk by the complainant, and passed to the warden of the opposite realm for action. It was his duty to bring the accused to defend himself at the day of truce. A 'foul bill' is one in which the accused is guilty. The opposite is a 'clene bill'. 'Fyling' a bill is the process of judgment of the guilt *or innocence* of the defendant. The word is often associated with 'foul' inasmuch as it was often assumed that the existence of a bill requiring judgment implied the guilt of the defendant. Consequently, the words are sometimes used interchangeably, but the meanings are distinct. The matter is fully and lucidly discussed in T. I. Rae's, *Administration of the Scottish Frontier*, pp. 52 ff.

INDEX

Index

complaints, 25, 51, 68, 114

Complaynte Aganis the Theivis of Liddisdail, 49, 53-6, 112, 191

Complaynt of Scotland, 80

Cospatrick, 167

Crew Tower, 70

Cruel Mother, The, 145-6, 186

Cruel Sister, The, 156-7

Daemon Lover, The, 13, 185-6

Day of Truce, 45; *see also* Warden's meeting

Days of March, 48; *see also* Warden's meeting

Death of Featherstonehaugh, The, 4

Death of Parcy Reed, The, 9, 19, 70, 84, 89, 93, 105, 111-18, 126 and Pl. 11

Debatable Land, 9, 42-3, 50, 53, 87; 14-15 (map)

Deloney, Thomas, 123, 169

Dick o' the Cow, 6, 39, 43, 65, 70, 74-8, 193

Dowie Dens of Yarrow, The, 144-7, 149, 171

Dryhope Tower, 126 and Pl. 15, 144, 199

Dunbar, William, 11

Earl Brand, 8, 136-9

Edlingham Church, 30 and Pl. 8, 34

Edward, 157-9, 172, 180

Elfin Knight, The, 178

Ellen Irwin, 102

Elsdon Church, 134-5

Elsdon Tower, 29, 30 and Pl. 7, 34, 126 and Pl. 13

Embleton (vicar's pele), 34

Erlinton, 139

Eure, Lord, 27, 39, 80

Evergreen, The, 3, 81, 119

Fair Annie, 170

Fair Flower of Northumberland, The, 168-70

Fair Helen of Kirkconnel, 101, 195

Fair Margaret and Sweet William, 142; *see also The Douglas Tragedy*

Fair Mary of Wallington, 170

families, 1, 10, 19, 22-4, 43, 56, 111-19; 46-7 (map)

Famous Flower of Serving Men, The, 149

Fause Foodrage, 154-6

feud, 19-21, 110-11

Fine Flowers in the Valley, 186; *see also The Cruel Mother*

Forster, Sir John, 23, 43, 45, 49, 119

Foulbogshiel, 27, 72

fray, 49, 72

Fray of Suport, The, 4, 5, 65, 95-8, 118

Gil Brenton, 167, 171, 180

Gilnockie Tower, 81, 82, 126 and Pl. 10, 199

Goldielands Tower (Gaudilands), 107, 199

Greenknowe Tower, 30 and Pl. 5

Gude Earl Brand and Auld Carl Hude, 136

Hangingshaw Tower, 34

Herd, David, 3, 129, 172, 194-5

Hermitage Castle, 5, 7

Heron, Sir George, 119, 120

Hildebrand and Hilde, 136, 139

Hobbie Noble, 27, 44, 50, 59, 65, 69-74, 84, 88, 94, 199

Hogg, James (The Ettrick Shepherd), 3, 11, 129, 130, 131, 135, 146, 149, 152, 153, 154, 164

Hole Bastle, 30 and Pls. 1, 2

hot trod, 45, 75

Hudibras, 125

Hughie the Graeme, 43, 70, 84, 87-9

Hunting of the Cheviot, The, 139

Jack of Newbury, 123, 169

James V of Scotland, 79, 81-4, 88, 149

– 216 –

Index

James VI of Scotland and I of
England, 17, 29, 56, 62, 144, 173
Jamie Telfer, 24, 44, 45, 49, 53, 59,
104-9, 115
Jellon Grame, 154, 156, 171
Jock o' the Side, 6, 57-61, 65, 68, 70
John Armstrong's last Farewell, 81
Johney Armstrong's Last Goodnight,
81, 84
Johnie Armstrong, 65, 70, 74, 78-
86, 88, 126 and Pls. 9, 10, 131,
149, 199
Johnie o' Breadislee (*Johny Cock*),
65, 99, 118, 146

Kemp Owyne, 176
Kershopefoot, 53, 71, 76, 95, 103
Kinmont Willie, 42, 43, 48, 57, 60,
69, 61-9, 94, 107
Kirkandrews Tower, 29
Kirkhope Tower, 143

Laidlaw, William, 4, 136, 146, 185
Laidly Worm of Spindlestoneheugh,
The, 176
Laird's Jock's Tower, 126 and
Pl. 9
Lament of the Border Widow, 149-
151
Lay of the Last Minstrel, 1
Lay of the Reedwater Minstrel, 112
Leesome Brand, 164, 168
Legend of Sir Owain, 150, 194
Lennoxlove Tower, 34
Leyden, John, 4, 38, 84, 151
Liddesdale, 4, 5, 7, 22, 40, 43, 53,
57, 68, 70, 71, 74, 76, 103, 104,
111
Lizie Wan, 158, 159, 171, 172
Lochmaben Harper, The, 44, 65,
78
Lockhart, John, 3, 129
Long Lonkin, 151-4
Lord Ewrie, 4
Lord Randal, 160-1
Lyke Wake Dirge, The, 193-4

Maitland, Sir Richard, 34, 49, 53,
57, 59, 112, 191
Mangerton, 57-9, 70, 73, 76, 77, 81,
199
Marches, 41-4, 71; 46-7 (map)
Marmion, 9, 12, 33
Mary Hamilton, 157
Melkridge Tower, 30 and Pl. 3
Mervinslaw Tower, 30 and Pl. 4
Minstrelsy of the Scottish Border, 3,
4, 8, 33, 57, 62, 69, 74, 88, 92, 95,
110, 119, 129, 131, 136, 139, 140,
144, 147, 152, 155, 156, 161, 185,
186, 193, 194
Motherwell, William, 7, 81, 82, 99,
131, 136, 145, 157, 161, 165, 187,
190, 191
Musgrave, Thomas, 18-19

Newark Castle, 110
nicknames: *see* to-names
Norham Castle, 9, 17, 29, 42

Oakwood Tower, 143
Otterburn, 124, 132, 134, 199
Outlaw Murray, The, 110

pele towers: *see* architecture, *and*
Askerton, Blackhouse, Crew,
Dryhope, Elsdon, Embleton,
Gilnockie, Goldielands, Green-
knowe, Hangingshaw, Kirk-
andrews, Kirkhope, Laird's
Jocks's, Lennoxlove, Mangerton,
Melkridge, Mervinslaw, Oak-
wood, Shilbottle, Smailholm,
Troughend, Tushielaw
Percy, Thomas, Bishop, 1, 2, 3,
149, 157, 159

Raid of the Reidswire, The, 44, 48,
95, 118-23, 126 and Pl. 12
Ramsay, Allan, 3, 81, 82, 101, 119
Rare Willie Drowned in Yarrow,
101, 147

Index